"What a help for local church prayer ... published manuscript of *The Prayer-Satur...* ... ...ar I
was taking. I was so taken by the co......... that I ended up tearing out
pages and teaching them instead of my material. The local church now
has a new and fresh construction manual for the House of Prayer."
— DR. TERRY TEYKL, prayer consultant, Renewal Ministries

"Thank God for Cheryl Sacks! *The Prayer-Saturated Church* is a must for
anyone involved in prayer ministry. It gives practical, balanced revelation
on how not to get distracted so you remain focused for breakthrough praying in your church. Cheryl not only has lived and led prayer but has now
written and explained how the prayer ministry evolves and matures."
— DR. CHUCK D. PIERCE, vice president, Global Harvest Ministries;
president, Glory of Zion International Ministries, Inc.

"Here's a simple fact: Some ideas just work better than others. Cheryl
Sacks helps leaders sort through the vast overload of information on
prayer to find those strategies that do work best in a local church. *The
Prayer-Saturated Church* will help you distinguish real answers from
theory for establishing a prayer strategy in your church."
— Ted Haggard, president, National Association of Evangelicals;
senior pastor, New Life Church, Colorado Springs

"*The Prayer-Saturated Church* is a major missing link between the church
and the transformation of congregations, cities, and nations. It is practical
yet deeply personal and warm. It gives us keys to the release of revival
and a great harvest of souls."
— CINDY JACOBS
founder, Generals of Intercession

"The dynamic prayer movement that God has been activating throughout
America has now reached a new level. *The Prayer-Saturated Church* not
only will help you understand what the Spirit is saying to the churches
concerning prayer, but it will also motivate you to jump into the stream
and move forward in the divine flow. I congratulate Cheryl Sacks for this
strategic and exciting book!"
— C. PETER WAGNER, president, Global Harvest

"When Cheryl Sacks speaks about prayer, people listen! She is a gifted communicator, and she is also uniquely anointed to call people and churches to a deeper, higher level of intercession. So this book isn't just full of good prayer ideas; it will ignite your spirit! Cheryl has been especially called by God to impart her passion to church leaders. I've felt it! I've seen the results! I'm Cheryl's pastor."

—DR. GARY D. KINNAMAN, senior minister, Word of Grace, Mesa, Arizona

"Cheryl Sacks has produced a resource that both pastors and prayer leaders have been waiting for years to put their hands on. She covers the A to Z's of birthing and building prayer into the ministry and mission of the local church. This handbook is essential for every prayer ministry I have ever known. Buy it, use it, and give thanks to God for Cheryl."

—PHIL MIGLIORATTI, facilitator, Church Prayer Leaders Network

"This book is one that is incredibly comprehensive yet thoroughly practical. Cheryl not only covers the "how" of prayer ministry but also the "why." For anyone interested in building or improving their church as a house of prayer, *The Prayer-Saturated Church* is a must-read."

—DR. GREGORY FRIZZELL, prayer and spiritual awakening specialist, Baptist General Convention of Oklahoma

CHERYL SACKS

The
Prayer
saturated
church

A Comprehensive Handbook for Prayer Leaders

NAVPRESS®

BRINGING TRUTH TO LIFE

Pray! Books • P.O. Box 35004 • Colorado Springs, CO 80935 • www.praymag.com

Pray! Books are published by NavPress. NavPress is the publishing ministry of the Navigators, an international Christian organization whose mission is to reach, disciple, and equip people to know Christ and to make Him known through successive generations.

Note: Some of the names of individuals and churches used in the illustrations have been changed to protect privacy.

Visit the *Pray!* website at www.praymag.com.
Visit the Church Prayer Leaders website at www.prayerleader.com.

ISBN: 1-57683-615-0

Printed in the United States of America
2 3 4 5 6 7 8 9 10 / 08 07 06 05 04

Cover illustration by Simon Shaw

DEDICATED TO

my loving husband and prayer partner, Hal,
AND
my precious daughter, Nicole,
whose prayers and those of her friends
have filled our home for many years.

contents

acknowledgments

This book was made possible by the prayers and support of many special friends. First, to my husband, Hal, your love, prayers, and spiritual input have been my constant strength. Also your work with pastors for more than twenty years paved the way for me to train church prayer leaders in many cities across the nation.

Nicole, my precious daughter, the image of you and the kids from Sacred Edge filling the floors, doorways, and stairwell of our home with heart-wrenching cries to the Lord for your generation has forever changed my perspective of the word "prayer."

I cannot say enough about my editor at NavPress, Rachelle Gardner, except that without you there would be no book. Your prayers, encouragement, and editorial direction are a gift from God. I'll never have another cup of Starbucks without thinking of you. To Jon Graf, my friend and publisher at *Pray!*, thank you for giving me this great opportunity.

To my assistant, Kathleen Graham, thank you for picking up my office duties and helping compile the resource list and disk materials. You're the best! Sandi Powelson and Caroline Erickson, your input on several sections of the book was invaluable.

To my pastor, Gary Kinnaman, I think you started this process when you opened the door for me to implement my prayer ideas at Word of Grace. Thanks for believing in me.

To my friend and "house of prayer" mentor, Terry Teykl, catching your vision has changed the course of my life. To my friends Steve and Mary Marr, thank you for all your hand-holding of a first-time author.

I am grateful for the intercessors, too numerous to name, who birthed this book. A special thanks to Deborah Tyrrell and my mother, Chris Mackin, who prayed me through the final weeks.

To the donors who gave so generously so I could purchase a new laptop computer, may the Lord richly bless you. And my dear friend Cindy Jacobs, your constant encouragement kept me from giving up.

To my spiritual Mom, Hazel Shelton, thank you for taking the time to teach me the power of prayer. There could be no greater gift.

Finally, I want to thank the Lord Jesus Christ for helping me complete this work. This book is first and foremost for and about You.

foreword

Ezekiel 47 is a prophetic passage about a river—the river of God—that flows from the altar in the temple of God. This river, as it flows, gets ever broader and deeper, and it brings life and enrichment. It teems with life and brings fruit wherever it flows.

That is also a picture of the church and the work of the Spirit of Jesus Christ. Out of the church flows the work of the Spirit on earth. The cover of *The Prayer-Saturated Church* captures that image. When a church is truly connected to the Spirit of God, His Spirit flows in ministry—first through the church and then out the doors into the surrounding community, bringing life and fruit wherever it flows.

How does a church become filled to overflowing with the Holy Spirit of God? There is only one way: through prayer. The Spirit's working doesn't come through gaining Bible knowledge, though that's important. It doesn't come through learning about leadership, though that's important. The Spirit's work doesn't come through dynamic small groups or the latest church growth ideas, though they are important, too. The transforming, life-giving work of the Holy Spirit only comes through powerful prayer. It comes through becoming a prayer-saturated church. How do I know this?

Luke 11:5-13 is an interesting passage on prayer. Usually this passage brings sermons on persevering in prayer. But there is a hidden little message in its powerful thoughts. At the end, Jesus says, "How much more will your Father in heaven give the Holy Spirit to those who ask him!" The passage wasn't about the Holy Spirit; it was about asking for what we need—ask and keep on asking, seek and keep on seeking, knock and keep on knocking. And what do we get as we pray more and more? Luke says we get the Holy Spirit! We get the river of God that flows in and through us.

Since the beginning of *Pray!* magazine, one of my greatest passions has been to see God use our ministry to fuel prayer in the local church. While that passion was never written into our mission statement, it has been a driving force under the surface, like a hidden river deep in the bedrock that brings life to parched ground.

Seeing prayer become foundational in the lives of believers and then in the life of every church is what we are about. It's in our blood! It seeps out of our pores. We get excited over every step forward in raising the prayer level in a church. We grieve over every roadblock, every setback we hear about from prayer leaders.

As a result of this passion, we have developed relationships with many prayer leaders over the years. Our relationship with Cheryl Sacks developed as she and I both sat on the advisory board of The National Association of Local Church Prayer Leaders (now the Church Prayer Leaders Network). A few years ago, we began feeling that it was time for a new, major work on raising up prayer in the local church. We wanted a practical, helpful, encouraging, challenging, and, above all, comprehensive book that would provide everything a pastor, church leader, prayer coordinator, or intercessor needed to develop his or her own church into a prayer-saturated church. After watching Cheryl and seeing the breadth of her experience in the relatively uncharted waters of local church prayer, we knew we had our author. Low and behold, when we approached her, we found out that she was already working on such a book.

I believe *The Prayer-Saturated Church* is bar none the finest, most complete work on church prayer that has ever been written. Multiple copies should be in every church. As you seek to grow prayer in your church, God's Word, the Holy Spirit, and then *The Prayer-Saturated Church* will guide you in making your church that Spirit-transforming, life-giving community God wants it to be.

—JONATHAN GRAF, founder of *Pray!* magazine, president of Jonathan Graf Ministries, Inc.

CHAPTER 1

The Church
That Prayer Built

If we call upon the Lord, He has promised in His Word to answer, to bring the unsaved to Himself, to pour out His Spirit among us. If we don't call upon the Lord, He has promised nothing—nothing at all. It's as simple as that. No matter what I preach or what we claim to believe in our heads, the future will depend upon our times of prayer. This is the engine that will drive the church.

Jim Cymbala
Fresh Wind, Fresh Fire

Many years of my life's journey were spent as a high school journalism teacher. I still pray regularly for the public school system. One morning I was up early praying.

"Oh God," I cried. "Please return prayer to the classrooms of schools across our nation."

Suddenly the Holy Spirit responded to my prayer. His words seemed almost audible as they rang through the air: "Why don't you ask that prayer will return to the church?"

At first I was stunned. Then I began to ponder the meaning of those words. Could it be that the Lord saw the church's doors closed to prayer—just as they are in our schools?

I knew our Christian community needed to pray more. For more than twenty years, while my husband, Hal, and I had been working with the pastors of our city, we also had been leading citywide prayer meetings. Attendance was up and down. I was always asking the Lord for a new strategy.

But now He dropped this new thought into my mind: *How can the city become a "house of prayer" when the local churches are not even praying? The citywide prayer movement will never be any stronger than the prayer in the local church.*

Thus began my journey of training local church prayer leaders to work alongside their pastors in building houses of prayer.

THE LOCAL CHURCH PRAYER MOVEMENT

The world is now in the midst of an escalating prayer movement—and the hot spot of the movement is local church prayer mobilization. Christian bookstores are filled with books on the whys and hows of prayer and the need to pray, but very few address the topic of local church prayer. Fewer still offer any actual plan for developing a church into a house of prayer.

Recently, the pastor of a church in my city sat in our office belaboring the woes of trying to mobilize his church to pray. He had put himself through a crash course on prayer in the previous two weeks, reading some eight to ten contemporary books on the subject. He was now convinced that he needed to get a prayer ministry up and running in his church and spiritually map his community. He seemed overwhelmed by the vast amount of work to be done on this important project, and he didn't know where to start.

This is the same place in which literally thousands of pastors and prayer leaders find themselves today. Their eyes have been opened to the need to make prayer a priority in their church, yet they simply don't know where to begin.

I am writing this book to help fill the gap—to provide comprehensive, practical, and strategic material for mobilizing prayer in the local church. Whether you're a pastor, church elder, prayer leader, or interested intercessor, if you have a heart to see your church draw closer to God in prayer, I have written this book for you. While I've aimed most of the material at the church prayer leader (whether that person is a pastor, staff member, or volunteer), I've also included "For Pastors Only" sections. You'll find these clearly marked within the chapters.

In the following pages you'll find help for establishing a prayer ministry and becoming more of a praying church. You'll learn how to assess your church's needs, build a prayer action team, and develop a comprehensive prayer strategy that involves the entire congregation—and how to avoid many pitfalls along the way.

This book is for churches at every level of prayer. I've seen churches that are full of prayerful people and God's tangible presence, yet they don't have many organized opportunities for prayer and desire to increase that. Then there are churches with plenty of programming but not much prayer. Many pastors and church leaders are tired of running endless programs without seeing much fruit. I am writing for any of you who see outward signs of success but feel empty because of the lack of the presence and power of God. This book is essentially a call for the church to return to her first love, with a road map to show her how to get there.

Why is this movement so important?

- Prayer is the priority for transforming our nation (1 Timothy 2:1-4).
- Prayer-saturated churches are capable of transforming their communities.
- Churches need a designated person to promote and mobilize prayer initiatives.
- Pastors, church staff, and prayer leaders need resources to help them succeed in this mission.

THE UPPER ROOM PRINCIPLE

If an outsider observed your church, would prayer be immediately visible? For many churches, the answer is no. Yet prayer is certainly what anyone would have noticed about the early church or any of the churches during the Great Awakenings. Their continual practice of prayer was the primary reason for phenomenal growth and evangelism.

In the book of Acts, the early church was awakened, equipped, and mobilized to pray. They prayed in the temple, in one another's homes, and in the streets. They even had a special room where they assembled for prayer: "And when they had entered [the city], they mounted [the stairs] to the upper room where they were indefinitely staying. . . . All of these with their minds in full agreement devoted themselves steadfastly to prayer, [waiting together] . . ." (Acts 1:13-14, AMP).

The Upper Room was filled with activity; people were always coming and going. Many believe that it was a place where prayer was going on continuously—24/7.

The Upper Room became a launching pad for the church's mission. The disciples emerged empowered to share the message of Christ with boldness and authority. Profound and exciting things happened after the Holy Spirit came upon them. This little group of disciples with no buildings, no money, and no tapes and books, turned the world right side up.

Terry Teykl, in his book *Making Room to Pray*, explains this prayer phenomenon in what he calls the Upper Room Principle. The principle is simple:

> When God gives us a great task, He expects us to seek Him with all our heart, soul, mind, and strength before we endeavor to do that task, because we must realize completely that His Spirit, not our might or power, will accomplish the work (see Zechariah 4:6).[1]

THE CHURCH THAT PRAYER BUILT

In 1993, Biltmore Baptist Church was in trouble. After a string of devastating events, this once-active congregation of 600 had diminished to 175. In the wake of dissension, factions, and power struggles, the only staff left was a part-time secretary. There was no pastor, only an interim worship leader.

"We were a desperate, broken people," recalls church member Carolyn Fuqua, "but we began to call out to God." The congregation went through a time of confession, repentance, and cleansing. "We asked God to send us a pastor with a vision that would lead us."

God sent a man by the name of James Walker. Together he and the congregation dreamed about what their church would look like in the future. Yet none of them could have even imagined what God was going to do.

"We began to pray that God would send people to help the pastor ful-fill the vision—God's plans and purposes, not man's," says Carolyn. "We asked the Lord to bar the door to people who would come with a hidden agenda or who were seeking power or position for themselves. We asked God to do something so big that no man could take credit for it."

Ten years later Biltmore Baptist Church is a growing, dynamic church. With a staff of close to eighty, including sixteen ministers, membership has reached nearly five thousand. According to Carolyn, the phenomenal turnaround is all because of prayer.

With the coming of the new pastor, seeking God together became the church's number-one priority. "The prayer ministry was born in the heart of the pastor," says Carolyn. "He believes it, he preaches it, and he gives leadership to it."

Carolyn now serves on staff as the prayer ministry coordinator. She and her nine-member leadership team coordinate the church's prayer activities. The expanding prayer ministry began as "God's 300," became "God's 600," and is now "God's One Thousand." At this time, 825 inter-cessors are involved in one of eighty-nine prayer groups.

Every person in leadership is a part of the prayer ministry. "Whether you're a pastor, deacon, or Sunday school teacher, you're either leading a [prayer] group or you're a committed member of one," says Carolyn. "We are a church dedicated to and excited about seeking God together."[2]

And what are the results of all this prayer?

Increased unity and harmony. "I always knew there could be a place where people got along—where egos were laid aside," says Carolyn. "In the last ten years I've seen this. I can honestly say that I don't see ego in our sixteen ministers. They love the Lord and they love each other."

Increased fruit in ministry. Every year the church baptizes from 300 to 400 people, and from 500 to 600 people join the church. "One Sunday we baptized ninety-six people in a nearby lake."

Increased presence of God. Jesus is exalted and praised in every worship service. God's Word is preached with authority. Many broken people, in difficult situations, have come to the church. "Because of the tangible presence of the Holy Spirit, we've been a place of healing," says Carolyn. One family shared how they pulled into the parking lot and right away knew something was different. They began to weep and said the presence of God was so evident they could have just sat in their car and worshiped.

"We believe what is happening at Biltmore Baptist Church is because people are on their faces praying for God to pour out His blessings and power upon the church," says Carolyn. Our constant prayer is, 'Help us to stay clean and obedient and blessable. Let not your Holy Spirit depart from us.'"

redefining success

The way we define success in the church is often influenced more by the world than by the Scriptures. It is easy to believe that if we are busier, we are more fruitful. If we have more people and more money, we are more successful. In some cases this is true. However, the real mark of success is obedience.

> *The definition of success is: finding out what is on Jesus' heart and then doing it, when and how He says to.*
>
> Steve Smith
> Australian church consultant

The question is, "Are our activities pleasing the Lord? Does His pleasure shine upon our work? Is God's tangible presence in the church?"

The following story told by one church leader illustrates this point:

Our church has been struggling with a sense of spiritual dryness and a lack of God's leading for more than a year, and the leadership has finally thrown their collective hands in the air and basically given up. They know that we need to get back to the basics and have decided to suspend all of the church's programming (the church numbers over nine hundred families, so that's a lot of programming!) and announced a time of fasting and prayer. They say that the fasting and prayer will continue for at least forty days and that if we are not able to get back to our First Love in forty days, then we will go eighty, or 120, or whatever God leads us to!

The most remarkable thing, though, is that when a group of prayer people from the different churches got together for a time of prayer and fellowship and found out what was happening at my church, they said that they had been hearing God say something similar at their own churches but had been afraid to act on it. They fear losing "sheep" to churches who have programming going on. What are you up to, God? We have decided to take Moses' words to God to heart: "We are not moving unless you come with us" (Exodus 33:15, my liberal paraphrase).[3]

Another church, Solid Rock in Colorado Springs led by Calvin Johnson, stopped all other activities to call the church to thirty days of prayer and fasting. Each staff member was asked to take at least three days off to pray and fast. Immediately murmuring and complaining ceased. People repented who had unforgiveness in their lives; people who had been disconnected returned to the church.

where are we?

When I think of the church in other nations around the world, words come to mind such as all-night prayer meetings, prayer and fasting chains, and multichurch and community-wide prayer and worship gatherings.

What is the American church known for? I think people might say we're known for great programs, effective small groups, excellent resources, or good administration. Most people probably wouldn't think of the American church as being known for dynamic prayer.

"A paradigm shift is needed in the minds and hearts of American church leaders if their churches are to become houses of prayer," says Frank Damazio, pastor of City Bible Church in Portland, Oregon. A number of years ago his church made that shift, and his experience led him to believe that if a church is to become a house of prayer, six areas need to change:[4]

1. The heart of the senior pastor.

Only the senior pastor can cast the vision on Sunday morning to the whole church. No one else has that place of visibility or authority. When the pastor's heart is captured, the whole church is affected.

2. The heart of the congregation.

A house of prayer is made up of living stones—the prayer lives of God's people. Through a pastor's example and prayers, a congregation's heart can be moved to spend more time with the Lord. In fact, it's important to see this happen even before establishing a prayer ministry.

3. The spiritual atmosphere of the church.

When the prayers of God's people focus upon the things that open the heavens over a church, the spiritual atmosphere will change. Damazio asks his congregation to pray over twelve specific goals, some of which are biblical truth to lead the church, strong prayer and intercession, awesome worship, liberal giving, healing, and miracles.

4. The worship service.

When prayer is a priority of the church, it will be visible in the weekend service. When Damazio realized the announcements were taking more time than the prayer time, he made a radical change in the service agenda. Now the church makes as much room for intercession as they do for worship.

5. Intentional prayer mobilization.

Start a prayer ministry—one that ignites the whole church to pray. Then select a pastor of prayer or church prayer coordinator to lead it. Even though the pastor is the church's primary motivator for prayer, it's helpful if someone other than the pastor is given the responsibility to lead the prayer ministry.

6. Outward, not just inward, focus.

In addition to praying for the church, it's important to include an outward focus of prayer. This includes prayer warfare for cities and nations. A house of prayer has a heart for the world.

WHY PRAY?

Some Christians today are not sure if prayer really makes a difference. They think, *Why would an all-knowing, all-powerful God need me to pray? Isn't God going to do what He wants to do anyway?* Because their view is "whatever will be will be," they say, "Why pray?"

A look at Scriptures throughout the Old and New Testaments reveal that although God is all-sovereign, He chose from the time of Creation to work on the earth through humans. He is in partnership with us, not independent of us. Scripture reveals no other way in which God intervenes in the affairs of earth.

Didn't Jesus tell us to ask that His kingdom would come and His will would be done (see Matthew 6:10)? Why would He tell us to ask for something He was planning to do anyway?

Didn't He tell us to ask for our daily bread (see Matthew 6:11)? Yet doesn't He know our needs before we ask?

Why would He tell us to pray for laborers to be sent into the harvest field? Doesn't the Lord of the harvest want this more than we do[5] (see Matthew 9)?

There is only one logical explanation: God does nothing outside the realm of prayer and intercession. Is it any wonder the Bible is filled with multiple entreaties, urgings, and invitations for us to pray?

In addition to those already mentioned, many other verses in Scripture answer the question "Why pray?"

- Because it is right (Luke 18:1)
- Because it is commanded (1 Thessalonians 5:17)
- Because it is sinful to neglect it (1 Samuel 12:23)
- Because neglect of it grieves God (Isaiah 43:21-22; 64:6-7)
- Because it is the medium through which God bestows blessing (Matthew 7:11; Daniel 9:3)
- Because it is essential to victory over the forces of evil (Ephesians 6:12-18)
- Because of the obligation imposed by Christ's example (Hebrews 5:7; Mark 1:35)
- Because of the emphasis given to it in the early church (Acts. 6:4; 12:5; Romans 1:9-10; Colossians 1:9)

With such importance upon prayer in God's Word, it should come as no surprise that the Father proclaims that prayer will be the priority activity of His church: "For my house will be called a house of prayer" (Isaiah 56:7).

Today God's Spirit continues to lead Christians into a lifestyle of prayer, a divine partnership of Jesus with His church, so that the things that have been prepared in heaven will become reality on earth.

WHY CHURCHES DON'T Pray

Recently, I asked a group of some two hundred pastors and prayer leaders to make a list of the reasons churches don't pray or pray more. Among the top reasons given were the following:

- **Busyness.** Overwhelmingly so, the number-one reason these leaders said churches don't pray is because of busyness. Jesus led a simple, unencumbered life. We too must avoid being weighed down by activities and the cares of this world that keep us from sitting at His feet. What would need to change in your church so that more time could be given to prayer?

> *The spiritual history of a mission or church is written in its prayer life.*
>
> R. Arthur Matthew
> *Born for Battle*

- **Apathy.** There was no tie for second place. Apathy took the slot, hands down. Many people in churches today have little desire to spend time with the Lord. Why is this? I think one Christian leader described it best: "If we're not hungry for God, it's because we've filled ourselves up with something else."

- **Self-sufficiency.** Another top reason given was that church leaders and those in the congregation are confident they can run things themselves. Even if this isn't really what they believe, they haven't become desperate enough to stop and change their mode of operation. Jesus had strong words about a church in this condition in Revelation 3:17: "You say, 'I am rich; I have acquired wealth and do not need a thing.' But you do not realize that you are wretched, pitiful, poor, blind and naked."

- **No leadership.** Both pastors and prayer coordinators said there was a lack of leadership to guide the vision for prayer in their churches. They said leaders were focused upon other ministry activities. Little time was given to supporting the prayer ministry. These were churches that had prayer leaders. I can only imagine what it would be like in those places where no one is assigned to lead the ministry of prayer.

WHAT A HOUSE OF PRAYER LOOKS LIKE

Jesus declared in Mark 11:17, "My house will be called a house of prayer for all nations." But what does a house of prayer look like? What did Jesus have in mind when He spoke those words?

Dr. Greg Frizzell explains, "If a restaurant is called a 'House of Fish,' that implies . . . that the predominant practice of that establishment is the cooking and eating of fish. When you call a place a "house of something," you certainly expect that 'something' to be the predominate practice of the establishment. In exactly the same way, if the church is to be a 'house of prayer,' God expects prayer to be its predominate ongoing practice. When a church chooses to become a house of

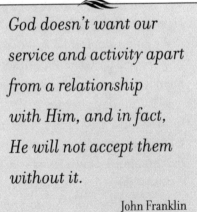

God doesn't want our service and activity apart from a relationship with Him, and in fact, He will not accept them without it.

John Franklin
A House of Prayer

prayer, the practice of prayer literally saturates all it does."[6]

In the context of describing a house of prayer, it is important to define *prayer* so that familiarity with the word doesn't cloud our vision. Oswald Chambers defines prayer as "coming into perfect fellowship and oneness with God."[7] Because a house is "a dwelling place," a house of prayer then is "a dwelling place for God—a place where we abide in perfect communion and intimacy with Him." Out of communion with

Him will come strategies, plans, and power to accomplish the mission of the church.

A Tour of a Virtual House of Prayer

It is 7:00 A.M. on Sunday and twenty-five men have gathered to meet their pastor before the church service. For the next hour they pray over their pastor—that he will preach not with the words of man but in the power of the Holy Spirit. Then together with their pastor, they move throughout the sanctuary praying for the person who will sit in each seat during the upcoming service. Already other intercessors have gathered in the prayer room where they will intercede throughout the entire church service.

When the worship begins, there is an atmosphere of faith and expectation of what the Lord is going to do. Soon after the service begins, the worship leader invites the people to break into small groups and pray for the community surrounding the church, including other pastors and churches in the vicinity. Following the service, people stream to the front of the sanctuary to make confessions of faith and ask for prayer for personal needs. Trained altar prayer ministry teams are already on the front row, prayed-up to help. Church members linger to talk about the Lord and pray with one another.

On Sunday afternoon, three couples meet for lunch. Amid the talk of football, kids, and busy schedules, much of their time is spent excitedly talking about what is happening in their church, miraculous answers to prayer, and testimonies of sharing Christ with strangers and neighbors.

At 9:00 Monday morning, the church receives a call that a nine-year-old boy has been admitted to the hospital for tests and observation. He is running a seriously high fever. Within the hour, the church prayer chain is fully activated and the call for prayer is spreading throughout the church. One of the crisis prayer teams has been notified, and its members are on their way to the hospital to pray on-site.

At 10:00 Tuesday morning, the weekly women's prayer meeting is getting started. One focus today will be interceding for the youth and their schools as the fall semester begins. Meanwhile, the church prayer coordinator is meeting with her pastor to discuss plans for the upcoming staff prayer retreat. Everyone is amazed at how well the staff meetings are going now that they have been spending the first thirty minutes praying over agenda items.

Before the Wednesday night corporate prayer gathering, the pastor meets with a group of fifteen children who serve as a part of his intercessory team. They are planning a trip to the sheriff's office to pray that the Lord would guide and protect him in his line of duty.

Thursday afternoon the church's prayer coordinator hosts a meeting for other prayer leaders from throughout the community. They will pray together and plan the next monthly multichurch prayer and worship gathering.

On Saturday morning the pastor meets with a group of twenty-five men for the monthly men's prayer breakfast. They pray together about being a Christian influence in the workplace. Tomorrow the men will meet their pastor in the sanctuary at 7:00 A.M. to pray for the church services.

Though this church is fictitious, the stories are all true. They come from a composite of churches that are finding new ways to incorporate more prayer into the life of their church.

BIBLICAL SNAPSHOT OF A HOUSE OF PRAYER

If Jesus were to visit your church next Sunday and were given complete freedom to conduct the service, what do you think He would do? This question is worth pondering for more than a few seconds. I'm not sure what would happen, but most likely our agenda would go flying out the window. I think the announcements would be very short.

Well, at least once, Jesus did visit a church and take over the weekend service. Actually it was the temple and it was on the Sabbath day. What did He do?

Matthew 21:12-16 contains this memorable story of Jesus kicking the money changers out of the temple in "righteous anger." I can only imagine what the scene was like. Artists' renditions of this episode depict Jesus with whip in hand, overturning tables and driving out those who were selling at exorbitant prices the supplies required for making temple sacrifices.

In this passage, we discover the progressive steps for building the house of prayer. The first thing Jesus did was cleanse the temple of impure motives and activities, making it a house of *purity* (verse 12). Sometimes before you build a new structure you have to tear down the old. God says He will not pour new wine in old wineskins. Old wineskins can't hold the new things. Don't be surprised if the Lord builds a new "structure" in your church by first demolishing the old.

National prayer leader Wes Tullis says, "When we invite God to dwell in our midst . . . it is an invitation for Him to dismantle everything that the Holy Spirit did not initiate."[8]

Next, in Isaiah 56:7, Jesus reminded us of His Father's words, "My house will be called a house of prayer" (verse 13). Isaiah talks about those who will come to the house of *prayer*. It's a place where the broken, the foreigner, the eunuch can come and worship. This is a place where you will find acceptance no matter what you look like, no matter what your station in life. A church doesn't get to this place unless our hearts are changed. That's one thing that happens when we pray.

What Jesus then demonstrated is that a praying church is a place of *power*. The lame and the blind came to Jesus in the temple, and He healed them (verse 14).

Finally, when the children saw the wonderful miracles that Jesus performed, they cried, "Hosanna to the Son of David" (verse 15). After the church became a house of *power*, it was transformed into a house of *praise* (verse 16). We know that God inhabits the praises of His people. At this point, we can be certain that God's presence filled the temple. I have noticed that praying people are most often worshiping people. Prayer and worship are all about focusing upon the Lord. When we open ourselves up to Him, He will clean us up, fill us up with His nature, and send us out to change the world. We'll see salvations, miracles, liberal giving to the poor, and Christlike living.

House of Prayer, or Prayer Ministry?

It is important here to distinguish between a church with a prayer ministry and one that is a house of prayer. Prayer ministry is a broad term defining a church's strategies for involving their congregation in prayer. A prayer ministry could be as simple or as complex as a church chooses to make it.

Traditional prayer ministries involve only a portion of the congregation, usually those with the greatest desire or burden to pray.

In a true house of prayer, we see prayer saturating every aspect of individual and corporate church life. Communication with our Father is the lifeblood of the church—an indispensable pillar—without which God-given dreams, giftings, and spiritual power lie dormant. In a house of prayer, talking and listening to God characterize worship services, business meetings, and even informal social gatherings. The whole congregation is involved in a lifestyle of drawing near to Him.

Establishing a prayer ministry can be a positive first step toward becoming a house of prayer. However, this can happen only when we realize that a prayer ministry is a means to an end, not an end in itself. God's purposes are hindered when we look at prayer ministry as just another program of the church. Prayer is communion with the living God. Without prayer, the life flow from Christ to His body is cut off; the church ceases to be a living organism and becomes little different from any other organization.

Jesus said in John 15:5, "I am the vine; you are the branches. If a man remains in me and I in him, he will bear much fruit; apart from me you can do nothing."

In the Old Testament, God's house, or temple, was built of stone, but in the New Testament it was built of His people (see Ephesians 2:19-22). The defining characteristic of that new house is that God's very presence would dwell among His people in a love relationship through prayer. No record exists in Scripture of another way God prefers to relate to His people.

Having a praying church is not just a good idea; it is the foundation from which everything else flows.

seven marks of a praying church

But how do we measure whether or not we have a praying church? What does one look like? The following are seven signs or marks of a praying church:

1. Most members have a strong devotional prayer life and are committed to praying for others.

> *I know it's easy for pastors to think, "Don't talk to me about another ministry I have to organize and promote. My plate is full already!" However, developing a strong prayer ministry will actually make your other ministries more effective.*
>
> Dr. Gregory Frizzell
> *How to Build an Effective Prayer Ministry*

2. Church members have a biblical understanding of who God is and how they can relate personally to Him through prayer.

3. Leaders are praying people and set an example of prayer for the congregation.

4. Prayer is a way of life throughout the church. Rather than being seen as an isolated program, prayer permeates every ministry within the church and every outreach of the church.

5. Corporate prayer meetings are given high priority in the lives of the church leadership and congregation.

6. Spending time in the presence of the Lord produces humility, purity, unity, compassion, and Christlikeness in the lives of leaders and the congregation.

7. God's presence fills His house. Perhaps the single most distinguishing characteristic of a "house of prayer" is that it is filled with the tangible presence of God. A lack of spiritual appetite in the congregation is replaced by spiritual hunger. Unbelievers' hearts are converted by the life-giving messages preached from the pulpit. The spiritual objectives of the church begin to move forward, not so much by human ingenuity and hard work as by the supernatural assistance of God's Holy Spirit. Striving ceases; it often seems more is accomplished with less effort.

Don't be discouraged if your church doesn't possess all of these qualities. Not many do. Instead, take a look at these characteristics and prayerfully and honestly survey the prayer life of your church.

MAKING ROOM FOR HIM

It was 8:30 Sunday morning. Hal and I were sitting in a service at Skyway Church in west Phoenix. The service was taking a "house of prayer" format—the whole service was going to be devoted to prayer. The guest speaker, Esther Ilnisky, spoke for a few minutes and then invited children and youth to join the adults on the platform to help lead the prayer meeting.

"Would you pray over all the hurting and abused children in the world?" Esther asked, handing the microphone to a five-year-old boy. With stammering lips and a shaking voice, the child began to pray. As he continued to pray over his generation, I was amazed at his clarity and focus.

"God, make the mothers and fathers stop fighting," he prayed. "Tell them it's hurting their kids."

Then with tears streaming down his face, he fell to his knees. He wept uncontrollably and finally laid prostrate on the platform with his face in his hands. Several young children moved to pray for and comfort him as the prayer meeting continued.

A young girl prayed, "God, tell the parents to stop killing our brothers and sisters through abortion."

Another child prayed for the salvation of young people who did not know Christ. Others prayed for revival in their schools and that our nation would return to Christ. The simplicity of their prayers accompanied by humility and brokenness brought tremendous conviction to our hearts.

It was now time for the second service. Pastor Greg Brown looked at the platform filled with some two dozen children, teenagers, and adults crying out for change in their world. He obviously was trying to decide whether or not to stick to the church's schedule.

Then he took the microphone and instructed the ushers to stand at the door and tell people who were coming into the second service what was happening.

"Tell them it will not be church as usual today," he said.

The first service melted into the second, and the extraordinary move of God did not end until after 2:00 P.M. When you ask God to make your church a house of prayer, be prepared for change. You may be wonderfully surprised by what He will do.

THE HOUSE OF PRAYER

Building a successful prayer ministry is an important goal for any church. However, this is only the beginning. God's heart is after something more. His desire is that your congregation will be known as a house of prayer—a habitation for His presence and glory that transcends the walls of your church.

The goal is for prayer to saturate every aspect of the individual and corporate life of the church. In this stage, the whole congregation becomes consumed with a passion for intimacy with Christ that spills over into the entire community.

It is like the dream the prayer leader at First Baptist Church in Boerne, Texas, shared with me: "All of a sudden it began to rain in the sanctuary. The people were rejoicing. They didn't seem to mind the rain at all! As the worship became sweeter and the prayer more fervent, the water kept getting higher and higher. Then someone opened the door and the water began to flow out of the church and into the street. It touched everything in its path—homes, other churches, people without Christ. And everywhere the water flowed, there was life."

I believe this dream is symbolic of what God is about to do with His houses of prayer. He is calling the church to a place of intimacy with Him. As we respond by inviting the presence of the Lord into our midst, we will see the power of God transform our churches, communities, and world.

I hear the Lord asking, "Who will help Me build this house of prayer?" Is it you?

---

1. Terry Teykl, *Making Room to Pray* (Muncie, Ind.: Prayer Point Press, 1993), p. 13.

2. Telephone interview conducted by Cheryl Sacks with Carolyn Fuqua, January 9, 2004.

3. From a personal e-mail from Rachelle Gardner from Cindy Moe, September 22, 2003.

4. Frank Damazio, "Restoring Prayer to the Local Church," NALCPL convention, Colorado Springs, Colo., June 2002.

5. Dutch Sheets, *Intercessory Prayer* (Ventura, Calif.: Regal, 1996), p. 29.

6. Dr. Gregory Frizzell, *How to Build an Evangelistic Church Prayer Ministry* (Nashville: Tennessee Baptist Convention, 1999), pp. 2–3.

7. Oswald Chambers, *My Utmost for His Highest* (Grand Rapids, Mich.: Discovery House Publisher, 1992), daily reading, September 16.

8. Conversation between Cheryl Sacks and Wes Tullis, Colorado Springs, Colo., April 25, 1995.

CHAPTER 2

The Role of the Church Prayer Coordinator

Darla Cruz lay on the old ragged carpet in the storage room of her church—praying. Tears rolling down her face, she cried out to God for her pastor, church leadership, and families in the congregation.

This evening on her way home from work, at the prompting of the Holy Spirit, Darla had stopped by the church to pray—something she had begun to do daily. Even with her busy schedule as a real estate agent, wife, and mother of two small children, Darla could not resist the call of the Holy Spirit to intercede for Pettisville Missionary Church.

She had looked for a room she could quietly slip into and pray unnoticed. However, it seemed every room in the church was taken. Finally she discovered a storage room located just to the side of the main sanctuary. This had become Darla's prayer room.

In the weeks that followed, praying after work just didn't seem to be enough. Darla found herself stopping by the church to pray between appointments and on her lunch hour. Soon the pastoral and office staff noticed Darla, and they began to stop by the storage room to ask for prayer.

Recognizing that God was calling Darla to spend more time in prayer for the church, Darla's husband suggested she quit her full-time job and take one that required her to work fewer hours. The couple realized this would put a financial strain on the family, but they stepped out in faith. Miraculously, God provided while Darla spent 50 percent of her work day at the church, volunteering her time as a prayer coordinator.

One day the pastor asked Darla to attend the upcoming church council meeting. There the board announced their approval to hire Darla to a part-time staff position. One and one-half years later, Darla became the full-time director of prayer ministries. While she still spent numerous hours in prayer each week, she also coordinated the ongoing prayer efforts of hundreds of church members and was instrumental in the training and motivation of countless new prayer warriors.

* * * * * *

In 1986, Fielder Road Baptist Church's prayer ministry consisted of a small prayer room and a handful of volunteers who prayed over a stack of prayer requests, sadly often many months old.

Like other prayer ministries in churches across the nation in the 1980s, this one needed attention, the kind of attention that could come only through a called and dedicated church prayer leader.

The call would be answered by a man who might seem an unlikely candidate: Tim Tremaine, a police officer for the Arlington, Texas, police department.

Tim had a long history of serving, teaching, and training others at Fielder Road Baptist Church, where he had been a member for eleven years. As he grew in his personal prayer life, Tim became more and more interested in praying for the city of Arlington and for the nation. Before long he was helping coordinate citywide prayer events, such as the National Day of Prayer.

As churches in the Arlington area began to catch the vision for prayer, Tim longed for his church to be included. He prayed that Fielder Road Baptist Church would become more of "a house of prayer" and would link arms in prayer with other churches in the city. One day Tim felt God was asking him to be the answer to his own prayer.

When he met with his pastor and volunteered to be the church prayer coordinator, the pastor wholeheartedly embraced the idea. During the next four years, Tim spent his evenings and weekends developing a model prayer ministry—"one that offered as many prayer options as possible so that no one would feel left out," he explains. Later Tim was hired to a part-time staff position while still holding his full-time job at the police department.

* * * * * *

These stories are not unique. All across America, God is calling people like Darla and Tim to become their church's point person for the ministry of prayer. They are assisting their pastors in successfully mobilizing their churches to pray.

In this chapter we will look at the role of the church prayer coordinator. Although some people differentiate between the terms "prayer coordinator" and "prayer leader," I am using the terms synonymously to describe the person given oversight of the church's prayer ministry.

You may be reading this book as a pastor, a newly appointed prayer leader, a prayer team member, or simply someone interested in building a house of prayer. Whatever your position, use this discussion of the prayer leader's characteristics to help guide your thinking and planning for the next step.

Webster's dictionary defines *role* as "character or function." In the following pages you will learn what characteristics to look for when selecting a prayer coordinator as well as what functions they perform in the local church.

THE CHURCH PRAYER LEADER

You may be asking, "Is a prayer coordinator really necessary?"

Yes! Just as every other ministry in the church has a leader, so the prayer ministry needs a designated person to coordinate prayer. Too often we think prayer will happen on its own. If we are to be a praying church, however, we must be intentional about mobilizing prayer. The selection of a church prayer

> *The prayer leader should be a member of the church who organizes, schedules, and provides general leadership for all the church's prayer activities. Together with the pastor, the prayer leader gives energy and direction to the church's prayer organization.*
>
> Bjorn Pedersen
> *Face to Face with God in Your Church*

leader is foundational to this process.

Prayer leaders ensure that intercession is raised up not only for pastors but also for children, youth, marriages, missions, and more. Their role is to see that prayer is integrated into the total life of the church.

Appointing and publicly recognizing a prayer coordinator is vital for any church that wants to establish a separate prayer ministry. Appointing a coordinator:

- signals to the church that prayer is important
- brings attention to the ministry
- ensures that prayer has an intentional place in the church
- ensures that the ministry will not fade or be forgotten
- provides a way to recruit ministry participants and to encourage greater participation in prayer[1]

The prayer leader's title may vary. I've seen everything from "prayer coordinator" to "director of prayer ministries" to "pastor of prayer." The position may be filled by a full- or part-time paid staff member, or a volunteer. (The smaller the church and the less developed the prayer ministry, the more likely your starting prayer coordinator will be a volunteer as opposed to a staff member.)

Because the position of prayer leader is new to many churches, I frequently hear the question "How do we select the right person?" The inclination when selecting a prayer leader is to choose a member of the congregation with the greatest gifting and desire to pray. However, this might not be the best person for the job. If that prayer warrior also has administrative gifts and the ability to mobilize others, the ministry has a better chance.

CHARACTERISTICS OF A SUCCESSFUL PRAYER LEADER

Studying the following qualifications will help a pastoral staff select a church prayer coordinator; or if you're thinking about volunteering yourself, this will help you discern whether you're the right person for the job.

CALLED BY GOD

The opening stories in this chapter illustrate how God is sovereignly calling specific individuals to the position of local church prayer coordinator. Perhaps being called by God is the most important of all the characteristics of a prayer leader.

The best way for a pastor to choose the right person for the job is to take time to pray and ask the Lord who He has set aside for the position. Just as you might call for an all-church time of prayer and fasting before hiring a worship leader, it's worthwhile to invest some prayer to discover who God is calling to lead your prayer ministry.

> *The first thing a potential prayer leader must do is answer this important question: "Is this just something I want to do, or is this something God is calling me to do?"*
>
> Joe Guinnip, prayer coordinator
> Covenant of Grace, Phoenix

Hopefully, a time of prayer will reveal the name of a potential coordinator. When you're ready to approach him, it may be helpful to share your vision and then ask the person to pray about whether or not God would have him accept the position. Asking the potential coordinator to pray about God's will before accepting the position ties his accountability ultimately to God.[2]

You may be a church member thinking about starting a prayer ministry, in which case you'll have to approach the pastor, rather than vice versa. Chapter 3 has more detailed information for you if you're in this situation; nevertheless, it's still wise to begin the process with personal prayer, seeking God's guidance and confirmation of what He wants you to do.

Remember when Moses had an encounter with God at the burning bush? The Lord said, "So now, go. I am sending you" (Exodus 3:10). And in Exodus 4:12, the Lord further tells Moses, "Now go; I will help you speak and will teach you what to say." If you're a prayer coordinator, you'll possibly encounter times of challenge, frustration, and burnout. If you can't go back to a burning bush experience, you'll be tempted to quit.

In some cases a potential prayer leader may not sense God's call personally, but other church leaders recognize the gifting and spiritual readiness of that individual. The pastor can explain to the individual why it seems he is the appropriate person and then (without pressure) let him decide whether he thinks it's the right decision or not.

If you are considering accepting the job of prayer leader, ask the Lord to search your heart and expose any wrong motives. Don't accept the position just to please others—even if it is your pastor, spouse, or trusted friend. John 12:43 speaks to this issue about the Pharisees: "for they loved praise from men more than praise from God."

Additionally, we always have to be wary of accepting a position in order to receive status or power: "And when you pray, do not be like the hypocrites, for they love to pray standing in the synagogues and on the street corners to be seen by men" (Matthew 6:5).

A HEALTHY PERSONAL PRAYER LIFE

Does the person have a passion for prayer? This is one sign that God has worked in the individual's heart to prepare him for this assignment. The prayer coordinator must have a strong personal prayer life in order to lead with authority. You can lead people only to a depth in prayer that you have explored yourself. People may think you are a great prayer warrior, but only you and the Lord know your true devotion to prayer.

Praying people are the building blocks to a "house of prayer." Therefore, the one who leads the prayer ministry must be first and foremost a person devoted to prayer—one who can set an example for others. A devotion to prayer for the leader is further important because the prayer ministry will not be built through creative ideas and strategies alone. God Himself must blow the breath of life upon the endeavor if it is going to work. God's Spirit and power are released primarily through prayer.

SPIRITUAL MATURITY

Spiritual maturity is an important qualification for a prayer leader. First Timothy 3:6 admonishes that anyone selected for church leadership should not be a recent convert or he may become conceited. The person should have been a believer for a while, but there is no hard-and-fast rule as far as length of time. Furthermore, it is essential that the leader is well-grounded in the Word of God. The prayer leader may be managing intercessors who have a passion for prayer but who lack knowledge of God's Word and are therefore susceptible to error. Leaders who understand the patterns and principles found in the Bible can keep pray-ers and prayer meetings on target.

Prayer leaders also need discernment, which comes through experience. Solomon prayed, "Give your servant a discerning heart to govern your people and to distinguish between right and wrong" (1 Kings 3:9). Wendy Ryan, prayer coordinator for Oro Valley Nazarene Church in Tucson, Arizona, shares the following examples regarding the need for discernment:

> *Each week I make up a prayer request/praise report sheet that is distributed to members of our congregation. One day I received a frantic call from a mother in our congregation asking me to include on the prayer sheet a request for prayer for her teenage son who had been picked up on a DUI charge. I asked whether or not to include her son's name in the request, and without reservation she said yes. After prayer I sensed I was not to mention the teenager's name. The request was posted, "Pray for someone in our church who has been charged with a DUI."*[3]

On another occasion, Wendy received a call from a woman asking for prayer regarding her marriage. The woman confided that she feared her husband was having an affair. Wisely, the request on the prayer sheet was worded, "Pray for a troubled marriage in the church."

LEADERSHIP GIFTS

As mentioned earlier, it is essential that a love for prayer in the prayer leader be coupled with gifts to lead, organize, and mobilize. Many prayer ministries have failed because the pastor has chosen the church's most visible prayer warrior as the leader. Confusion in this area can be alleviated when we understand the difference between the gifts of the intercessor and the prayer coordinator.

Though every Christian should desire to spend extensive time with the Lord, intercessors feel called to prayer as their personal ministry. While other people are serving in the nursery or leading a men's group, many intercessors see their service to the Lord and to the local church as time spent in prayer. When pastors see this extraordinary gift in an individual, they understandably desire to see her used to the fullest.

Though spending hours in the prayer closet is a high calling, this alone does not make for a good prayer coordinator. When an intercessor leads the prayer ministry, she often has tunnel vision, seeing the prayer ministry as a weekly prayer meeting rather than a multifaceted, churchwide ministry. Prayer coordinators are most effective when they possess gifts not only to pray but also to mobilize people, organize events, lead meetings, and represent the church in communitywide prayer efforts.

If the person you are considering for the job doesn't have the necessary leadership skills, then either God is not calling that individual, or his skills will have to be developed.

ABILITY TO SPEAK/TEACH

A prayer coordinator's role is enhanced when she feels at ease in teaching and speaking before people. If the prayer leader is not gifted in this area, then it will be important to invite someone with the gift of teaching to serve on the prayer ministry leadership team.

The speaking/teaching gift is important because training is key to mobilization. Many Christians admit that the real reason they don't attend prayer meetings and other prayer events is because they don't feel comfortable with their personal prayer skills. Children, youth, intercessors, new converts, and many others in the church family need more training in the basics of prayer. One role of the prayer coordinator is to ensure that those teaching in other ministries of the church receive resources and training to equip them to teach on prayer.

A TEAM PLAYER

Much of the success of the prayer ministry will depend upon the prayer coordinator's ability to develop and work with a prayer leadership team. From my experience, the single most critical mistake the church prayer leader makes is attempting to do the job alone. Developing a strong leadership team is critical so that responsibilities are shared and all the giftings needed to run the prayer ministry are present.

One quick look at the list of prayer leader responsibilities would cause anyone in his right mind to shy away from the job—unless he realizes his job is not to perform all the tasks but rather to find and equip others to lead those areas of ministry.

A GOOD REPUTATION

Another quality required of a prayer leader is a good reputation and the confidence of the church leadership. Leaders who walk in integrity earn the trust of others. Does the person being considered for the position influence others by his lifestyle as well as his words?

Because of the sensitive prayer requests prayer leaders handle, they also must be able to hold a confidence and teach others to do so. Prayer ministries have been ruined because someone betrayed a confidence in prayer. David prayed, "Set a guard over my mouth, O LORD; keep watch over the door of my lips" (Psalm 141:3).

THE ABILITY TO LEAD PRAYER

The prayer coordinator must have the ability to lead or learn to lead small-group and corporate prayer. Dynamic prayer meetings usually don't just happen. They require leaders who are prepared and equipped. If a prayer coordinator leads prayer meetings successfully, she'll have the respect of the other intercessors.

Leading prayer is primarily learned through experience and sitting under good role models; therefore, a leader who is sensitive, discerning, and assertive can learn the principles of leading prayer.

A SERVANT'S HEART AND A TEACHABLE SPIRIT

Good prayer leaders facilitate development in others through being a servant. They take more of their share of the blame and less of their share of the credit. One prayer leader I know suggests leading by example.

"I never ask anyone to do something I wouldn't do myself," she says. "For example, I wouldn't ask one of my team members to take the 2:00 A.M. prayer slot while I take the one at 10 A.M. I wouldn't ask him to write prayergrams while I take the day off."

Prayer leaders also must demonstrate a heart for submitting to authority, receiving correction, trying new things, and receiving further training. We are reminded in 1 Peter 5:5, "God opposes the proud but gives grace to the humble."

TIME TO COORDINATE PRAYER ACTIVITIES

It takes time for the church prayer leader to coordinate the activities of the prayer ministry and attend key prayer events in the church and the community, so it's important to select a person who has the time available. Of course, job responsibilities must be realistic and volunteers cannot be expected to work full-time—though some may choose to. Those with full-time jobs outside the church may find it difficult to handle the position, especially if they have families and other commitments. However, God has many ways of working things out, so if the best candidate has numerous time limitations, that person may need to be even more reliant on a team. Larger churches with well-developed prayer ministries will want to consider hiring the prayer leader at least on a part-time basis.

Sometimes an associate pastor is asked to take on the responsibilities of prayer coordination. Usually his plate is already full, and prayer becomes something that is "tacked on" to the job description. At other churches, prayer ministry coordination is assigned to the pastor in charge of hospital visitation because he has a heart to pray for and care for the flock. Still, he may not have the time, desire, or gifting to lead the church's prayer ministry. At some point, you'll want to go through the process of praying and making a well-thought-out appointment of your prayer coordinator.

When a "pastor of prayer" is called, gifted, and given sufficient time to lead the church's prayer ministry, then he can be a great choice for the job. Usually the pastor of prayer is an ordained minister and this alone elevates the position in the eyes of the congregation. Still, to make certain that prayer saturates every area of the church, the pastor of prayer will find it advantageous to build a prayer action team (described in chapter 4). In addition, appointing a church prayer coordinator to work alongside the pastor of prayer may be the best scenario for ensuring that prayer becomes the highest priority in your church.

DISPELLING THE MYTHS ABOUT
PRAYER COORDINATORS

Wendy Ryan shares three things she has discovered are not her responsibility as a church prayer coordinator. In talking with other prayer leaders,

I have found that many have fallen prey to the same fallacies that made their way into Wendy's thinking. Let's dispel these myths.

Myth #1: *The prayer coordinator is the person who prays for all of the congregation's prayer requests.*

You are not to carry the prayer load of the entire church on your shoulders. This misconception is held by many prayer leaders and their pastors as well. Wendy shares how easy it is to fall into this subtle entrapment:

"As the prayer coordinator, I would have people come up to me in the church courtyard on Sunday morning and say, 'Wendy, would you pray for me? My husband is having a biopsy next Tuesday.' This would be just one of many requests I would get throughout the week. It was the very way they formulated the question that caused me to adopt this belief that it was my responsibility to carry the whole prayer load for the church, the city, and the nation.

"I had to change the way I processed the request. I began to tell myself to put this request on the prayer sheet that goes out to everyone in the church and pass along the request to the captain of the prayer chain and make the intercessory prayer groups aware of this prayer need."[4]

Myth #2: *The prayer coordinator is responsible for "getting" people to the prayer meeting.*

The prayer leader may encourage people to pray, make opportunities for them to pray, and educate them in how to pray, but ultimately it is the work of the Holy Spirit to draw people to the place of prayer. Ezekiel 36:27 says, "And I will put my Spirit in you and move you to follow my decrees and be careful to keep my laws."

Motivating people to pray is much the same as leading someone to Christ. We may share with another the plan of salvation, give our personal testimony, and pray for her to come to Christ; however, salvation is a spiritual transformation that only God can bring forth.

First Corinthians 3:6-7 tells us, "I planted the seed, Apollos watered it, but God made it grow. So neither he who plants nor he who waters is anything, but only God, who makes things grow."

It is good to remember that no matter what you do, you cannot make the prayer ministry grow, nor can you perform enough acrobatic tricks to get people to attend a prayer meeting. Only God can make things grow. This is the reason that first and foremost you and your team must spend extended time praying for God to give you favor, anointing, and direction for the job, and that He will make your church "a house of prayer." Trying to do the work of the Holy Spirit is a sure formula for burnout.

Myth #3: *It is the role of the prayer leader to finance his own training, resources, travel, supplies, and materials.*

If you have been appointed as your church prayer coordinator, it is the responsibility of the church to pay for your training and materials. This is true whether you are paid staff or a volunteer.

The best way to make sure that this happens is to put together an annual prayer ministry budget and submit it to your pastor and appropriate church committee or board. The budget may be only $300–$500 the first year, but it helps your church leadership plan ahead. Presenting a budget helps your leaders and congregation see the whole vision for the prayer ministry rather than getting piecemeal requests for small budget items throughout the year. (Chapter 7 explains the planning and budgeting process in detail.)

Asking the church to pick up your expenses makes leaders aware that the prayer ministry takes money to run, just like any other ministry in the church. It reminds them that your time is valuable even if you're a volunteer.

If your church is really struggling financially and unable to purchase the materials you need or the admission to a training conference, it would be better to make a donation to the church and let them write the check than to go on paying for everything out of your own pocket.

Prayer Leader responsibilities

A prayer leader's job description is best developed by the pastor and prayer leader jointly. The following list of prayer leader responsibilities is given as a guide rather than a checklist.

Don't let this list overwhelm you. If yours is a new prayer ministry, you may be able to take on only two or three of these activities. It will probably take years for a prayer leader to develop such a comprehensive prayer ministry.

In addition, remember that this list of responsibilities does not belong to you alone but to your team as well. The following are responsibilities the prayer leader may fulfill, delegate, or oversee (see appendix A for a sample prayer coordinator job description):

- Identify key people in the church who are willing to pray or serve in leadership of the prayer ministry, and enlist their support.
- Establish a prayer action team and serve as the team leader. The leadership responsibilities of the prayer ministry can be divided among the members of the prayer team.
- Act as a liaison between the pastor and church leadership and the prayer action team.
- Assist the pastoral staff to raise up their personal intercessory prayer support teams.
- Colabor with the prayer action team and church leadership to establish prayer for corporate services.
- Work with the pastor and prayer team to develop a mission statement for the prayer ministry and a prayer strategy for the church.
- Aid the development of a prayer chain.
- Create a resource library on prayer.
- Provide Sunday school teachers and small-group leaders with training, materials, and resources for prayer.
- Help plan and organize special prayer events in the church (such as prayer conferences, workshops, and National Day of Prayer events).
- Train and equip prayer leaders who can establish and lead small-group prayer.
- Set up (with prayer team and church leadership) a prayer room in the church.
- Create an information network that keeps everyone informed of prayer concerns.

- Serve as a liaison between your local church and churches citywide to foster cooperative prayer efforts.
- Ensure that prayer is mobilized and integrated into every ministry and department of the church.

QUESTIONS PRAYER COORDINATORS MOST FREQUENTLY ASK

I don't feel qualified to serve as my church prayer coordinator. Should I resign? If not, where can I go for more training?

Most prayer coordinators I have talked with don't feel qualified for the job. However, it is a good thing to ask yourself this question. Read carefully again the characteristics of a prayer coordinator, and prayerfully take inventory. Identify the specific skills and qualifications you lack and let your pastor know you'd like to become better trained. If you feel deficient in many areas, it's possible you're not the right person for the job. You may be better positioned as a member on the prayer leadership team, overseeing one aspect of prayer rather than leading the whole ministry.

Only a few materials exist that are designed specifically to help church prayer leaders fulfill their roles. This book has been written as a response to the cry for help from many prayer leaders such as yourself. At the end of this book, you'll find a list of additional helpful resources.

Pray! magazine is an excellent resource for local church prayer leaders. Every issue contains inspirational, practical stories and ideas that will prove indispensable in mobilizing your church to pray. The *PrayKids!* section of the magazine offers excellent prayer curriculum for you and your children's workers. *Pray!'s* popular booklet titled *My House Shall Be Called a House of Prayer* is another great help for church prayer leaders.

Join the Church Prayer Leaders Network (CPLN), which is managed by *Pray!*. It hosts national and regional conferences for local church prayer leaders annually. Its website (www.prayerleader.com) and book and tape library will provide you with teachings from the best speakers in the nation on the subject of local church prayer mobilization.

Finally, I recommend that you connect with or start a Local Church

Prayer Leaders Network in your city. This will allow you and other prayer leaders the opportunity to network, share resources, pray together, and receive training from local and national prayer leaders and speakers. We started a network in Arizona in 1996, and today several hundred local church prayer leaders are involved from throughout the state. Information on how to start a local network can be found in appendix B and on the Prayer Tools CD.

I'm frustrated because I can't seem to get the people in my church interested in prayer or in the prayer ministry. What can I do to motivate them?

How exciting it would be to walk into your church and discover that it is packed, not just for a church service but for a prayer meeting. We would all like to host prayer meetings like the one Jim Cymbala, pastor of the Brooklyn Tabernacle in New York City, holds every Tuesday night. As described in his book *Fresh Wind, Fresh Fire*, the meetings are often standing room only.[5]

However, holding an all-church corporate prayer meeting is not the only way to get your congregation praying. The key is to offer a variety of prayer options. Set meetings at different times of the day to accommodate work and family schedules. Offer opportunities to pray in large groups, in small groups, with prayer partners on the telephone, for requests taken from the Internet, and in church meetings the people already attend.

Many Christians say they don't pray or attend prayer meetings because they don't feel adequate to pray. Training is, therefore, an integral part of motivating people to pray. The seed of God's Word must be planted in the hearts of the people. This can be accomplished through the pastor preaching on prayer and by offering prayer training in Sunday school classes, seminars, and conferences.

Link opportunities for prayer with everyday situations in life, and the interest level of your congregation will rise. Examples of this are seminars on such topics as How to Pray for Your Children, Praying with Your Spouse, or Praying for Success in the Marketplace. For more on how to teach and motivate your church to pray, read chapter 9.

1. Bjorn Pedersen, *Face to Face with God in Your Church: Establishing a Prayer Ministry* (Minneapolis: Augsburg, 1995), p. 60.

2. John Franklin, *A House of Prayer* (Nashville: LifeWay Press, 1999), p. 18.

3. Wendy Ryan, "The Role of the Church Prayer Coordinator," PrayerQuake, Phoenix, 2002.

4. Ryan.

5. Jim Cymbala, *Fresh Wind, Fresh Fire* (Grand Rapids, Mich.: Zondervan, 1997), pp. 53, 184.

CHAPTER 3

The Pastor/Prayer Leader Relationship

I have been training hundreds of church prayer coordinators and prayer team members throughout America for the past several years. Frequently, I ask prayer leaders and their pastors to share their greatest frustrations in working together.

Prayer leaders inevitably share their need for more pastoral support. They say it's disheartening to work alongside a pastor who says prayer is a priority but in reality is too busy to offer time and resources to prayer events and the prayer ministry.

Pastors talk about feeling pressured by expectations in the face of already-packed schedules. Many feel as though they're tagged as "unspiritual" by prayer leaders and intercessors. They say the overall well-being of the church is damaged when prayer leaders exhibit an attitude of superiority because of their dedication to prayer. Instead of feeling supported and blessed by the prayer leader and prayer ministry, the pastor often feels put down or alienated.

The success of any church ministry is dependent upon the positive working relationship between the pastor and the ministry leader. Pastors and prayer coordinators need each other, and the prayer ministry's chance of succeeding is better if they genuinely demonstrate mutual support for one another.

Most pastors need their prayer leaders to add an element of organization to their visions. Statistics show that 80 percent of pastors don't have gifts of administration. The pastor needs someone to implement and manage the church's prayer strategy, do research on what is happening in the prayer movement and keep him informed, and pray for him personally.

Prayer leaders need pastors to broadcast the prayer vision to the entire congregation. Prayer leaders don't have pulpits. Their ideas are likely to get stuck in a little committee unless the pastor owns the prayer vision and is willing to promote it to the broader body. Only the pastor can stir hunger in the entire congregation by teaching on prayer and sharing powerful answers to prayer in the worship services. In addition, pastors carry the authority to help prayer leaders obtain funding and facilities for the prayer ministry.

For pastors and prayer leaders to develop this kind of strong partnership, communication lines need to be kept open and expectations clearly defined. Scheduling an initial meeting is a good place to start.

THE INITIAL MEETING BETWEEN THE PASTOR AND PRAYER LEADER

Soon after the prayer coordinator has been appointed, it will be important for the pastor and prayer coordinator to meet to share their visions and set a course of action. If you're the newly appointed prayer leader, don't wait for your pastor to call the meeting—be proactive and take the initiative.

As the prayer coordinator, ideally you'll want several important things to happen in this initial meeting. Following are some guidelines to help you structure your discussion.

COMMUNICATE SUPPORT

Your first order of business is to find out what's on your pastor's heart, how you can pray for him, and what you can do to lighten his load in carrying the existing prayer agenda. Let him know that you are interested in learning more about his vision for prayer and for the church. Assure him that you want to help him fulfill the vision God has given him—that you're not out to promote your own agenda.

Communicate excitement about the future of the prayer ministry.

This is not the time to pour out your frustrations about the prayer ministry, lack of a prayer emphasis, and everything you see that's wrong in the church. Let your pastor talk, and take note of what he feels is important. At some point you will have the opportunity to share your dreams, and if your pastor asks you to do so in this meeting, it would be appropriate.

DEFINE ROLES AND EXPECTATIONS

Discuss your pastor's expectations of you as prayer coordinator. Find out how many hours a week he expects you to be present at the church or working at home, and to whom you are to report. Discuss your job description, taking notes on his ideas. You can type up the job description later, and you both can sign it. (A sample job description is available in appendix A.) Make a note that you'll want to reevaluate your job description at least annually.

It is equally important to discuss what the pastor sees as his role in leading the church body into a deeper place in prayer. Defining both your role and his will help alleviate future confusion and disappointment. It is important to establish that this endeavor is a partnership.

AGREE UPON PRIORITIES

Early in the process you will want to discuss the need to establish a prayer leadership team and to develop a church prayer strategy. You will want to secure your pastor's commitment for budget support for the prayer ministry as well. It is easier to secure support for these needs in this early stage rather than later. (Later chapters give more information on how to build a prayer action team, prepare a prayer ministry budget, and develop a prayer strategy.)

Because it will take time to complete these goals, it will be important for you and your pastor to agree upon immediate priorities as well.

SET A REGULAR MEETING SCHEDULE

Most likely you will need more than one meeting to lay the foundation for a working relationship with your pastor. Even after the groundwork is in place, you'll need to communicate with your pastor on an ongoing basis. Ask what the possibility is of meeting regularly with your pastor. The meeting could be biweekly, monthly, or bimonthly, and last from thirty minutes to an hour. In the busy life of a church, unless meetings are on the calendar, they often fall through the cracks.

CONSIDER THE IMPORTANCE OF SUPPORT FROM CHURCH LEADERS

The first meeting is a good time to discuss with your pastor some ways for getting all of the church leadership united in the vision of becoming a praying church. Most pastors and church leaders desire that their churches become houses of prayer; however, they may be too overwhelmed by their demanding schedules to give the vision any attention.

John Franklin, in his book *A House of Prayer,* calls prayer leaders to make a realistic assessment of how much support they can expect from their church leadership. With full support of the pastor and church leaders, the vision of prayer for the church has a great chance of thriving. In the long run, the Lord may use your faithfulness to sway the hearts of your church leaders, but the process will take much longer.

> *For many churches, one of the biggest roadblocks to increased prayer is the indifference of—or even opposition from—its leaders (elders, deacons, board members). Many leaders simply do not recognize the importance of prayer to the life of a church.*
>
> David Butts
> *My House Shall Be a House of Prayer*

WHAT IF CHURCH LEADERS DON'T SHARE YOUR VISION?

First, it's important to discern why your leaders don't have a heart for prayer. Is it apathy, burnout, busyness, lack of vision, spiritual coldness, or spiritual warfare? Maybe all the good things the church is accomplishing are crowding out the priority of prayer in the church or its leadership.

The first thing you can do is pray. Ask God to help your pastor and church leaders catch the vision for prayer—not your vision, but the Lord's. As you do so, you'll want to keep a careful watch over your heart and mouth so that your own attitude stays pure.

Second, you could suggest your pastor and church board plan a retreat to pray and talk about what it would take to make your church more of a praying church. Bring in someone they all respect to share the vision of a praying church.

Third, you can encourage your leaders to read a book or attend a conference on prayer. Many pastors across the nation are gaining a renewed interest in prayer as they attend weekly pastors' prayer meetings and pastors' prayer summits in their city. You also can plan a prayer conference in your church and invite a pastor or prayer leader with a powerful vision for local church prayer to come and speak.

Lastly, if you sense your pastor is overwhelmed with his workload, a strategy for lightening his load is needed. This may require the involvement of other church leaders, the church board, and lay leaders who can help shift the pastor's workload. Prayer leaders must not go around their pastor's back to make this happen, but they can pray and even make suggestions to their pastor where there is mutual respect and receptivity.

"FOR PASTORS ONLY"

PASTORS SPEAK UP ABOUT WHAT NOT TO DELEGATE

The story is told of a busy businessman who hired a landscaper to design and plant a garden for the backyard of his new home. The homeowner commissioned the landscaper to select plants that required no attention and requested a completely automatic sprinkler system. (He didn't want to be bothered with watering.) The man repeatedly told his landscaper that he wanted a lawn that was maintenance-free. In addition to being too busy to give attention to his garden, the homeowner was not even available to help make selections or give input in the decision-making process. Finally, in frustration, the landscaper said to the homeowner, "Let's get one thing straight: If there is no gardener, there is no garden."

Pastors who desire to establish praying churches can delegate many responsibilities to their associates and prayer leaders; however, scores of pastors across the nation confirm that some things just can't be delegated.

After talking with pastors about their role in calling their church to prayer, the following guidelines emerged:

1. **Develop an authentic prayer life.** Statistics indicate that many pastors pray about five minutes a day. As pastors, our efforts to establish a praying church will be in a strong position from the beginning if we have started the building process with our own lives. A personal belief in the power of prayer is fundamental.

2. **Take ownership for the prayer ministry.** We are the primary initiators of the vision, and motivators of the people. Our efforts at becoming houses of prayer will be spurred by our own ability to have a clear vision, preach about it, promote it in the church, and celebrate it through prayer events and activities.

3. **Mentor and disciple the prayer leaders.** When we become invested in their lives, they are strengthened and enabled to carry out our church's vision for prayer. Mentor them in prayer, mentor them in the values of the church, and mentor them in leadership.

4. **Build and maintain rapport with the prayer leaders of your church.** It's not a task—it's a relationship. The prayer ministry will grow out of these connections. Try not to delegate the entire ministry to a prayer coordinator with the words, "Call me if you have any problems." Your prayer leaders will be motivated and inspired to the extent that you take a real interest in them.

Leonard Griffin, pastor of Covenant of Grace, tells the story of how he learned this lesson. His prayer ministry was experiencing conflicts, power struggles, and accusations.

"At first I just wanted to close down the prayer ministry. Then I realized this was happening because I had spent no time with the prayer leaders. I didn't take time to get them on board with the church's vision. It's no wonder they developed their own agenda."

Leonard does things differently now. "Two years before I appointed my present prayer leader, I recognized he was a potential prayer leader candidate. My wife and I began spending time with him and his wife. I took him through a discipleship program. More than the information that was being imparted, I realized that the greater value was the time we spent talking about the vision of the church and praying together."[1]

ways pastors can support prayer Leaders

- Give the prayer coordinator the same level of respect as you do your worship leader, youth pastor, or Christian education director, even if your prayer leader is a volunteer.
- Publicly affirm and recognize your prayer leader and her role in the church. This signals that prayer is a core value to the church, brings focus and intentionality to the prayer ministry, provides a way to recruit intercessors, and encourages greater prayer participation from the congregation.
- Develop a job description and clarify to whom the prayer leader will report.
- Encourage and assist your prayer leader in building a prayer team, developing a prayer strategy, and establishing a budget. Prayer ministry takes manpower, planning, and money, just like any other ministry.
- Set regular appointments with your prayer leader to pray with him and evaluate the progress of the ministry.
- Draw your prayer leader into the leadership circle of the church. This will ensure that prayer becomes not an isolated ministry but a part of the fabric of the church.
- Teach on and model prayer from the pulpit, and promote the many times and ways in which your church members can get involved in prayer. Even when a church has a top-notch prayer coordinator, the senior pastor should be visibly and solidly involved in the prayer ministry.
- Offer training for your prayer leaders. Support them financially if they want to attend a seminar, workshop, or conference for church prayer leaders. Sometimes local church prayer leaders are called to lead but are afraid to step out because they feel uninformed, unsupported, and inadequate to do the job.

WAYS PRAYER LEADERS CAN SUPPORT THEIR PASTORS

- Pray daily for your pastor and his family. Make mobilizing prayer for the pastor a top priority.
- Always speak well of your pastor, other ministry leaders, and their families. Do not entertain gossip. Avoid the hook of the Enemy to draw you in with remarks such as, "Our pastor just isn't interested in the prayer ministry."
- Allow the pastor to lead the process, impart vision, and set the pace for prayer mobilization.
- Develop a prayer strategy that complements the vision of the pastor and supports the ministries in the church. Remember, you'll lead best by serving.
- Keep your pastor informed about what you are doing through meetings, memos, e-mails, and letters. Be sure to seek pastoral advice and endorsement before asking anyone to serve in a leadership role.
- Be patient with your pastor and the process of becoming a praying church. Developing a comprehensive prayer strategy can take three to five years. Don't give up!

> *Praying my pastor's vision overcomes division among the congregation and affirms unity on what our pastor has heard from God. It warns principalities that we stand united.*
>
> Margaret Caldwell
> Grace Community Fellowship
> Smyrna, Georgia

WHEN THE PRAYER LEADER IS COMMITTED TO THE PASTOR'S VISION

A prayer ministry can be a pastor's greatest blessing or a "thorn in the flesh." In large part, the outcome depends upon the attitude of the prayer leader. His positive attitude will be caught quickly by others in the prayer ministry as well as the congregation. Supportive prayer leaders also help intercessory prayer groups stay focused on blessing rather than criticizing or correcting the pastor.

Understanding and supporting the pastor's vision for the church is key to the role of prayer leader. The word *division* simply defined means "two visions." When the prayer leader has a vision for the church different from that of the pastor, you have the makings for dissention and possibly even a church split. If a prayer leader's vision for the church is so different from that of the pastor that it hinders his ability to be supportive, it might be best to resign.

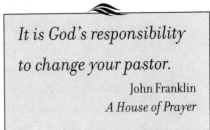

> *It is God's responsibility to change your pastor.*
>
> John Franklin
> *A House of Prayer*

Delphine Floyd, former prayer coordinator of Solid Rock Church in Colorado Springs, gives this testimony regarding her role of strengthening the pastor's vision through prayer:

> As a local church prayer leader, I strongly believe in submitting to the authority of the local church. One of the ways that I make sure the prayer ministry is in line with the vision of my church is by listening attentively and taking notes of the things my pastor says as he addresses the congregation during his Sunday morning messages or leadership meetings. Then during our church corporate prayer meetings as well as during my personal times of prayer, I use these notes as prayer points. When we do this, we are praying back to the Father the things that He has placed on the heart of our local pastor.[2]

QUESTIONS ABOUT PASTORS MOST FREQUENTLY ASKED BY PRAYER LEADERS

What if my pastor doesn't seem as interested in prayer as I am?

There are several reasons that your pastor may not be showing a high level of interest in the prayer ministry. First, many pastors today are overwhelmed by their job assignments and the expectations of their boards and congregations.

Sometimes a prayer meeting just feels like one more thing on their to-do list.

Second, it is the pastor's job to make sure that all the scriptural mandates to the local church are fulfilled, including worship, discipleship, evangelism, preaching of the Word, hospital and prison visitation, and outreaches to the poor. While he recognizes the importance of prayer, he sees it in the larger context of the numerous important ministry goals. Your pastor may be feeling pressure from the leaders of all these ministries who see their area as the most important.

Third, a spiritual need may exist in your pastor's life. Maybe it's been a long time since he's experienced miraculous answers to prayer, so he's not passionate about it. It could be that he's a "can-do" type of guy who feels more comfortable being proactive in his ministry rather than "just praying." Perhaps he is disillusioned or experiencing burnout.

Lastly, remember that your pastor is a target of spiritual warfare. Satan wants to keep your pastor too busy to pray, and spread too thin to give leadership to the prayer ministry. The Enemy may be driving your pastor to believe he must just "work harder" if the church is ever going to flourish.

For these reasons and more, the first place to start in mobilizing prayer in the local church is with prayer for the pastor and his family. If your pastor is open to this idea, then start a campaign to mobilize prayer for him. Even if he tells you he's not interested in your mobilizing intercessors on his behalf, you can make praying for your pastor a daily priority in your own life. (Chapter 8 explains in detail how to raise up personal intercessory teams for your pastor.)

Whatever you do, always remain supportive and publicly affirming of your pastor. If that ever becomes an impossibility, then it may be time for you to resign your position.

How do I gain my pastor's support?

Communicate to your pastor that you desire to submit to his leadership and that in no way do you want to work contrary to his vision for the church. Look for ways to become a blessing rather than a burden to your pastor. When your pastor can't meet with you, send him short reports and e-mails to keep him informed of what's happening in the prayer ministry. Put together a prayer ministry schedule before the year begins and submit it to your pastor. Let him know the events that you feel would be most important for him to attend so he can put them on his calendar. Avoid making him feel guilty when he can't be involved.

Plan ahead. Nothing is more frustrating to a pastor than finding out the National Day of Prayer is next week and you want his help in pulling off an event at the church at the last minute.

It takes time to build trust. Be patient. Showing your pastor respect, remaining faithful to the assignments you're given, and keeping a servant's heart will make it easier for your pastor to return the trust and support. However, even if you never see your pastor's support outwardly, render your service as unto the Lord and remember that it is He who will reward you.

> *I appreciate my prayer leader's support. She doesn't come across like "Pastor, there's something wrong with you, and God has sent me here to fix you!"*
>
> Byron Banta, Corona Baptist Church
> Chandler, Arizona

I have a prayer language and believe in spiritual warfare, deliverance, and "the gifts" of the Holy Spirit, but the leaders in my church do not believe in these things. What should I do?

There is no one sure answer to this question because this same scenario plays out differently depending upon the personalities and theological persuasions of those involved. However, I have seen those with differing theological persuasions work together well. It takes honor and submission on the part of all involved, but mostly on the part of the one who believes in and operates in "the gifts."

While there may be exceptions, I believe that if you hold a leadership role in your church, you should let your pastor know where you stand on these issues. If he still desires you to hold leadership, then find out exactly what your boundaries are. For example, in order to lead prayer meetings it may require that you withhold your prayer language for use in your own prayer closet. Still, this is not the only issue that may arise. Ask how the church leadership feels about your sharing your view on these subjects when questions come up, which is almost certain to happen.

Most everyone recognizes the need to be submissive to and work under the authority of the pastor of the church where you serve. "However," says one prayer leader who found himself in this precarious situation, "you may need to ask your pastor to define what submission means to him. If it means abiding by the desire of the pastor within the scope of his vision for the ministry—without either of you making demands on the other to change—then true cooperation and respect will be the result."

Once you know you are welcome and feel comfortable with your boundaries, then commit to your church and make walking in the law of love your primary concern.

Beyond You and Your Pastor

A gifted prayer leader can do much by coming alongside the pastor to build a successful prayer ministry. But if you desire to involve the greatest number of the people in your congregation in prayer, you will want to build a leadership team and develop a prayer strategy. The next chapter is designed to help you select and lead your prayer action team. Once your team is in place, you will be ready to begin assessing your church's needs and developing a strategy for building your church into a house of prayer.

---

1. Leonard Griffin, "The Pastor's Role of Mobilizing Prayer," PrayerQuake, Phoenix, 2001.
2. Delphine Floyd, *Empowered*, Fall 2001, p. 16.

CHAPTER 4

Building Your Prayer Action Team

There it was again—that uneasiness in the pit of her stomach—a feeling Kathleen Graham couldn't shake. After ten years serving as her church's prayer coordinator, it seemed the Lord was asking her to do something unthinkable. How could this be?

"Lord, when I cried out to you for answers, I didn't expect this answer," Kathleen pleaded. "You couldn't be asking me to *resign!*"

Yet, apparently it was true. The Lord was asking her to step down. During Kathleen's tenure, she had led many successful prayer initiatives. The prayer room she pioneered had become a model for other churches. She held the respect of the congregation and the confidence of her pastor to a degree shared by few other local church prayer leaders.

Still, Kathleen yearned to see more of the congregation participating in the prayer ministry. Yet she was already stretched thin with prayer ministry responsibilities. How could she do anything more?

"What can I do to get more people involved?" she had prayed.

The Lord's response had surprised and baffled her. Was she truly hearing the voice of the Holy Spirit? One such confirmation surely would be the surfacing of her replacement. Yet, several months later, no replacement was in sight.

So Kathleen met with her pastors to seek their counsel. After much prayer and deliberation, with still no replacement found, the pastors reluctantly accepted Kathleen's resignation. Together, Kathleen and her pastors laid the prayer ministry on the altar, released it to God, and waited to see what He would do.

The next season of prayer ministry at Fountain of Life Church would look much different than that of previous years, for Kathleen was to be replaced, not by a person but by a team. Although it took over a year, eventually God brought together four church members who together could be much more effective leading the prayer ministry than would ever have been possible for Kathleen alone.

> No truly effective ministry can live on the talents of only one person.
>
> Carl George
> *Leading and Managing Your Church*

And what happened to Kathleen? Well, to her surprise, she was the fourth member of the new team. Her organizational gifts made her the perfect person to fulfill this role, only now she was complemented by others with different gifts. Even though Kathleen and the church leaders were baffled when God asked her to step down, in the end they were all thrilled with God's perfect plan.

Just like Kathleen, maybe you're feeling your prayer ministry needs something more—something you're not certain you have. If you review the list of prayer coordinator responsibilities in chapter 2, you'll see that even a "superstar" prayer leader could not successfully keep up with all the requirements. That's because the job description was designed to be carried out by a team, with the prayer coordinator serving as team leader.

The best advice a church prayer coordinator could receive is this: Don't try to do the job alone. If you've already started as a solo leader, it's not too late to stop and build a team.

You may be thinking, *My church is too small. How can I build a team?* or *I've never led a team, I don't know how.* Don't let these thoughts discourage you. God has set aside people to help you, no matter what size church you are in. This chapter is designed to help you discover and lead a prayer action team that can call your whole church to prayer.

WHAT IS a Team?

Many people mistakenly think of teams as being synonymous with work groups or committees. Work groups are collections of people who come together for a duration of time to accomplish a particular task. A committee is a group of people who meet for discussion or to make recommendations regarding policy, programs, or plans.[1]

Leadership teams are much different. Typically a group will consist of four to six people. A group any larger gets bogged down and nothing gets done. According to researcher George Barna, a leadership team is a small group of leaders who:

> *Leadership works best when it is provided by teams of gifted leaders serving together in pursuit of a clear and compelling vision.*
>
> George Barna
> *Building Effective Lay Leadership Teams*

- possess a balanced mix of spiritual gifts and skills
- are committed to each other's growth and success
- lead a larger group of people in pursuing a common vision, specific performance goals, and a plan of action
- will hold themselves mutually accountable[2]

BIBLICAL endorsements OF Teams

The use of leadership teams is not new. In fact, the New Testament concept of the body of Christ illustrates the need for many parts working together as each performs its unique purpose. Many Scriptures in both the Old and New Testament endorse the value and significance of teams. One example is found in the leadership model of Moses. Hampered by severe limitations, Moses was reluctant to lead from the start. His response to the call of God upon his life was to ask for associates who could compensate for his weaknesses. While Moses remained the senior leader, God sent Aaron and Joshua to serve on his leadership team.

Even with the help of his teammates, Moses was still holding on to too many supervisory and counseling responsibilities. From morning till night the children of Israel were lined up waiting for Moses to hear their problems. When Moses' father-in-law, Jethro, came for a visit, he was appalled at Moses' leadership style: "Moses' father-in-law replied, 'What you are doing is not good. You and these people who come to you will only wear yourselves out. The work is too heavy for you; you cannot handle it alone'" (Exodus 18:17-18). Jethro then offered Moses a simple plan to alleviate the problem: Divide the responsibilities into manageable portions and delegate duties to other qualified leaders.

The Bible also speaks of teams led by Nehemiah. When he was assigned the monumental task of restoring the walls of Jerusalem, Nehemiah organized teams of laborers with various skills to accomplish the project. Each team built its section of the wall. If Nehemiah had attempted to do the job alone, the walls never would have been rebuilt.

The apostle Paul is another example of a team leader. In the book of Acts, we find Paul traveling and ministering in teams—accompanied by such leaders as Barnabas, John, Simeon, Lucias, Timothy, Silas, and Judas. Of course, Jesus Himself set the most profound example of team leadership in raising up the twelve disciples.

THE Importance OF Teams

The use of teams is important in both large and small churches. The larger a church gets, the more it must rely upon team leadership to stay healthy. Teams also work well in small churches. Barna's research shows that "not only can teams work in a small church environment, but the better they work, the more likely it is that the church will not remain small for long."[3] He suggests that it is important for all directors of church ministries to see themselves as team leaders rather than solo practitioners.

Following are several reasons your prayer ministry will benefit from building a leadership team. Teams:

- offer gifts and skills beyond what one person will possess
- provide division of responsibility and shared workload

- increase the ministry's sphere of influence
- offer synergy of working and thinking together

WHY LEADERS DON'T USE TEAMS

With so many compelling reasons for building teams, why don't more churches and prayer ministries take advantage of them? Though many reasons exist, here are a few:

- **It is easier to do the job alone.** In the short run this may be true; however, in such cases, the success of the ministry is limited to the abilities and capacity of one person.
- **The leader would feel less significant.** Those who have a deep-seated need to be needed or whose insecurity causes them to desire to be center stage, will resist building teams.
- **The leader lacks the ability**. Many leaders have never been trained to build or lead a team.
- **There is an absence of vision.** If the church at large does not have a clear and compelling vision, then the leaders within the church may lack purpose and direction as well.

THE ROLE OF THE PRAYER ACTION TEAM

Some churches refer to their prayer leadership team as a *prayer council* or *prayer committee*. The current trend replaces these words with *prayer team*. I like the designation *prayer action team* because it distinguishes this team from that of prayer groups in the church. The prayer action team is the group of leaders called to oversee the prayer ministry and bring a focus upon communion with God into every aspect of church life.

I often ask pastors and prayer coordinators to tell me about the makeup of their prayer leadership team. Invariably, they describe the Wednesday night or Tuesday morning intercessory prayer group. Intercessory prayer groups are vital to the life and health of a church because they *pray!* The intercessory group, however, is not synonymous with the prayer action team.

While the prayer action team must pray in order to lead with authority, authenticity, and vision, their primary role is not to pray. The role of the prayer action team is to call the rest of the church to prayer and to equip them to pray. Their job consists of the ongoing process of:

- evaluating the prayer ministry's effectiveness
- setting goals for raising the level of prayer in the whole congregation
- following through with projects to achieve these goals

Accomplishing these tasks requires that the prayer action team possess gifts to lead and administrate as well as pray.

If as a prayer leader you think your job is solely to pray or even to lead an intercessory prayer group, then your church's prayer ministry may never grow beyond a small group of intercessors.

One day I was talking with a pastor friend of mine on the phone.

"How is your prayer ministry going?" I asked.

"Not well at all," he responded.

I was disturbed to hear this because it had been at my suggestion that he had selected a church prayer coordinator. I was hoping to hear a better report.

After further discussion, I learned that the prayer coordinator had no team or prayer organizational plan. His sole objective was to lead a prayer group each week in "The Upper Room." Unfortunately, not many people were involved.

Many churches' prayer ministries never grow beyond a single prayer group. The prayer ministries in such churches could become much more fruitful if the prayer coordinator would do just one thing: build a team, one that provides a variety of prayer opportunities for everyone in the church.

Most often each member of the prayer action team will lead one or more of the prayer ministries of the church. Some churches refer to the leaders of their prayer ministries as prayer captains. Larger churches and more developed prayer ministries may have both a small prayer action team and prayer captains who serve under the prayer action team.

Gifts and competencies needed by prayer captains include staying organized, relating well with people, handling and resolving conflict, managing projects, teaching, leading prayer meetings, and praying effectively with and for others.

Smaller prayer ministries may utilize only one or two captains, where more advanced ministries may have five or six captains. The long-term goal is to have a prayer captain over every prayer ministry in the church. As mentioned earlier, members of the prayer action team may double as prayer captains, and in smaller churches and prayer ministries this quite often is a necessity.

To illustrate the utilization of prayer captains, let us consider a church with a well-developed prayer ministry. Such a church might enlist the following prayer captains:

Prayer captain in charge of corporate prayer.
He leads intercessory prayer meetings to pray over the weekend services. He also is in charge of recruiting and scheduling intercessors to be present for these meetings.

Prayer captain in charge of the prayer room.
She handles prayer room tours, the ordering of supplies and furnishings, and the scheduling and training of prayer room intercessors.

Prayer captain in charge of pastors' prayer shields.
He assists the pastoral staff in recruiting, training, and maintaining pray-ers for their personal intercessory teams.

Prayer captain in charge of the prayer chain.
She organizes and implements the churchwide prayer requests and praise reports through a telephone prayer chain.

Prayer captain in charge of training.
He teaches on prayer in Sunday school classes and prayer seminars, trains prayer leaders and intercessory groups, and facilitates and invites outside speakers for all-church prayer conferences.

Prayer captain in charge of care prayer.
He puts together teams that make hospital visits to pray for the sick and their families, prays with others facing critical issues, and writes prayergrams of encouragement and support.

The specific job description of prayer captains will differ from church to church depending upon its number and type of prayer ministries. (A sample prayer action team organizational chart is provided for you in appendix C and on the Prayer Tools CD.)

It is important to remember that developing a prayer action team is a process, not an overnight task. Moving from a solo prayer coordinator to the leader of a team may be a big jump for you, especially if you're just getting started. Consider beginning by soliciting a secretary or administrative assistant who is willing to serve on a volunteer basis. As your ministry unfolds, you'll begin to put together your prayer action team.

QUALITIES TO LOOK FOR IN A LEADERSHIP TEAM MEMBER

Not everyone who volunteers to serve on your leadership team will make a good team member. The following are some important qualities to consider when selecting your leadership team. This is not a checklist but food for thought as you begin to evaluate possible members of your team.[4]

Character.
Qualities that make up good character include honesty, integrity, self-discipline, teachability, dependability, perseverance, and conscientiousness.
Influence.
Leaders know where they are going, and they are able to persuade others to go with them.
Positive attitude.
People with a positive attitude draw the best out of other people.
Excellent people skills.
Some people skills can be learned. However, at the core of good people skills is a genuine concern for others—a heart attitude that people recognize.
Evident gifts.
Every person is created with gifts from God, though not every

person is gifted for the task at hand. It is important to try to match gifting with job opportunity.

Confidentiality.

Because of the sensitivity of many prayer requests, it is critical that leaders in the prayer ministry are able to hold a confidence. Lack of confidentiality in handling prayer requests can kill a prayer ministry faster than most anything else.

Effective communication.

Good written and verbal communication skills help leaders work together well as a team. Clear communication helps leaders share the compelling ministry vision effectively.

THE GIFT MIX OF TEAMS

Building a team with a balanced gift mix will help you raise the level of enthusiasm and effectiveness in your prayer ministry. Start by assessing your own gifts. Ask yourself, *What has God called me to do?* Because God has gifted you to perform certain ministry functions, you have a responsibility to spend the majority of your time and efforts in accordance with those gifts. When you focus upon your areas of giftedness, two things will happen: You will enjoy your work and you will become more effective in ministry.

Though we can't function in our primary gifting 100 percent of the time, the rule of thumb is that people should spend at least 60 percent of their workweek operating from their strengths. Utilizing the gifts of others frees us to minister out of our gifting.

After assessing your own God-given motivations, make a list of gifts that are needed to lead a prayer ministry. Which gifts do you possess? Which must other team leaders possess? The answers to these questions will guide you in selecting the right team members. If you already have a team in place, it will be important to help them identify their gifts and to release them to lead in their areas of strength. To assist in this process, I recommend that you give your team the book *Your Spiritual Gifts Can Help Your Church Grow*, by C. Peter Wagner.

Barna suggests that the ideal team consists of four leaders, each possessing a different aptitude.[5] Here is a description of the four types of leaders:

- **Visionary**—one with the ability to motivate people to get involved in the vision
- **Problem Solver**—one with the ability to identify and solve problems
- **People Person**—one who works well with people and can build teams
- **Administrator**—a detailed person with organizational skills

Not only will a leadership team contribute to the ministry's success through their complementary abilities and skills but team members each bring the additional asset of their sphere of influence. While one team member may be involved with retirees, another is connected with the marketplace. One member may have influence with the men of the church and another with young moms. The broader the sphere of influence of your team, the more people the prayer ministry has the potential of serving and impacting.

Building a team takes time, and you may not readily find people to fill all these roles. In the beginning you may have to wear several hats, some of which may not fit very well. The key is to start with the leaders you have while you continue to pray for God to send you people with the giftings your team lacks.

selecting the prayer action team

You may be asking, "How can I get excellent leaders like these to volunteer to lead the prayer ministry?" The answer is that they probably are *not* going to volunteer. You usually have to go after good leaders.

Prayer coordinators often choose their prayer action team from the members of their prayer group, simply because these are people known to have a heart for prayer. One or two members from your prayer group may be good choices. However, you're not limited to traditional prayer circles when searching for your leadership team. Members of other ministries, small groups, Bible studies, Sunday school classes, or the choir might be possibilities.

Don't rely upon just who you know. Talk with other leaders in the church and ask for recommendations. This may open up a whole new sphere of influence to you. If you can, make arrangements to visit the meetings of several small groups in the church, letting them know of your need. Include an announcement in the church bulletin for several weeks.

When you begin to make a list of possible candidates, don't rely on your own understanding; instead seek divine guidance. One scriptural example is Jesus' model for selecting the twelve disciples. As the authors of *Growing a Healthy Church* point out, "Because Jesus was a master at discerning what was in the hearts of men, you might think He would rely on His own wisdom to select these men. But He did not do it without prayer!"[6] Luke 6:12-13 tells us, "Jesus went out to a mountainside to pray, and spent the night praying to God. When morning came, he called his disciples to him and chose twelve of them, whom he also designated apostles."

Ask the Lord to set aside your prayer action team and to prepare their hearts and schedules. Then trust Him as you seek confirmation through godly counsel and Scripture. Confer with your pastor regarding those people you feel may be qualified to serve on your team, and ask for his input. Never invite anyone onto your leadership team without first obtaining your pastor's approval.

> *When choosing team members, try to ensure that you recruit individuals who can contribute a complementary mix of skill sets. Look not only for those people who currently possess the skills the team needs but also for those who have the potential to develop needed skills.*
>
> Sarah B. Campbell
> *Leading a Team*

You or your pastor will want to go to each individual and invite him personally. Be prepared to share the compelling vision God has given you for your church becoming a house of prayer. Busy leaders must be convinced that their investment of time and talents is going to make a difference in the life of the church and in the kingdom of God.

"FOR PASTORS ONLY"

commissioning your leadership team

The amount of support your prayer leader and team receive from ministry leaders and your congregation rests on you, the senior pastor. If your church knows you value this team highly, they will, too. Here are some ways you can hep to raise the team's level of support.

Publicly introduce and commission your team. This shows the congregation that they're operating under the authority and with the blessing of church leadership. In some churches, the prayer team is looked upon as "superspiritual" and people have the idea that they're out there doing their own thing. We want to dispel that notion.

During a weekend service, call the prayer team to the front of the church, pray and lay hands on them, and say something like, "We believe God has called our church to be a house of prayer. These are the people who are going to help make this happen."

Explain the role of the team and its individual members. Let the congregation know how the team is going to serve them. Then share ways the church family can get involved in the church's prayer training and prayer gatherings. To add some inspiration, you might include some testimonials of answered prayer.

Leading your team

Many prayer coordinators have little or no leadership training. Leading a team may be a new and even stretching experience for you. There are many ways you can pick up the leadership skills that you lack—either through a mentor, leadership seminars, books, or other teaching materials. The stronger leader you become, the stronger leaders you will be able to draw around you.

This book is not designed to teach all the leadership skills you will need. However, I suggest you consider giving priority attention to leading well in the following three areas:

VISION

God inspired Solomon to write in Proverbs 29:18, "Where there is no vision, the people perish" (KJV). The ability to lead your team toward God's vision will be central to your role as team leader, for only if you have a firm grasp upon where God wants the ministry to go can you take others with you.

> *Since a leader must motivate, mobilize, and direct people, on what basis would you accomplish such outcomes without casting a compelling vision?*
>
> George Barna
> *Building Effective Lay Leadership Teams*

BUILDING RELATIONSHIPS

Take time to meet with your leaders one-on-one and get to know them as people. Pray with them often. Listen to their ideas, opinions, suggestions, and frustrations. Become an expert at discovering the needs of your team. Whether they need encouragement, resources, training, or time off, make it your aim to give them what they need.

Set an example for your team of speaking positively about others, avoiding gossip and demeaning statements. Exhibit a humble and submissive attitude toward church leadership, even if they don't carry your vision for prayer. In this way you will model a caring, Christlike attitude that will help your team build positive relationships with one another and others in the church family.

TEAM MEETINGS

Leading your prayer ministry will require bringing your team together for meetings. Your presence is needed in meetings in order to keep the vision before the team and help them stay focused. In addition to the presence of a team leader, meetings need a scribe or recorder to keep written records of team meetings.

The first step to leading an effective meeting is preparing a simple agenda. Include only items that are truly important to accomplish, and list the items in the order of their importance. Make copies for all team members. Be certain to make prayer an agenda item and give sufficient time to pray over any items that require a decision. When plenty of time is allowed for prayer, the meeting usually exhibits more unity and a sense of God's purpose. Following the meeting, highlight on the meeting notes any action steps on which a member is to follow up, and then distribute the notes.

IT'S TIME TO GO TO WORK

Once your team is in place, you can begin the process of assessing your church's prayer ministry needs. The next chapter will take you and your prayer action team step-by-step through the process of evaluating your church's personality, analyzing your church's prayer level, understanding your congregation's interest level, evaluating the health of your current prayer ministry, and identifying barriers to the presence of God. With this information in hand, you will be prepared to design a strategy to take your church to the next level in prayer.

---

1. George Barna, *Building Effective Lay Leadership Teams* (Ventura, Calif.: Issachar Resources, 2001), p. 24.

2. Barna, p. 12.

3. Barna, p. 27.

4. John Maxwell, *Developing the Leaders Around You* (Nashville: Nelson, 1995), pp. 47–60.

5. Barna, p. 81.

6. Dann Spader and Gary Mayes, *Growing a Healthy Church* (Chicago: Moody, 1991), p. 102.

CHAPTER 5

Assessing Your Church's Needs

Once when I was driving home late at night from a speaking engagement, I became desperately lost. After driving in circles for two hours, I spotted a policeman in a parking lot at the side of the road. I pulled over to ask for directions.

"I know how to get where I'm going," I said. "I just don't know where I am."

When we're driving to an unfamiliar destination, we use a map and trace our route, but of course we need to know our starting point. At the mall when we're looking for a store on the directory, the first thing we do is find the "you are here" arrow.

It's the same in the church. We may have a clear vision of our destination, but in order to get anywhere, we have to know where we are. If we are to arrive at our destination of becoming a house of prayer, it makes sense to start by assessing the current state of prayer in our church.

The following steps are designed to help you gather the information you will need to take your church to the next level in prayer. As you walk through these steps, you will begin to get a picture of your church's unique needs. With this information you will be able to design a prayer strategy that releases the power of God and neutralizes the plans of the Enemy in your church.

STEP 1: EVALUATE YOUR CHURCH'S PERSONALITY

What kind of prayer ministry should your church have? That's the first question you must ask yourself. Your prayer ministry plan must reflect your church's personality.

Each church has unique "character traits"—from mainline churches in which prayers are read from a prayer book to highly expressive churches where people pray Korean style, hands raised and voices calling out to God in unison.

Your pastor and your congregation are different from any other church, even churches of your same denomination. Everything from the spiritual gifts of your pastor and key leaders to your church's location in the city will have a bearing upon how you develop your prayer strategy. Though you can learn much by studying other churches' prayer strategies, your house of prayer plan will be one-of-a-kind.

> *In many respects, the way a church develops its prayer ministry will depend upon its size, its localized context, its focus and functions and its denominational or theological flavor.*
>
> Dawn Ministries
> *Developing a Prayer Strategy*

It may not take you long to discover that your pastor or congregation sees the plan differently than you do. One mistake some prayer coordinators make is designing a plan that fits their personality rather than that of the church. One example of this would be including a deliverance ministry in your plan, when the concept is outside the theology of your church or the congregation is simply not ready for it. The only good plan is one that works. For some, that may mean starting with a prayer ministry that is smaller or more basic than you originally had in mind.

The development of a prayer strategy, to some extent, is dependent upon the overall strategy of the church. It should flow from the vision and purpose of the church, serving the overall strategy, not be seen as a challenge to it.[1] Fortunately for my prayer leadership team, our church has a clearly defined mission and vision.

Every year in January, Pastor Gary preaches his annual "bus" message.

It's a sermon on the vision and spiritual direction of the church. Using the illustration of a "bus," he explains that every church is going somewhere in particular. Most church members, however, never read the sign on the front of the bus to know where their church is headed. My pastor wants to ensure that everyone in our church understands the unique vision and purpose of Word of Grace Church.

After hearing the message, a few people may want to get off the bus, but overwhelmingly the majority of the members of Word of Grace are excited about where we're going—and the church keeps growing.

> *Prayer, like a plant, needs to grow over a period of time. Each church has a unique soil (receptivity), climate (spiritual atmosphere), and mix of gifts.*
>
> Dawn Ministries
> *Developing a Prayer Strategy*

If your church has a written strategy detailing its vision, mission, and goals, then begin to study that plan. Ask the Lord how a prayer ministry can come alongside to help your church fulfill its God-given purposes. Of course, not every church has developed a strategic plan. This, however, should not keep you from designing a plan for prayer. Just think: The prayer strategy may set a course for better organization in the whole church.

STEP 2: analyze your church's prayer level

When I consider the typical prayer levels in various churches, I see most fitting into one of three models: the prayer "lite" church, the prayer ministry church, or the house of prayer. As you study the diagrams on the next page, try to identify the model that best portrays your church. Perhaps your church falls somewhere in between.

The prayer-lite church is a church that nominally recognizes the importance of prayer to its ministry but has not developed prayer in any strategic way. It may open meetings in prayer, include a pastoral prayer in the worship service, and hold special prayer meetings from time to time for important issues. Prayer, however, is largely unstructured.

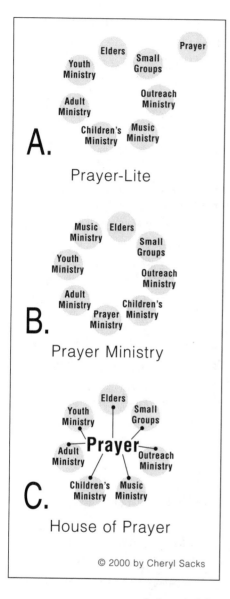

A.

Elders
Youth Ministry
Small Groups
Prayer
Adult Ministry
Outreach Ministry
Children's Ministry
Music Ministry

Prayer-Lite

B.

Music Ministry
Elders
Small Groups
Youth Ministry
Outreach Ministry
Adult Ministry
Children's Ministry
Prayer Ministry

Prayer Ministry

C.

Elders
Youth Ministry
Small Groups
Adult Ministry
Prayer
Outreach Ministry
Children's Ministry
Music Ministry

House of Prayer

© 2000 by Cheryl Sacks

There may be a few people praying for the church and its ministries, but they are not given specific requests and are not recognized as a ministry of the church.

The prayer-ministry church recognizes that prayer is important. It wants to see things prayed for and wants to provide passionate intercessors with a place to plug in. It recognizes prayer as a ministry of the church, much like youth or music. A minister of prayer or prayer leader may be in place. However, most of the burden to call the church to pray falls upon this one person. People who have an inner burden for prayer are involved in the prayer ministry, but not many others.

The house of prayer believes that nothing lasting will happen apart from communion with God. Leaders are praying people and set an example of meeting with the Lord every day. This church believes that in order to be empowered for service by the Holy Spirit, people must spend time in His presence. This congregation desires that prayer permeate every aspect of church life. Every ministry is prayed for, and prayer is a significant part of each ministry. There is teaching on prayer from the pulpit and priority is placed on prayer by the pastor. While the prayer leader oversees the prayer ministry, the pastoral staff comes alongside to ensure that everyone has the opportunity to get involved in prayer. There is a fresh flowing atmosphere of the Holy Spirit in the services due to the whole church moving into a deeper relationship with Jesus Christ.

STEP 3: UNDERSTAND YOUR CONGREGATION'S INTEREST LEVELS

In most congregations, you'll find people at one of three interest levels when it comes to prayer: the passionate intercessor, the interested seeker, and those not yet awakened to the purpose and power of prayer. A successful church prayer ministry will develop strategies to meet the prayer needs of all three groups.

Understanding Your Congregation's Interest Levels

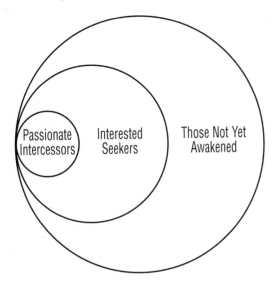

Passionate Intercessors

Interested Seekers

Those Not Yet Awakened

PASSIONATE INTERCESSORS

It is easy to identify the passionate intercessors. Usually you will find them involved in the church prayer ministry at some level. You may want to study the demographics of this group. This will yield important information regarding the age, gender, marital status, and so on, of those involved in the inner circle of prayer in your church. This can be helpful in drawing more people to the prayer ministry. For example, if young mothers aren't involved in the Tuesday morning prayer group, maybe it's because there is no babysitting available.

Intercessors have a vital ministry to the church. If their gift is not recognized and utilized, they might look for another church that has made room for them. Developing a prayer ministry will offer those with the greatest passion for prayer a place to pray, connect, and serve their church with their gifting. These people most likely will be the ones who pay the price to lay the prayer foundation in your church.

INTERESTED SEEKERS

It is important for churches to offer prayer opportunities that are inviting and unintimidating for those who are just learning to pray. Seekers are looking for classes, workshops, and resources to help them begin or deepen their prayer life. An effective prayer ministry will offer training and opportunities not only for those who love to pray but also for those with an interest in learning how to pray or how to pray more effectively.

THOSE NOT YET AWAKENED

If you attempt to call people to prayer who have not yet been awakened to the power and purpose of prayer, they will not respond. Holding a prayer conference will not reach them because they will not attend. In order to change the mindset or heart attitude of this third group of people, it's wise to encourage and train them in places they are already connected within the church, such as a weekend service, a small group, or a married couples' class. These people are not going to come to the prayer ministry; the prayer ministry must be taken to them.

Those who serve on the prayer leadership team will best serve those who fall into this category by encouraging Christian education classes to include prayer in their curriculum. Another option is to train Sunday school

> *I recommend acknowledging that most church members will not become involved in an intensively focused, high-commitment prayer program. However, that does not mean the responsibility of leading the church to pray ends there. Instead, a different strategy ought to be developed for mobilizing all the church body to pray.*
>
> John Franklin
> *A House of Prayer*

or small-group leaders how to teach others to pray.

One way to discover your congregation's interest in prayer is to conduct a survey. Ask church leaders what they are observing about the prayer life of the congregation. Use nonthreatening surveys that allow people to respond anonymously to questions about their prayer life and that of their family. Perhaps you will want to put a questionnaire in the church bulletin to ask what classes or seminars church members would be interested in attending.

"Don't assume anything," suggests Dr. Alvin Vander Griend, author of *How to Coordinate Your Prayer Ministry*. "For example, don't assume that when members are asked to pray about something they actually do. Don't assume that everyone present is praying when someone leads in public prayer, or that every member has a personal devotional life, or even that most people understand the importance of prayer."[2]

STEP 4: EVALUATE THE HEALTH OF YOUR CURRENT PRAYER MINISTRY

If your church currently has a prayer ministry, how is it doing? Talking with leaders and participants in the various prayer ministries can yield valuable information. Here are some questions that may help you evaluate your prayer ministry's effectiveness:

Are your church leaders prepared to lead and model prayer?
Talk with staff and lay leaders to better understand their attitudes and disciplines regarding prayer. Interview the head of every ministry in the church. Find out what they are doing, what their challenges are, and how the prayer ministry can assist them.

One prayer coordinator I know surveyed the leaders in her church, assuring them that their answers would be held in confidence. She asked such questions as "How would you rate your personal prayer life? How comfortable do you feel leading corporate prayer? Teaching on prayer?" What she discovered was that most leaders lacked confidence in all these areas of prayer. In light of this valuable information, the prayer action

team was able to draft a strategy to meet the needs of their
leaders.

Is your church prayer meeting working?

Is it "the place to be"? Are people coming out of duty, or is it
the visible powerhouse for what God is doing?

How effective are the other prayer ministries?

Is the prayer chain missing some vital links? Is the pastor's
prayer shield (a team of people praying for him) still up and
functioning? Are you the only one praying in the prayer room?

**If something's not working, should you scrap it, reshape it,
revitalize it, or replace it?**

Should you reschedule the meeting time? Instead of 6:30 in the
evening, how about 6:30 in the morning? Instead of spending
one hour, how about two, or vice versa? Does the ministry or
meeting need a new focus, new name, or new leader? Does the
style or format need an adjustment? Is a fresh mobilization
strategy needed?

Are there obvious holes in the prayer ministry?

Maybe an important aspect of prayer ministry has been missed
altogether. Your research may have brought to light the need to
train your church leaders to more effectively lead corporate
prayer. Perhaps you've just realized that parents are looking for
creative ways to lead their family in prayer or that church
members want to know how to pray for friends and family who
don't know Christ.

What is the strongest element of the prayer ministry?

Just as important as discovering what's not working is finding out
what is. What is God blessing? What are the people most excited
about? Don't let it slide just because it's working. It may be best to
pour in more energy here and let something that's not working die.
This is the basic principle espoused by Dr. Henry Blackaby in
Experiencing God. Find out what God is doing and jump on board.

To help you evaluate your current prayer ministry, refer to
the evaluation surveys found on the Prayer Tools disk. While
the list is not exhaustive, it covers most major areas of prayer
ministry.

STEP 5: IDENTIFY BARRIERS TO THE PRESENCE OF GOD

Author and researcher George Otis Jr. poses the following thought-provoking questions: "If God is not present, why not? The Holy Spirit comes where He is invited; where He feels welcomed. If God is not present, we must ask ourselves the question, 'What have we done to offend Him?'"[3]

Many congregations today, perhaps even yours, tolerate corporate sins. Dr. Neil Anderson, in his book *Setting Your Church Free*, defines corporate sin as patterns of behavior in a church or a significant group within the church that are displeasing to our God and contrary to His revealed will.[4] Busyness, gossip, competition, division, denominational pride, control, and sexual impurity are examples of corporate as well as individual sin.

Like families, churches have histories, some of which we might rather keep hidden in the closet. Over time, undisclosed and unconfessed sin (past or present) will take its toll on a church. You can't just sweep corporate sin under the carpet.

Anderson says that "this pattern of sinfulness within the group life of the church calls for corporate action on the part of its leaders in order to deal with it."[5] The Bible is filled with passages of Scripture in which an individual repented not only for his own sins but for the sins of a group or nation.

> *Realize that if you were to add only extra prayer into your current situation, without addressing the underlying causes for your present condition, the results would be minimal at best. It would be like putting a bandage over a sliver without removing the sliver first.*
>
> Glen Martin and Dian Ginter
> *PowerHouse*

A few biblical examples include Daniel, Nehemiah, and Ezra. Daniel confessed the corporate sins of his ancestors even though he probably never participated in them. We find his prayer recorded in Daniel 9:4-19. Nehemiah repented of his personal sins as well as the sins of his people (Nehemiah 1:5-7). After hearing God's law read, Ezra and those gathered with him confessed their sins, both individual and corporate, including the sins of their ancestors: "They stood in their places and confessed their sins and the wickedness of their fathers" (Nehemiah 9:2).

These leaders understood something our generation may have forgotten: the power of confessing corporate sin. They knew that following their brokenness and sorrow for sin, God promised healing, cleansing, and help in their most desperate circumstances (see 2 Chronicles 7:14; 2 Corinthians 7:10).

The following questions will help you and your church leaders identify corporate sins that hinder the presence of God in your church. Once hindrances are identified, you will want to develop strategies for making them targets for prayer.

What are our sins of omission?

Ask the Lord to help you discern any areas of disobedience in your church. Ask, "What are our failures?" "What should we be doing that we are not doing?"

What are the sins of church leadership?

How well do staff meetings and board meetings run? Is it easy or difficult to make progress? Ask the Holy Spirit why. Are there sin issues in the lives of leaders that have not been addressed or repented of?

What sins of our denomination are affecting our church?

Do denominational pride or isolationism characterize your denomination or church? What traditions are you holding on to that no longer bring life to the services? Do we avoid talking about these and other issues that need change?

What are our historic sins?

Answering the following questions will be helpful in identifying sins of the past: Were the organizing leaders under authority? Did your church have a healthy planting? Was it birthed by default or division? For what reason did the founding pastor and subsequent pastors leave the church? Were there misunderstandings, power struggles, or moral discrepancies? Has your church ever had a church split?

What are the top three barriers that keep us from being a praying church?

Can we identify specific hindrances?

What areas of our church are under attack from the Enemy?

Look to see where the Enemy is attacking your church for the things you are doing right—the areas of your church's strengths. Also look to see where the Enemy is attacking the weak areas— where the walls are down. Ask yourself, *Where does the Enemy come in time and time again? Is there a rash of divorces, back-slidden youth, loss of jobs, or serious health issues?* Answering these questions will help you identify patterns and root problems in your church that need to be considered when you develop your prayer strategy.

It might be helpful to chronicle the important events in the life of your church—both good and bad. The following chart gives you the idea. It may clue you in to situations that might need confession, restoration, or healing.

Noteworthy Events in the Church's History	
1984	Church founded after a split
1985	Called first pastor
1989	Moved to bigger facilities
1994	First pastor forced to leave
1996	Second pastor called
1997	Pastor sets new vision for the church
1998	Church split
2000	Second pastor called to large ministry

YOU'VE ASSESSED YOUR CHURCH'S NEEDS . . . NOW WHAT?

Now that you've identified the current state of prayer in your church, you are ready to develop a plan to take your church to the next level. Whether you are a large church or a small one, just getting started in your prayer ministry or well on your way, the next chapter is designed to help you enlarge your house of prayer.

---

1. Dawn Ministries, *Developing a Prayer Strategy* (Forest Hills, London: Challenge 2000, 1994), p. 3.

2. Alvin Vander Griend, *How to Coordinate Your Prayer Ministry* (Grand Rapids, Mich.: Church Development Resources, 1997), p. 7.

3. George Otis Jr., PrayerQuake, Phoenix, 1998.

4. Neil Anderson and Charles Mylander, *Setting Your Church Free* (Ventura, Calif.: Regal, 1994), p. 212.

5. Anderson and Mylander, p. 212.

CHAPTER 6

Taking Your Church to the Next Level

I can remember when my daughter first began to crawl. Within a few days she was scrambling all over the house, obviously pleased with her new-found freedom. It's exciting to see our children tackle this important milestone. However, it would be sad if they never progressed beyond that stage of development.

Most churches have some level of prayer ministry, and many have experienced the excitement of seeing a small ministry emerge where previously one did not exist. But no matter where your church is on the spectrum of prayer ministry development, I can almost guarantee you it's time to move to a new level. Just as a body of believers grows in other aspects of their spiritual lives, so God expects the prayer life of a church to grow. First we crawl, but at some point we begin to walk and then to run.

God's methods for growing and maturing each church are unique. As you study the following levels, keep in mind that this is not an exact science. Please don't feel compelled to follow the levels in the order presented. I encourage you to jump in wherever you feel your congregation is. You'll likely see yourself making progress at several levels and in need of work at a few others. Remember that no church has arrived. Growing closer to the Lord through communicating with Him is a life-long process.

FOUNDATIONAL LEVEL:
UNIFIED CHURCH LEADERSHIP SETTING THE COURSE

I once heard a simple definition of the word leader: "You go first." This definition certainly holds true when it comes to building a house of prayer. Throughout Scripture, we find how easily leaders influenced the people of God for both good and evil. When a congregation sees that their leaders' determined purpose in life is to become more intimately acquainted with their Savior, they likely will follow the example.

Usually the first building blocks in a church's house of prayer are the prayers of the pastor himself. Some pastors hesitate to take the lead in calling their church to spend time with the Lord because their own prayer life is weak. This can be remedied when the pastor openly acknowledges his struggle and asks others to intercede for him. Then he and his congregation can begin the exciting journey of seeking God together. An excellent resource that has at its core the desire to help pastors in their personal prayer lives is www.prayingpastor.com.

The church's prayer foundation is strengthened when all of the church leadership make spending time with God a priority. The pastor and leaders can join together in praying that the desire for intimacy with Jesus would saturate the church. This is important regardless if you're a new or smaller church, even if your church leadership consists only of you and your spouse or worship leader. Because the Enemy will resist any move in your congregation to draw closer to God, it is essential that the leadership be unified before approaching the congregation with a corporate vision to become a house of prayer.

If you find yourself in a church where your pastor and leaders seem satisfied with a superficial level of church prayer, continue to ask God to awaken your leaders' hearts with deeper longing for Him. Know that He wants to see this happen even more than you do.

MOTIVATIONAL LEVEL:
AWAKENING THE CONGREGATION

Northside Church is a three-year-old church plant with two hundred people in attendance—of which 80 percent are new believers. As babes in Christ they have little understanding or direction when it comes to talking and listening to God. Most of the members are busy businesspeople and parents of young children. The church has no prayer coordinator to organize prayer, no Sunday school classes or small groups to utilize for prayer training. The pastor would like to raise up a praying congregation. Recently he came to me and asked, "What should I do?"

The key to moving this church forward is the pastor. He may begin by promoting a passionate pursuit of Christ in the congregation through his pulpit ministry. The pastor can begin to share with the congregation how the Lord longs for His people to explore and experience the depths of His love by spending time in His presence. The pastor can give the church body a shared vision for what happens when God's people seek Him together: The Lord promises He will draw near to those who draw near to Him.

Here are several other ways pastors can prepare the hearts of their congregations to spend time with their Creator:

- Model a powerful and intimate relationship with Christ.
- Pray with and for the congregation.
- Communicate the exciting rewards that come to those who seek, knock, and ask in prayer (see Luke 11:5-13).
- Preach and teach the Scriptures that give personal prayer instruction.
- Offer nonthreatening ways to pray in the worship service.
- Prepare the church family for the need of a ministry that focuses on prayer—one that helps more people present their adoration, thanksgiving, repentance, and petitions to the Lord.

PREPARATION LEVEL:
TRAINING PRAYER LEADERS

After the hearts of the people in the congregation begin to be stirred with desire to pray, it is important to find the people God has prepared for leadership and then bring them together for training. The pastor does not have to do all the training if someone else in the church, such as the prayer coordinator, is gifted to do so. You may have only a handful of interested people. Still this training level is important.

Reproducing prayer leaders is biblical. For example, Jesus spent time teaching His disciples to pray. Moses invited Joshua into the tent of meeting (his prayer room) to prepare him to be the next leader of Israel (Exodus 33:11). Keep in mind that your church is going to need some powerful prayer groups. Usually it is recommended that you don't start a prayer meeting until a trained leader is in place.

One pastor noted that when he attended prayer meetings led by others, the meetings quickly went into a ditch. Since he didn't want to end up leading all the prayer groups, he decided to hold a boot camp to train others to lead effective prayer meetings. Ongoing training is necessary when raising up a praying church.

Initiation level: Establishing a Beachhead

As soon as you have a trained leader in place, it will be time to start a prayer meeting. Don't be discouraged if at first this is only a small group. Their role is significant: They will establish a "beachhead" for a praying church.

A beachhead is a military term used in warfare to describe the first territory taken from the enemy. This territory is secured only with great sacrifice, often the loss of life. Securing a beachhead is strategic in warfare because from this place all other military operations are launched.

Perhaps the best biblical model for establishing a beachhead is in Acts 2, where we find that the church was established in Jerusalem with a praying company in the Upper Room who prayed until God's Spirit showed up. Then 120 Spirit-filled believers stepped out with great boldness to preach the gospel, and 3,000 were saved in a single day. The mission was the nations of the earth; Jerusalem was the beachhead. Yet it all started with a small number praying in the Upper Room.

Some churches' prayer groups make the mistake of spreading themselves too thin, trying to pray over all the church's prayer requests. Any group desiring to establish a beachhead must maintain focus upon God's strategic goals for the church rather than upon all the congregation's personal requests. To help with this, the prayer leader may ask the pastor to submit his vision statement and church goals to the group for them to pray over. A primary purpose certainly will be for the expansion of the prayer ministry and becoming a house of prayer.

Begin by asking God to bring vision and appoint leaders to expand the church's prayer ministry. Pray for the congregation's spiritual appetite to increase, for a spirit of prayer to saturate the entire congregation. Beseech God consistently and continually until you see His strategic goals established in the church. Increasingly you will want to call out to God for others to join you in holding your beachhead and in taking new ground.

Realize that only a few members may have the desire or preparation to be a part of this initial prayer group. When Gideon was preparing to fight the Midianites, God had him first qualify his army, releasing nearly all of the thirty-two thousand soldiers to go home and keeping only the three hundred that were prepared to go to war (see Judges 7). To establish a beachhead, bring together those who are ready, equipped, and willing to pray the price.

The Enemy will do everything he can to stop your church from establishing a beachhead. He doesn't want you to have an effective ministry that becomes the command and communications center for prayer and spiritual warfare. Recognize that your group's prayers are a huge threat to the kingdom of darkness and that any discouragement you may be facing is just the Enemy's attempt to retake ground. Don't give up!

Through common passion and purpose, covenant with each other not to quit praying until your church becomes a house of prayer that transforms lives, churches, cities, and nations.

IGNITION LEVEL: STARTING UP THE PRAYER MINISTRY

When Dan Bowen took over as prayer coordinator, his church had only an emergency prayer chain. Dan quickly identified a number of people in his church who had a desire to be involved in prayer ministry and in praying with others. However, with myriad prayer options available, Dan was asking, "Where do I start?"

At some point your church will be ready to move from having a single prayer activity or group to having an organized prayer ministry that offers several opportunities for prayer. What you do first will depend upon the specific needs of your church. Some churches begin by mobilizing prayer for some urgent need, such as finding a youth pastor or worship leader.

Where you begin also will be determined by your available resources: leaders, pray-ers, space, and finances. For example, if your church's first prayer coordinator is the pastor's wife, church secretary, or someone else with many time constraints, you will need a simple start-up plan. If your church meets in a school facility, holding prayer meetings during the week may be a challenge.

Especially in the beginning stages, the methods that are most helpful tend to be those that are simple. Dann Spader and Gary Mayes offer the following advice: "The more complicated or time-consuming the method, the less actual prayer takes place. Keep things simple, and you will involve the greatest number of people in the greatest amount of actual prayer.[1]

Prayer leader Cheryl Addabbo uses the principle Dr. Henry Blackaby shares in his book *Experiencing God:* Find out where God is moving and join Him there in His work. As she has followed this wisdom, Cheryl has found willing participants for the pastors' prayer chain, weekly intercessory group, and prayer training classes. When a member of her team came to Cheryl and mentioned the need to raise up prayer for the worship services, she knew it was time to add a new aspect to the prayer ministry.

Here's what a start-up-level prayer ministry might look like:

Leadership: Pastor
Personnel: A part-time volunteer prayer coordinator
Plan: List of prayer activities and a calendar of prayer-related events
Activities:
- Pastor's Prayer Shield
- Prayergram writing
- Telephone or e-mail prayer chain
- Prayer calendar with daily prayer targets
- Prayer library
- Prayer partners meeting in homes or by phone
- Weekly small-group prayer

EXPANSION LEVEL:
BROADENING THE PRAYER MINISTRY

Expanding your prayer ministry means more than adding additional prayer meetings to the calendar. Keep in mind that every successful prayer ministry will include activities to accomplish the following goals:

- **Motivating people to pray or to pray more.** We often call people to come to prayer meetings but spend no time motivating them regarding the rewards of spending time with God and in praying with others. Sharing testimonies of answered prayer and the power of corporate prayer is a strong motivator.
- **Training people to pray more effectively.** When you teach people to pray, you teach them to triumph. It's the prerequisite to a victorious, overcoming Christian life.
- **Developing opportunities for people to become involved in prayer.** One way to expand the prayer ministry is to offer multiple entry points for people to get involved. Don't forget to create ways to connect new members and new believers with the prayer ministry. For example, consider making a tour of the prayer room a part of the new members' class. Then enlist them to come in and pray during the week there. Or start a prayer group that models basic prayer for new believers.

Here's what an intermediate-level prayer ministry might look like:

Leadership: Pastor
Personnel: A part-time or full-time staff or volunteer prayer coordinator and a prayer action team as discussed in chapter 4.
Plan: A written plan with one-year goals
Activities:
- Prayer for the worship services
- Prayer curriculum for all classes
- A prayer room
- Prayer seminars
- Prayerwalking the church campus, schools, businesses, the community

INVASION LEVEL:
FOCUSING THE PRAYER MINISTRY

As your prayer ministry grows and matures, it can become a "hub" for prayer—a command and communications center for prayer mobilization. This will require a God-given strategy. The following story illustrates the importance of a strategic plan.

Several years ago, international prayer leader Cindy Jacobs became deeply concerned about the condition of the church. Everywhere around her, she saw Christians living in defeat, yet God's Word promised so much more.

"How can this be?" she asked the Lord. For several days she agonized over this question as she prayed and fasted. Finally the answer came. "I shall never forget the words that the Holy Spirit impressed upon my heart: 'Cindy, Satan has a strategy, but my people do not!'"[2]

Webster's dictionary defines the word *strategic* as "planning and implementing military operations to defeat an enemy."

Here's what a strategic-level prayer ministry might include:

Leadership: Pastor
Personnel: Paid staff and prayer action team
Plan: Written strategic plan with one-year and five-year goals, objectives, and timeline
Activities:
- All-church corporate prayer
- Crisis and healing prayer teams
- Prayer conferences
- School of prayer
- Twenty-four-hour prayer
- Prayer and fasting periods
- Citywide multichurch prayer gatherings
- Prayer to transform cities and nations

SATURATION LEVEL:
BECOMING A HOUSE OF PRAYER

Trinity Chapel has a well-developed prayer ministry. The centerpiece is a well-run prayer room with a 24-hour manned telephone prayer hotline. Requests from the congregation as well as requests from hundreds of people in the community are prayed over daily. Yet only about 10 percent of the congregation is involved in the prayer ministry. John Moore, the director of prayer ministries, is asking, "What must we do to truly become a house of prayer?"

If Trinity Chapel is to be saturated in prayer, the leadership must take the ministry broader. In a traditional model, the prayer ministry becomes a separate ministry much like any other ministry in the church. In a house of prayer model, prayer is also integrated into the life of the church—the Sunday worship service, Christian education classes, staff, and board meetings. Prayer is woven into the very fabric of the church.

I have discovered a few churches that have attempted to integrate prayer into all aspects of church life without ever establishing a separate and distinct prayer ministry. There is definitely more than one way to accomplish the desired results. However, my personal observation is that the best results are achieved when a church develops a prayer ministry and, from that base of operations, motivates and equips the whole church to pray.

Here are a few guidelines to help you turn a traditional prayer ministry into a house of prayer model:

- Prayer is integrated into all aspects of church life.
- All church leaders take responsibility for prayer envisioning and motivating.
- Prayer training and opportunities are designed for people at all levels of their spiritual journey.
- The prayer ministry moves outside its circle to impact everyone in the church.
- The prayer ministry's vision is to call, prepare, and mobilize the whole church to prayer.

"How will I know when my church is truly a house of prayer?" That's a question prayer leaders often ask. The greatest distinguishing characteristic of a house of prayer is the tangible presence of God. As we draw near to Him, He draws near to us. We can sense and feel His presence.

This pursuit of the Master takes our prayers beyond the superficial. We are no longer satisfied with a surface relationship with our Lord. We want to go deeper. As individuals and as a church, we move from being self-centered to God-centered. Petty differences and divisions disappear. We become empowered to witness; our love for Jesus and one another is evident to all. Something phenomenal happens when a congregation begins a passionate pursuit of God: They find Him.

Breaking the Prayer Level Barrier

In working with hundreds of churches across America, I have discovered that many have little understanding of the spiritual battle involved in becoming a house of prayer. They may sense resistance but lack clarity about what is going on. Others realize the Enemy is working against them but don't know what to do. In other cases, the Enemy quite simply has rocked the church to sleep.

In this section we will discuss how you can break through the invisible barriers that keep your congregation from experiencing new levels of intimacy with Jesus Christ.

Barrier Breaker One:
Removing Hindrances to God's Presence

Church prayer coordinator Linda Jacobs tells the following story of how her church discovered and dealt with hindrances to God's presence:

> One morning I was prayerwalking the property where my
> church was to plant a new work. As I walked I prayed about
> many things I was concerned about in the church—there was
> strife among the church members, the presence of God was
> lacking in our services, and finances were so low we couldn't
> even meet payroll.

As I walked, I asked the Lord again and again, "Why are we not seeing Your power in our church?"

The Lord's answer came like a bolt of lightning: "My people are not holy!"

The words pierced my heart like a jagged sword, and I fell to the ground, weeping.

I would hear these words at least twice more—each time while a church leader was praying for God to manifest His presence in our church. One such instance occurred while my husband and I were praying in a church service. The worship leader was on the platform inviting the Holy Spirit to come in a tangible way into the service.

"If I came in the condition you are in," I heard the Lord say, "you would not live, for I am a consuming fire."

After praying for several days, I shared the experience with my pastor, who promptly took the matter to the Lord. It was not long before the Lord showed the pastor that he was compromising the preaching of God's Word out of a fear of man.

As Pastor John prayed, God began to give him messages on holiness, with a mandate to speak them to the congregation. After repenting of fear and a desire to please man more than God, He found himself preaching with new boldness and authority. He took the church through a series of searching questions that revealed issues of heart. Soon a spirit of repentance fell upon the church.

Many things came to light during this time, among them that the worship leader was living in sexual sin. The church went through a time of cleansing, purging, and repentance.

Within six months the church was not only paying its bills, it was paying off huge portions of the mortgage on the new property. Today the church is growing and the new church plant is thriving as well.

How well that story illustrates how corporate sin hinders the blessings of God from being released in a body of believers. Your church may look good on the outside, but if internally things aren't right before God, you have only a facade. Jesus tells us in Matthew 12:25, "Every kingdom divided against itself will be ruined, and every city or household divided against itself will not stand." Interestingly enough, when a church begins to pray more fervently, one of the first things that happens is that hidden sin is revealed. When we ask the Lord to take us deeper and further with Him, He shows us the things that are standing in the way—things such as pride, prayerlessness, tradition, ambition, and busyness. This is the Lord's invitation to deal with the sin so that we can draw closer to Him. Unfortunately it's sometimes easier to remain status quo than to deal with uncomfortable situations.

Pray! magazine editor Jon Graf tells the story of a church that canceled a prayer initiative because of the light it shed upon a hidden sin issue in the church. Church leaders had started an adopt-a-kid prayer program that at first was met with enthusiasm. A short time later, however, a skeleton was exposed in the family closet of one child. Dealing with it became very messy for the church. Soon afterward, the church stopped the prayer emphasis, fearing that something like that would happen again.[3]

In chapter 5, you began to identify individual and corporate sins in your church that give ground to the Enemy and hinder the movement of God's Spirit. You looked at corporate sins of your congregation, church leadership, and denomination. You examined historic sins as well as those in the present.

To continue this process, you may want to suggest that your church leaders and their prayer partners set aside a day of prayer and fasting, asking God to reveal all hidden sin in the church and give you courage to deal with these issues. Don't be surprised at what is revealed, and be prepared to deal with anything.

It is important that as many as possible of the elders, board members, and full-time pastoral staff be present. It also can be helpful to invite an unbiased outside facilitator to lead the time of prayer and discovery.

It is vital for leaders to take time to search their hearts for personal offenses before embarking upon a time of repentance for corporate sin. I recommend two excellent resources to help with this process. Neil Anderson includes a comprehensive personal guide to freedom in his book *Setting Your Church Free*. Another effective resource is *Returning to*

Holiness, by Dr. Greg Frizzell. The book includes a series of heart-searching questions to help leaders identify and renounce thoughts and actions that are displeasing to the Lord.

After a time of personal repentance, ask the Lord to impress upon your hearts the corporate sins of the church or any significant group within the church. Write down only those sins that have group consensus. Confess (naming each sin individually) those things you have listed. Ask the Lord's forgiveness for each sin. Then ask Him to cleanse, renew, fill, and guide you into truth.[4] Be willing to make things right at any cost.

When leaders have been spiritually cleansed themselves and repented of the corporate sins of the church, they can take the whole church through the process. As you ask the Lord to open the hearts of your church leaders and congregation to this journey to holiness and wholeness, He may give you additional ways to address these issues.

For a forty-day period, Orangewood Nazarene Church prayed for a new revelation of holiness to permeate their congregation. Using the Acts 2 model, they confessed the sins of the church and prayed for a release of God's Spirit. Every Sunday night they distributed pages from the church directory around the sanctuary and prayed the following over every person in the church:

1. Awareness of sin
2. Brokenness
3. Release from sin
4. Christ-shaped character in place of sin pattern
5. A renewed passion for the unchurched

Some prayer coordinators may feel inadequate to talk to their leaders about the need for dealing with corporate sin in the church. One way to present the concept to your pastor is by putting a copy of *Setting Your Church Free* or *Returning to Holiness* in his hands. Another excellent resource is Chris Hayward's book *God's Cleansing Stream*. Church leaders around the world have used these books successfully to guide their church body through the cleansing process.

Barrier Breaker Two:
THE SHIELD anD SworD —
OFFensive anD Defensive Prayer

Several years ago I met a former pastor who told me a sad story. He once had pastored a dynamic, growing church with a heart for the community. The innovative evangelism program he initiated had resulted in more than five hundred new believers being added to the church in a single year. The church was the talk of the community. Even the local newspapers were giving the church positive coverage.

Then at the height of success, the pastor had a moral fall. The Enemy found a hole in the pastor's armor due to an emotional trauma he had experienced as a child, and his world collapsed. Though this man was restored to Christian work, he never pastored again. The church never recovered from the scandal.

This pastor, like so many others I know, went on the offensive with an aggressive evangelism initiative without first raising up his own personal prayer shield. I have noticed that many churches highly focused on missions and evangelism are so intent in their mission that they fail to cover their own lives, families, and congregation in prayer.

> *Most churches extend the ministry of the church beyond the boundaries of their prayer cover.*
>
> Mark Fuller, pastor
> Crossroads Nazarene Church

If your church is going to break through to the next level, you'll need prayer cover in advance of the battle. The bigger the target, the more covering it needs. Experience shows that weaker targets require more protection if they are to resist the attacks of the Enemy. Protection is needed not only for the pastor but for children, youth, marriages, and any area of the church that is especially vulnerable. If you're saving souls in Turkey but families are breaking up in your own church, you need to take another look at your defensive prayer strategy.

Glen Martin and Dian Ginter, in their book *PowerHouse*, say that "a strong prayer covering can help deflect and neutralize most if not all of what the Enemy sends to stop effectiveness for the Lord."[5]

On the other hand, some churches focus all their energies upon praying for the church's needs. Their prayers maintain rather than advance God's kingdom. Offensive prayer relates to fulfillment of the church's mission: winning men and women to Jesus Christ. If you're mostly focused upon the problems of those in the church but making little impact upon the community and the world, then consider mobilizing intercession for schools, government, and unreached people groups. Keep in mind that offensive prayer is most effective when it is coupled with the preaching of the good news and personal witness.

In his book *How to Coordinate a Prayer Ministry*, Dr. Alvin J. Vander Griend says, "A church with a vibrant, proactive ministry takes prayer on the offensive. It releases God's grace for growth and upbuilding as well as healing. Its prayers move beyond the walls of the church building into neighborhoods, workplaces, dormitories, and prisons. It contends as well as defends. It builds the kingdom of God as it breaks down the kingdom of darkness. It storms the gates of hell."[6]

Barrier Breaker Three: Concentration of Force

Generals, tacticians, and warfare strategists have studied and understood the principles of physical warfare for centuries. In the Scriptures, many metaphors and parables compare the Christian life to war. We can see how many precursors to victory in warfare parallel biblical principles. These include knowing your objective, going on the offensive, establishing a strong defense, mobility, communication, adequate resources, and obedience to the commander in chief.

In his classic book on military strategy, B. H. Liddell Hart says that "the principles of war . . . can be condensed to one word—concentration."[7] The word *concentration* comes from the Latin root *com*, which means "together" and *centrum*, which means "to focus one's thoughts and actions upon; to increase the strength and density of."

The principle of concentration then has two components: the first is unity, and the second is the focusing upon a predetermined target. Often in the heat of battle, troops will be pulled from several battlefronts in order to concentrate military force upon a single front or target.

Sometimes in our desire to grow a prayer ministry, we can spread our troops and resources so thin that we defeat ourselves and achieve no breakthrough. Hit-and-run prayer actions can be helpful, but it is better to develop a strategy that saturates a particular area with prayer.[8] There are times the Holy Spirit will direct you to bring the whole church together to pray and fast, concentrating upon a single target. It is important to spend time with the Commander in Chief and discover where He wants you to focus your resources at any given time.

Looking again at Acts 2, let's see how the element of concentration played a role in establishing the church. When Jesus gave the Great Commission, the apostles were not sent immediately to the outermost parts of the earth. They were told to remain together in Jerusalem until they were "clothed with power from on high" (Luke 24:49). Notice the elements of concentration:

- They were all together.
- They all continued together in prayer.
- They were all in agreement.
- They all preached the wonderful works of God (see Acts 2:11).

Barrier Breaker Four: Renouncing the Enemy's Attack

Earlier we mentioned the need to repent for the weaknesses in the church that give the Enemy access. It is also important to ask the Lord to help you discern accurately the attacks of the Enemy upon your church, its leadership, and your congregation that occur because of what you are doing right. The apostle Paul reveals that we should not be ignorant of Satan's devices (see 2 Corinthians 2:11).

C. S. Lewis's book *The Screwtape Letters* gives us a glimpse of the boardroom of hell. Here we see Satan dispatching his forces to hinder the work of God upon the earth. The Bible paints a similar picture of the Christian's battle with the demonic realm. The apostle Paul wrote in Ephesians 6:12, "For our struggle is not against flesh and blood, but against the rulers, against the authorities, against the powers of this dark world and against the spiritual forces of evil in the heavenly realms."

Some churches get beat up, even destroyed, because they are missing the ingredient of fighting the battle in the heavenlies—the realm of prayer. Often as churches, we're fighting only in the earthly realm.

Some of the attacks of the Enemy against us are obvious; others are so subtle we don't even realize who is behind the problem. Neil Anderson suggests that leaders pray together and ask the Lord to help you discern accurately the attacks of the Enemy upon your church, its leaders, and its people. When leaders reach consensus that a situation or situations are spiritual attacks, not just people's ideas, then a time of united fervent prayer is in order.

Anderson suggests that as church leaders we can renounce and disown all influence and authority of evil forces that would resist Christ's work in the church. Then acknowledge the lordship of Christ in the church and spend time exalting and worshiping Him.[9] The following prayer is recommended:

As leaders of this church and members of the body of Christ, we reject and disown all influence and authority of demonic powers and evil spirits that cause resistance to Christ's work. As children of God we have been delivered from the power of darkness and brought into the kingdom of God's dear Son.

In the name and authority of our Lord Jesus Christ, we renounce Satan's attacks of (or by, on, with, through) [each of the identified attacks]. We resist them in Jesus' all-powerful name. We announce that we have been bought and purchased by the blood of the Lamb.

We worship You, O God, and You alone. You are the Lord of our lives and the Lord of our church. We present our lives and the church body to You as a living sacrifice of praise.

We pray protection of our pastors, leaders, members, families, attenders, and all of our ministries. We dedicate our facilities to You and ask You to protect all the property that You have entrusted to us.

Lord Jesus Christ, You are the Head of the church, and we exalt You. May all that we do bring honor and glory to You. In Jesus' holy name we pray. Amen.[10]

If we're to break through to new levels of ministry and God's purposes, we will need to engage in battle. Beginning with clean hands and pure heart, let us lift up holy hands in persevering prayer as we petition our Father for His empowerment to move to new levels with Him.

---

1. Dann Spader and Gary Mayes, *Growing a Healthy Church* (Chicago: Moody, 1991), p. 103.

2. Cindy Jacobs, women's conference, Phoenix, 1998.

3. Jonathan Graf, "Warning: Expect Side Effects," *Pray!* January/February 2004, p. 7.

4. Neil Anderson and Charles Mylander, *Setting Your Church Free* (Ventura, Calif.: Regal, 1994), p. 227.

5. Glen Martin and Dian Ginter, *PowerHouse* (Nashville: Broadman, Holman, 1994), pp. 39–40.

6. Alvin Vander Griend, *How to Coordinate a Prayer Ministry* (Grand Rapids, Mich.: 1997), p. 3.

7. B. H. Liddell Hart, *Strategy* (New York: Meridan, 1991), p. 334.

8. Marc vander Woulde, "Kingdom Development," *Joel News, International Bulletin for Prayer and Revival.*

9. Anderson and Mylander, pp. 318–319.

10. Anderson and Mylander, pp. 318–319.

CHAPTER 7

Designing a House of Prayer Strategy

Just as you wouldn't build a house without a blueprint, so you cannot build a house of prayer without a plan.

A number of years ago I was burdened with a desire to see a comprehensive strategic plan for prayer implemented at Word of Grace. Though our church had several prayer groups and an emphasis upon prayer from time to time, like most other churches, we had no articulated vision or written plan.

After months of prayer and research, I made an appointment with Pastor Gary to share my vision. I came to the meeting with a pounding heart and an armful of books and resources.

Sitting in the reception area before the meeting I wondered, *Will my busy pastor be able to hear my cry for something new, something that's going to take even more of his precious time? Will he agree with me that the Holy Spirit is knocking on the door of Word of Grace with an incredible opportunity to receive more of Him? Or will I be just another appointment, something else on his never-ending to-do list?*

As I poured out my heart to my pastor, I released the outcome to the Lord. I determined I would not push or pressure. During the meeting, my pastor listened intently. He agreed we needed to be intentional about making prayer a priority in our church. To accomplish this goal, he suggested that we build a team and develop a strategy. I was appointed to serve as team leader. Pastor Gary committed to staying visibly involved in the process.

Our team met independently twice a month to formulate the prayer ministry plan. Pastor Gary requested that we meet with him once a month to allow him to pray with us, review our progress, and give his input. This made it possible for our pastor to guide the process while we did the majority of the work.

Later Pastor Gary asked us to seek input from other church leaders and staff. It took us more than a year to complete the process, but in the end the *Word of Grace Strategic Prayer Manual* became the written document that gave direction to the church's prayer ministry for the next several years.

Whether you are a part of a large church or a small one, a written strategy for prayer is essential because it:

> *Prayer is not a program. It's a movement beginning in the heart of God. Still your prayer ministry will benefit from structure because "God is not a God of disorder but of peace" (1 Cor. 14:33).*
>
> Onie Kittle
> *But I Don't Know How to . . .*
> *Start a Prayer Ministry*

- **helps others catch the vision.** A dynamic, living plan calls people into a unity of purpose. Habakkuk 2:2 tells us to "write down the revelation and make it plain on tablets so that a herald may run with it."

- **lets people know what's expected of them.** A plan produces order, brings understanding, and minimizes conflict. Without a vision, the people cast off restraint. In other words, unless everyone knows what's expected of them, there will be misunderstanding.

- **gets people moving.** A plan mobilizes prayer because it states your purpose clearly, outlines strategies to accomplish your purpose, and makes opportunities for people to get involved.

- **sustains prayer.** It sets long-range goals, anticipates measurable outcomes, and establishes ongoing evaluation. It's often more difficult to sustain prayer ministries than start them. A plan helps leaders measure progress and make adjustments when necessary.

- **provides a structure for the pastor to give prayer leadership.** A written plan intentionally keeps prayer on the front burner of the pastor's schedule as well as that of the entire church leadership.

After assessing your church's needs as described in chapter 5, you'll be ready to assemble your team and get started.

ASSEMBLING THE Team TO Draft THE Document

A suggested prayer strategy development team will consist of the pastor, prayer coordinator, and, if your church has one, a prayer action team as discussed in chapter 4. You also may choose to invite other ministry or business leaders in the church who have a heart for prayer and understand strategic planning.

The number of team members may vary, but a suggested team size is from four to six. While it is possible for a church prayer strategy to be assembled by one or two people, the document may never find its way out of a file folder without much broader involvement and acceptance.

PHases OF Prayer STrateGY Development

Once the pastor is committed to the process of developing a strategic plan and the team is in place, it is time to begin. While each situation is unique, most strategy development consists of the following four phases:

PHase One: Prayer and Preparation

It should come as no surprise that the first place to start in raising the level of prayer in your church is with prayer. Simply pray that God would begin to bring about such a shift. Pray for a "grace of prayer" to fall upon your congregation. Ask the Lord to guide you in developing a strategy that will help your congregation become more of a praying church.

God will do much in this season of prayer and preparation. As you spend time in His presence, you will be changed. Don't rush this process. As you spend time in prayer with others, the Lord will knit your hearts together and build your team. He will rid your hearts of disunity, pride, and impure motives. He will prepare the hearts of others He is calling to join

> *Prayer allows God to prepare our hearts, the hearts of all those who will be part of the prayer ministry, and the hearts and lives of those we will be praying for. The more time we spend in prayer preparation, the more effective our prayer ministry will be. It is as simple as that.*
>
> Bjorn Pedersen
> *Face to Face with God in Your Church*

you in this endeavor.

A strategy is not a mental plan. It is in God's presence that successful plans and strategies are born. No amount of planning can build a house of prayer unless it is first *birthed* through fervent prayer.

PHASE TWO: DEFINING YOUR VISION

Every great plan begins with a vision. Vision is a picture of how an organization will look, act, and minister at some point in the future. It is a conceptual plan with little detail that still addresses most areas that ministry will encompass.[1]

Any lasting vision is not just a human idea; it is a gift from God. A vision may first come to you as a dream or an inspired idea. Perhaps a Scripture begins to stir your heart. Reading a book or listening to a sermon may evoke passion about a particular need in the body of Christ. You will feel compelled to meet this need even though you may feel inadequate to do so.

When God gives you a vision, He may bring a picture to your mind repeatedly. Even when we try to push it away, the vision persists and sometimes even becomes stronger. The more you spend time in the presence of the Lord, the more He is able to "download" His heart into yours.

A vision must be clear so that it can be easily communicated. Lack of clarity may be an indicator that you are not ready to move ahead. Write down the vision as you see it at this time. Then pray over it and ask God to fill in the missing pieces. The best plans usually come when we collaborate with others. You may never see the vision clearly until others get involved.

One way to personalize your prayer ministry is to take time to study and pray over your church's mission statement and ministry goals.

Although all churches are called to advance Christ's kingdom, each one will have a different way of fulfilling that mission. If your church doesn't have a clear mission, this will be one of the first things you will want to pray for.

It may take time before a vision becomes clear, but it is worth waiting for. Habakkuk 2:3 tells us, "For the revelation awaits an appointed time. . . . Though it linger, wait for it; it will certainly come and will not delay."

More than twenty-five hunded years ago the Father God declared His vision for His church: "My house will be called a house of prayer for all nations" (Isaiah 56:7). Why not stop right now and ask Him to open your heart to receive His powerful prayer vision for your church?

PHASE THREE: INVOLVEMENT OF CHURCH LEADERSHIP

Though possibly only one or two staff pastors will be involved directly in drafting the prayer strategy, it is important that all feel a part of the process.

You may want to start with a brainstorming session of your church leadership team. A retreat setting would be ideal. The pastor might share his heart to see a praying church and teach briefly regarding the priority of prayer laid forth in Scripture. In an interactive session, ask your leaders to trace the history of prayer in your church. Help them to analyze the place prayer currently holds.

> *Our duty is to reflect the orderliness of God in all we do.*
>
> J. Oswald Sanders
> *Spiritual Leadership*

Allow time to discuss what your church would look like if it were a house of prayer. *The Church Prayer Discovery Guide*, developed by Prayer Transformations Ministries, is a powerful tool to help you take your church leadership through the process. You may print a copy of the guide from the Prayer Tools disk.

PHASE FOUR: DRAFTING A WRITTEN DOCUMENT

An effective written plan will include the following elements:[2]

1. A compelling mission statement
2. Practical goals

3. Clear objectives
4. Specific action plans
5. Adequate job descriptions for key responsibilities
6. A basic organizational chart showing who is responsible to whom
7. A simple budget

The remainder of this section will elaborate on these key elements.

Step #1: Write a clear and concise mission statement.

The mission statement is a short statement of purpose and direction for the ministry. Drafting the mission statement is the single most important planning activity because the mission statement communicates the vision in one or two simple, clear sentences, and all the other basics flow from it.[3]

Every church mission statement usually includes three components: win, build, send. For the prayer ministry this translates into motivation, training, and prayer opportunities.

Let's look at a few examples of prayer ministry mission statements:

Our purpose is to encourage and support all believers at Grace Chapel to communicate confidently and joyfully with God through all areas of prayer.

This mission statement is clear and to the point; however, it mentions only one of the key areas of prayer ministry: motivation. It does not specifically address training or prayer opportunities.

The mission of Joy of Life prayer ministry is to create opportunities and avenues for all believers at Joy of Life to enter into the presence of God through all areas of prayer. Through prayer, our people will be encouraged to strengthen their relationships with each other and reach the community with the message of Jesus Christ.

In its first sentence, this mission statement mentions that creating opportunities for prayer is one of its purposes. It does not mention motivation or prayer education. The second sentence does offer additional information on how prayer is going to enhance the life of the believer.

The mission of the prayer ministry at First Baptist Church is to pray, motivate, and teach others to pray, and to provide prayer opportunities for our church's members, inspired by the Holy Spirit.

The third mission statement is the clearest and most comprehensive, mentioning prayer, inspiration, training, and prayer opportunities all in one sentence.

Some prayer ministries have found that in addition to creating a mission statement, it is beneficial to develop an abbreviated mission statement or tagline that people can easily remember. An example of a tagline is "Every member, a praying member."

Step #2: Develop short-term and long-range goals.

Goals are broad statements describing what the ministry intends to accomplish. They describe the vision in more detail than the mission statement. One goal should come from each key word or idea in the prayer ministry mission statement. The goal and mission statement should be linked so clearly that prayer team leaders will be able to quickly see the relationship between the two.

National prayer mobilizer and strategist Bjorn Pedersen suggests that only two or three goals are needed for the first year. One major goal might be to develop a team of personal intercessors for your senior pastor. Another first-year goal might be to establish a team of intercessors to pray for the worship services.

When developing each goal, ask yourself, *How will we motivate people to pray? What training will we offer them? What opportunities (times, places, options) will be offered?* Then include these in the plan.

Prepare a detailed one-year strategy, and also include major three-year and five-year goals. Some teams find it easier to start with a five-year plan and then back up. Presenting several long-term goals lets your leadership know that you are starting small but that you have a big vision from God. It will also prepare them for next year's expanded ministry plan and possibly larger budget.

An example of a three-year goal might be to develop a video of testimonies that inspire your congregation to pray and to get involved in the prayer ministry. An excellent five-year goal is to hold a citywide multichurch prayer conference.

Step #3: Develop objectives.

Objectives are even more specific than goals. Objectives describe specific tasks that must be accomplished if the goal is to be met. Objectives should be realistic and measurable and include a timeline. For example, if one of your goals is "to raise up a team to pray during the worship services," your first objective might be "to mobilize ten people in two teams of five each to pray during worship by August 31."

One word of caution regarding the use of numbers and dates in goal setting is that they can be discouraging. God blesses plans, but we must be flexible and patient. He has ways of working in our plans and in us, and changing both. This takes time. I know of no church that has become a "praying church" in less than five years.

Step #4: Develop action plans.

Each objective is accompanied by a number of action plans, as each step in the process becomes more specific. Let's continue with the planning process starting above, this time adding objectives.

Goal: To raise up a team to pray during the worship services.
Objective #1: To mobilize two teams of ten people to pray during the worship services by August 31.

Action plans:
1. During July, pastor preaches on the power of praying churches
2. The prayer coordinator visits Sunday school classes on August 1 to recruit people to pray during services on a rotation basis
3. Hold an orientation and training session on August 15
4. Appoint team leader by August 15
5. Prepare prayer agenda for intercessors by August 20
6. Launch worship service intercession on August 27

These days, another important part of developing an action plan is to incorporate a plan for times of crises. Our hearts must be awakened to the times in which we are living. In addition to the threat of terrorism, our nation experiences earthquakes, droughts, fires, floods, tornadoes, and hurricanes of devastating proportions. Without warning, the lives or property of thousands of people in your city may be threatened or destroyed.

Individual churches face crisis when they suddenly lose a pastor, or a church member is hanging between life and death. We must be prepared to respond to any crisis that may arise. When you develop your prayer strategy, it is important to include a crisis strategy. In essence, your strategy says, "If our church, city, state, nation, or world has a crisis, we will respond in the following ways."

The leadership of one church announced to their congregation that in the event of a terrorist attack or other national or citywide disaster, their church would hold a prayer vigil at 7:00 P.M. the same day. In such an event, no other notification of the prayer meeting will be needed. Other churches depend on the churchwide e-mail list to quickly alert members of an emergency. Other examples of crisis prayer strategies include such ideas as twenty-four-hour prayer and fasting chains, around-the-clock on-site prayer teams, prayer booths at the site of a natural disaster, a website with up-to-date information on how to pray, and a prayer hotline.

Step #5: Develop adequate job descriptions for key responsibilities.
Those who serve in leadership function best when they know what is expected of them. For this reason, it is important to develop job descriptions for key leaders within the prayer ministry. A comprehensive job description for a prayer ministry leader would include the following categories: general information, prerequisite qualifications, skills and abilities, and specific ministry responsibilities.

General Information:
Following are some examples of what might be included in the opening portion of a job description. The information needed here will depend upon the level of leadership the position requires, the size of the ministry, and the expectations of the pastor and board.

- Name of the ministry along with its mission statement or purpose
- Job title: (for example, Director of Prayer Ministries, Prayer Action Team Member, or Prayer Captain)
- Job summary: (A sample job summary might be: The prayer

coordinator's role is to organize, schedule, and provide general leadership for the church's prayer activities.)

- Job classification: (for example, volunteer, part-time staff, full-time staff)
- To whom the leader reports (for example, senior pastor or pastor of worship and prayer)
- Position's duration of time: (for example, a prayer captain might serve for one year, a member of the pastor's prayer shield for six months, the director of prayer ministries for an indefinite period based upon evaluation of job performance)
- Expected hours per week: (for example, a part-time paid staff member may work twenty hours per week, a volunteer may have an estimated ten hours per week working at home or at the church)

Prerequisite Qualifications:

General prerequisites might include: a member in good standing with the church, attendance at the church membership class, a financial supporter, a love for prayer, well-grounded in the Word of God, spiritual maturity, moral purity, and honesty.

Skills and Abilities:

Examples of skills needed are the ability to lead, organize, and delegate; ability to lead small-group and corporate prayer meetings; ability to teach and train others in prayer; and the ability to work with a team.

Specific Responsibilities:

These will vary from church to church depending upon the degree of the prayer ministry's development. The following will give you food for thought:

- Responsibilities to the immediate supervisor: how often and in what ways the prayer ministry leader reports to his supervisor; how accomplishments will be tracked.
- Others within the church and the community the leader is expected to relate to and in what way: (for example, assist the head of each department in making prayer a part of the ministry, serve as National Day of Prayer liaison to the community).

- Meetings the ministry leader is expected to lead and/or attend: (for example, attend the staff prayer meeting, lead the Wednesday night all-church prayer meeting).
- Specific areas the leader is responsible for developing or maintaining: (for example, the prayer room, school of prayer, prayer conferences, or the pastor's intercessory team).
- Those whom the ministry leader will oversee.
- What the ministry leader is expected to do to increase skills (for example, attend an annual conference on prayer).

It is important to ask both the ministry leader and his supervisor to sign the job description. This ensures that everyone understands expectations and gives each a deeper sense of commitment to the ministry. Job descriptions will remain relevant when they are reevaluated and updated at least annually.

Step #6: Develop an organizational chart.

An organizational chart is a graphic or illustration that shows how the ministry is organized and to whom each leader is responsible. Developing an organizational chart helps people understand the authority structure and alleviates confusion and misunderstandings.

Because ministries grow and change, the organizational chart should be updated regularly. For more information about how the prayer leadership team relates to each other and fits into the overall church organizational structure, refer to the sample Prayer Team Organizational Chart in appendix C.

Step #7: Develop a budget.

When we think of prayer, we don't often think in terms of a budget. But if prayer is going to move into our church and eventually permeate every aspect of church life, we are going to end up paying for some things. Author and prayer leader David Butts suggests seven categories you may want to include in your prayer budget:

1. **Training for the whole church.** You may want to work with Sunday school classes and set aside an entire month when everyone teaches on prayer. This may require the ordering of

materials and curriculum, or inviting a special guest speaker.

2. **Resources.** These include those needed to set up a church library and/or a book table: fliers; *Pray!* magazine; and *Pray!'s* prayer guides, tapes, and videos.

3. **Prayer room.** In so many churches, the prayer room has become a nerve center. It is an exciting place where people are always coming in and out. Some offer a quiet place to pray. Others have computers where you can connect with other prayer rooms and missionaries. The prayer room will need furniture, supplies, and pictures.

4. **Prayer ministry brochure.** This will include your vision, mission statement, and list of prayer training and intercessory prayer opportunities. Printing and design costs will be involved.

5. **A video of thirty-second testimonies.** This will be a valuable tool for recruiting new people into the prayer ministry. Testimonies may include those who have been healed or saved through the prayers of the prayer ministry, or testimonies of how rewarding it is to pray an hour a week in the prayer room. If you use a video company, this can be expensive, so check to see if someone in your congregation can do this professionally.

6. **Prayer ministry team training.** You may want to take your team to a conference to receive training, or bring in a speaker to train your leaders in a specific area. Airfares and conference registration costs will need to be covered.

7. **Annual prayer conference.** Holding an annual prayer conference or seminar will raise prayer awareness and offer training for the entire congregation. If your church is not ready for a prayer conference, consider taking small groups on a personal prayer retreat. Speaker honorariums, printed materials, and retreat lodging are budget items.

Depending upon the size of your church, you may be able to include only one or two of the above items in your budget the first year. However, as you wisely use the resources God gives you, He will increase your storehouse so that you can do more. (See appendix E or go to the Prayer Tools CD for a Sample Prayer Ministry Annual Budget.)

prayer strategy checklist

Studying the following questions will help guide you and your leadership team through the process of developing a life-giving prayer ministry plan:

- ❏ Has the strategy development been bathed in prayer?
- ❏ Have we involved the church leadership in developing the strategy? Are they in agreement with the plan?
- ❏ Has the senior pastor's role in carrying out the strategy been defined?
- ❏ Has the role of other key church leaders been defined?
- ❏ Does the prayer strategy reflect the unique personality of our church?
- ❏ Does our plan ensure that prayer is a visible priority in the church?
- ❏ Does it include goals for the three essential elements of a strategy: motivation, training, and mobilization?
- ❏ Does the strategy seek to raise the level of prayer in every church member and attendee? Does it include all age groups with respect to their spiritual maturity and season of life?
- ❏ Have we attempted to make prayer a part of the fabric of the church rather than an isolated silo? Does the strategy seek to serve not only the prayer ministry but also the prayer needs of every other ministry in the church?
- ❏ Does the strategy reflect a balance between prayer for the church and its members and prayer for the community and the lost?
- ❏ Does the strategy include a communications system for dispersing prayer requests and answers to prayer?
- ❏ Does the strategy include a budget and organizational chart?
- ❏ Have we kept the desired end result in mind: to see the power and presence of God displayed in the midst of our church, community, and world?

TIPS FOR DRAFTING THE DOCUMENT

- The person or persons drafting the strategic plan must be commissioned by the pastor to do so.
- Don't be in a hurry to complete the written document. If you follow all the steps suggested in this chapter, the process could take a year or more.
- Keep it simple. Start with less complicated strategies and those that are most likely to succeed. Don't spread your resources too thin.
- Use language and a format that reflect the culture of your church. If you want to catch the attention of your leadership, you must speak their language. Is your board made up primarily of business leaders? Are you using "intercessor lingo" they won't understand? Ask your pastor for samples of other high-quality church ministry strategic plans, and study their style and content.
- Visual impact is important, too. Show you have put some time into not only the content but the presentation of the document. Make sure that the presentation is inviting and the document is free of misspellings and grammatical errors. Though it doesn't need to be long or complicated, the written document must be a work of excellence.

YOU'VE COMPLETED YOUR HOUSE OF PRAYER STRATEGY. CONGRATULATIONS! NOW WHAT?

PRESENTING THE STRATEGY FOR ADOPTION

In most churches, there is a process for approving ministry plans and budgets. They must be presented to a church board or someone in authority for approval. The purpose of presenting the strategy is twofold: first, to receive input on how to improve the strategy, and second, to ask for endorsement.

Begin your presentation by explaining the vision, and then move into the strategy. Ask church leaders for input. Listen carefully and take notes. If there is wide acceptance, ask for a formal endorsement of the plan.

Sometimes objections may arise. In such case, ask what specific changes need to be made in order for the plan to be adopted. Your goal is to have the leaders formally adopt the plan before you present it to the congregation.

SHARING THE STRATEGY

Schedule a weekend to share the strategy with the congregation and launch the prayer ministry. You may want to invite a special speaker to share a message on the power of prayer, or consider asking your pastor to preach a series on prayer preceding the launch.

Prior to the day of the launch, make sure you have put in place a sign-up system to enlist volunteers and a scheduled orientation to train new recruits.

IMPLEMENTING THE STRATEGY

Before implementing any ministry idea ask yourself, *Is God leading us to do this? Is the timing now?* Wait until you are certain you have heard from God regarding His timing and that you have sufficient manpower and resources to launch the initiative. Presenting a series of prayer ministry ideas to the congregation that go nowhere will cause you to lose momentum and the confidence of the congregation.

RENEWING THE STRATEGY

It is easier to start a prayer ministry than to maintain one. After starting a prayer ministry, people might begin to drop off after a while. There may be a lot of reasons for this, many of which are beyond your control. However, prayer leaders can minimize the problem by developing renewal strategies.

Sometimes it is necessary to take time off to regroup. Over time, ministries may become cluttered with excessive activities that are draining time and resources and that no longer have God's blessing upon them. Resting and refocusing can help put priorities into perspective. During this time, energy is renewed and team members are enabled to begin again.

In a meeting of more than two hundred key leaders in our church, Pastor Gary Kinnaman presented the strategic plan that we'd spent many months formulating. I shared our team's vision and heart to see Word of Grace become a powerful house of prayer. It has been ten years now since that meeting, and while many of our goals were realized right away, others came to pass years later. Some have been reevaluated and others are still coming to fruition, yet the vision for prayer has grown stronger, and the goal of being a house of prayer has been sustained because we took the time to write it down.

---

1. Walt Kallestad and Tim Schey, *Total Quality Ministry* (Minneapolis: Fortress, 1994), p. 48.

2. Bjorn Pedersen, *Face to Face with God in Your Church*, p. 27.

3. Pedersen, pp. 27–28.

CHAPTER 8

Raising Up the Pastor's PIT Crew

(Personal Intercessory Teams for Pastors and Church Leaders)

In physical warfare the enemy is told, "If you see a man giving instructions, take aim, shoot him."
—Marine Lt. Col. Tom Hemmingway

A. M. Hills recounted this amazing story about Dr. Wilber Chapman, who was a Presbyterian minister in the late 1800s and early 1900s and the cofounder of Winona Lake Bible Conference Center:

> Dr. Wilbur Chapman often told of the following experience when he went to Philadelphia to become a pastor of Wanamaker's Church. After his first sermon, an old gentleman met him in front of the pulpit and said, "You are pretty young to be a pastor of this great church. We have always had older pastors. I am afraid you won't succeed. But you preach the gospel, and I'm going to help you all I can."
>
> "I looked at him," said Dr. Chapman, "and said to myself, Here's a crank."
>
> But the old gentleman continued, "I am going to pray for you that you may have the Holy Spirit's power upon you,

*and two others have covenanted to join me." Then Dr.
Chapman related the outcome.*

"I did not feel so bad when I learned that he was going to
pray for me. The three became ten, the ten became twenty,
and the twenty became fifty, and the fifty became two hundred, who met before every service to pray that the Holy Spirit
might come upon me. In another room, the eighteen elders
knelt so close around me to pray for me that I could put out
my hand and touch them on all sides. I always went into my
pulpit feeling that I would have the anointing in answer to the
prayers of over 200 men.

"It was easy to preach, a real joy. Anybody could preach
with such conditions. And what was the result? We received
1,100 into our church by conversion in three years, 600 of
which were men. It was the fruit of the Holy Spirit in answer to
the prayers of those men. I do not see how the average pastor,
under average circumstances, preaches at all.

"Church members have much more to do than go to
church as curious, idle spectators to be amused and enter-
tained. It is their business to pray mightily that the Holy
Ghost will clothe the preacher with power and make his
words like dynamite."[1]

Dr. Terry Teykl, author of *Preyed On or Prayed For,* says that commit-
ting to pray for your pastor "means more than dashing off a few prayer
phrases once in a while on the pastor's behalf." He defines a pastor's intercessory team as "a hedge of people recruited, planted, trained, aimed, and
motivated to consistently pray for the pastor."[2]

One of the first places to start in building your church into a house of
prayer is with prayer for your pastor and his family. The size and structure of
your pastor's intercessory teams can vary from a small group of five or six
people who pray in the church's weekly prayer meeting to one hundred or
more people who pray daily for the pastor in their own personal prayer time.

My pastor, Gary Kinnaman, has been especially successful in mobilizing
personal intercessory teams. He not only has recruited teams of people to
pray for himself but also has encouraged his worship leader, youth pastor,

and Christian educators to mobilize their own Personal Intercessory Teams—or PIT Crews, as they are fondly referred to at Word of Grace.

WHY DOES THE PASTOR NEED A PIT CREW?

I've discovered that most laypeople don't have any idea that their pastors face incredible difficulties daily. In his book *Partners in Prayer*, Dr. John Maxwell discusses this myth:

> *Many think pastors have few problems, and they mistakenly believe that people in full-time Christian service have special favor with God that protects them from the ordinary difficulties of life. But nothing could be further from the trut. Pastors experience all the same difficulties as . . . [their church members] do, plus they have the incredibly demanding job of leading a church.*[3]

In addition to being on call twenty-four hours a day, a pastor is often plagued with unrealistic expectations and criticism from his flock. Pastoring a church is often a lonely and thankless task. Focus on the Family estimates that fifteen hundred pastors leave their assignments each month due to moral failure, spiritual burnout, or contention within their local congregations.[4] Satan knows that if he can strike a shepherd, the sheep will scatter, and the impact of the ministry will be diminished.

In his book *Pastors at Risk*, H. B. London reports that 40 percent of pastors say they have considered leaving their pastorates in the last three months,[5] and one-half of pastors' wives are severely depressed.[6] "Indeed," London says, "The pedestal is not all it's cracked up to be."[7]

In addition to battling loneliness, stress, feelings of inadequacy, and depression, pastors are also direct targets of spiritual warfare. Most of us have no idea pastors are under satanic attack, and many have never even thought to pray for their pastor. However, Dr. C. Peter Wagner says in his book *Prayer Shield* that pastors and Christian leaders need more personal intercession than others for at least five reasons:[8]

1. God gives pastors more responsibility and accountability than others.
2. Pastors are more susceptible to temptation. The higher one goes in Christian leadership, the higher one goes on Satan's hit list. The heat is turned up, particularly in the areas of money, power, and sex.
3. Pastors are more direct targets of spiritual warfare. It has been widely reported that Satanists, occult practitioners, witches, New Agers, and others have covenanted with each other to conjure up satanic forces specifically to break up the marriages of Christian leaders.
4. Pastors have more influence on others, so when they fall, they take more people with them.
5. Pastors receive more scrutiny, gossip, and criticism. People like to pull them down to their size, and the Enemy uses these openings to move in and destroy.

Without the supernatural power of God released through a praying congregation, pastors and churches often never reach their potential in God. However, when pastors are prayed for, they are equipped to carry out God's plans.

The great preacher and author E. M. Bounds writes,

> What preacher does not recognize when he walks to the pulpit whether the people have been praying for him or not? How hard they have found it to preach in some places. This is because the way had not been made in prayer. They were hampered in their delivery, there was no response to their appeals. On the other hand, at other times, thought flowed easily, words came freely; there was liberty. It takes prayer in the pulpit and prayer in the pew to make preaching arresting, life-giving, and soul-saving.[9]

Iverna Tompkins, head of a national ministry based in Scottsdale, Arizona, felt so strongly about the power of intercessory prayer for Christian leaders that her staff developed a five-hour training course to teach intercessors how to pray for pastors and other ministry leaders. They were given eighteen areas of a leader's life on which to focus prayer. Willing intercessors were assigned a ministry person to pray for during the year. (See appendix F or go to the Prayer Tools CD for this powerful prayer model.)

Sometime later, a survey was conducted to determine if the results of these prayers could be quantified. The survey of 130 pastors, evangelists, and missionaries revealed that prayer makes a dynamic difference— eighty-nine percent indicated a positive change in ministry effectiveness when one of these trained intercessors prayed for them only fifteen minutes a day for an entire year.[10]

One of the most frequent prayer requests I hear from pastors is "Please pray for my family." Pastors realize that spiritual attack is often aimed not only at their ministry but at their family as well. Pastors don't want their children or spouse to get caught in the cross fire.

The following story, published in *The Arizona Republic*, illustrates the power of intercessory prayer over the life of a pastor's son.

> It was 11 a.m. and the women's intercessory prayer meeting at The Father's House was just getting underway. Suddenly at 11:30 a.m. the group leader interrupted the general prayer time. Based on the Holy Spirit's prompting, she instructed everyone to focus their immediate attention upon praying for their pastor's seventeen-year-old son, Jerrod. "We must stop right now and pray for a 'spirit of death' to be removed from Jerrod Logan," she exclaimed.
>
> For the next forty-five minutes, five women earnestly beseeched God to protect Jerrod from death. At 12:15 p.m. the burden for prayer lifted, and the women stopped praying.
>
> Unbeknownst to them, several miles away Jerrod was riding in the backseat of his friend's vehicle, returning to West Valley High School after an off-campus lunch with several other students. Their car collided with another vehicle. Tragically, one of Jerrod's classmates was killed.
>
> Jerrod has no memory of the accident or the fast-paced events that led to it. However, the paramedics and police

report show the accident happened at 12:15 p.m.

"Within the boundaries of human means of communication, there was no way that these ladies could have known that Jerrod and those with him would be in an automobile accident or that his life would be threatened," said Jerrod's father, Pastor Logan.

These situations are difficult to explain. Why was one child's life spared and the other taken? "I don't claim to have all the answers," Pastor Logan said. "One thing we do know. The Holy Spirit Himself issued a call to prayer for Jerrod Logan—and He found yielded vessels ready and willing to respond.[11]

prayer shields—are they biblical?

The idea of personal intercessory prayer teams for pastors and Christian leaders is not new. Moses, Aaron, and Hur served as an intercessory prayer team for Joshua in the battle with Amalek (see Exodus 17). In this passage, Israel was in a battle with the Amalekites. Joshua, the ministry leader, was down in the valley in the heat of combat while Moses, Aaron, and Hur were interceding on the hilltop overlooking the battlefield.

The Scripture tells us that as long as Moses' arms and hands were up, touching God in intercession, Israel was winning the battle. However, when his arms were down, Israel was losing the battle. So Aaron and Hur came alongside Moses and held up his arms until the sun set. It is recorded that Joshua defeated Amalek with the sword. An intercessory prayer team made the difference between victory and defeat for Joshua and for the nation of Israel.

Many other Scriptures reference the power of intercessory prayer for leaders. In Acts 12 we find that King Herod is determined to destroy two Christian leaders, James and Simon Peter. Scripture is not explicit about why one leader was killed and the other spared, but the Word of God does tell us something concerning Peter that is not mentioned about James. When Peter was in prison, the Word tells us "the church was earnestly praying to God for him" (verse 5).

We also find in the New Testament that Jesus prayed for Simon Peter. Jesus said, "Simon, Simon, Satan has asked to sift you as wheat. But I have prayed for you, Simon, that your faith may not fail" (Luke 22:31-32). Today Satan still desires to sift our pastors and Christian leaders like wheat. As Jesus did, we must pray for leaders that they will not become discouraged or disheartened. Pray that their faith will not fail.

THE PIT CREW—GOD'S PLAN OF DEFENSE

Though we have an Enemy who is out to destroy our pastors, God has a plan of defense—the power of intercessory prayer. All over the world He is alerting His people about the need to pray for their Christian leaders. Pastors, too, are waking up to the fact they need the prayer covering of their church family now and more than ever.

For the best prayer coverage, it is recommended that pastors recruit more than one group of intercessors, as described by Cindy Jacobs in her book *Possessing the Gates of the Enemy*:[12]

1. **Inner Circle.** This is a small inner circle group knit together by God. Moses had Aaron and Hur. Jesus seemed most intimate with Peter, James, and John. In the same way, some intercessors will be especially faithful in praying for you.

2. **Outer Circle.** These committed intercessors can be likened to Christ's other nine disciples. Though they may not pray as often, they will pray for their pastor on a regular basis.

3. **Congregation.** These are members of a congregation who pray for their pastor frequently but with whom a pastor does not have close personal contact. They are nevertheless important to mobilize as a pastor describes his needs from the pulpit or platform every Sunday.

4. **Crisis Intercessors.** There are times when pastors have a ministry assignment that is particularly trying. At other times they are undergoing spiritual or physical attack and need more intercession than usual. God will raise up crisis intercessors to pray until the assignment is finished or the attack ceases. Crisis intercessors can be mobilized by a newsletter, media appeal, or other announcements.

A PASTOR'S TESTIMONY

When Dr. John Maxwell was pastor of Skyline Wesleyan Church in San Diego, California, he mobilized one hundred men to serve as his personal prayer partners. Each Sunday at 7:00 A.M. on a rotating basis, one-fourth of the men met Maxwell at the church sanctuary to pray over him and for every person who would sit in the service that morning.

Maxwell also recruited intercessors to pray during the Sunday services. His prayer coordinator assigned at least two prayer partners for every service and designated one as the captain. Most members served just once a month, but how often each person prayed depended on the size of the intercessory prayer team.

When Max Lucado visited Maxwell's church, he was so impressed by Maxwell's example that he went home and rallied 120 intercessors to pray for him. Within just six months of mobilizing prayer, Lucado's church experienced the following:[13]

- The church finished the year with its highest ever average for Sunday school attendance.
- Several significant healings were witnessed.
- Six new elders and three new staff members were added.
- Much of the congregation and staff fasted forty days, resulting in amazing blessings.

The discovery of Maxwell and Lucado about the power of intercession is not uncommon. Surveys show that pastors who are prayed for regularly by trained intercessors experience a positive impact on a ministry's effectiveness.

THE ROLE OF THE PASTOR'S INTERCESSORS

Problems sometimes arise between pastors and intercessors simply because the role of those serving on the intercessory prayer team has not been clearly defined. The following guidelines will help define the personal intercessor's role:

Pray daily if possible.

The intercessor should be faithful to pray for the pastor on a regular basis. However, intercessors should not be under bondage or fall into condemnation when they're unable to pray. The length of time each intercessor on the team can spend in prayer will vary greatly depending upon his schedule, circumstances, and gifting.

Pray as the Holy Spirit leads you.

Many intercessors find they pray for one particular area of their pastor's life more than other areas. For instance, some intercessors feel inclined to pray mainly for the leader's spouse or children, others for some particular aspect of the leader's life, such as integrity and moral purity. Feel free to pray whatever the Holy Spirit directs you to pray.

Pray—don't counsel.

Intercessors need to resist the urge to counsel the pastor or give direction to the ministry. God, however, does often reveal His plans to those who pray. If you receive a Scripture or prophetic word for your pastor in prayer, ask the Lord if you are to share it with your pastor or just pray about it. Ask the pastor or prayer coordinator what the best way is to pass on information of this nature. Unless it is an urgent matter, one suggestion is to drop your pastor a note.

Avoid expecting pastors to pray for you personally.

It's the pastor's responsibility to faithfully pray for his prayer team, although he cannot make the same commitment in prayer to his personal intercessors as they make to him. It, therefore, is not appropriate for an intercessor to ask the pastor to pray over his prayer requests, except for critical requests.

Never talk about or entertain anyone who talks about your pastor or his family.

Set the example. Never repeat anything your pastor asks you to pray about. If you're uncertain about the confidentiality of the request, ask for permission to share the request with others. Prayer team members who speak critically about the pastor or the pastor's family or share confidential information have ruined prayer ministries and brought pastors much pain.

Expect intercession to be a sacrifice of love.

If you expect to receive special recognition from the pastor, you may be greatly disappointed. Let your prayers be a sacrifice of love, and the Lord will reward you.

Stand in the gap.

The Enemy is looking to attack the leader in a place of weakness. God's defense is when intercessors stand in the gap where the wall of protection is crumbling down. Ask the Lord to rebuild vulnerable places in the leader's life. Be on guard that if you do not understand your role, you may become disillusioned, disappointed, and even critical of the leader.

Don't be an overcommitted intercessor.

Agree to serve as a personal intercessor only if you are directed of the Lord and have enough time to pray adequately for that pastor or ministry leader. Some intercessors say they pray for ten, fifteen, or even more ministries a day. This may be true. However, to commit to that many ministry leaders as a personal intercessor would take more time than most people have.

Be patient for pastors to reveal personal requests or needs.

Pastors are under no obligation to share prayer requests until a trust relationship is built.

An Intercessor's Testimony

Deborah Tyrrell has served as the personal intercessor for the same team of ministry leaders for twenty years. Her words regarding the relationship of an intercessor with a Christian leader speak more than mine ever could:

Sometimes I am asked how I learned to pray for a ministry leader. The answer is, "Just by doing it." The Holy Spirit teaches us how to pray. God's grace is sufficient for all that He requires from us. Though I sometimes use prayer guides, primarily I pray what the Holy Spirit directs me from the Bible.

Sometimes when I am praying, the Holy Spirit gives me a Scripture or an impression regarding one or both of the

*leaders for whom I pray. I have learned to be sensitive to
whether or not I'm supposed to share it with them, or just
pray it for them. Usually if it's a word that I share with
them, it is one of edification or encouragement instead of
direction or correction.*

*We must especially deal with our need for recognition,
approval, and affirmation from those we're praying for. If we
embrace the unconditional approval and acceptance from
God, we won't feel rejected. There can be no conditions on
our investment of time. It must be solely to please the Lord,
not to gain the approval of man or his ministry. If we give of
our time as a sacrifice to God for a ministry, then that work
will become our glory and our joy, too.*

*Lastly, intercession is a commitment to imperfect people.
To appropriate the discernment that is in the mind of Christ,
we first must have the love that is in the heart of Christ. A
judgmental or critical spirit is a foothold for the enemy that
will bring division and destroy the relationship. We need
God's love concerning leaders' character defects.*[14]

Here's a final word of encouragement for those who feel inadequate for
the task. Remember that faith regards neither sight nor feeling but rests in
the assurance that the Spirit is praying in and through you. The Spirit of life
in Christ can free you from failure in prayer. What you see no possibility of
doing, God's grace will do by enabling you to pray the effectual and fervent
prayer that avails much.

ORGANIZING THE PIT CREW

The following are some suggestions to help prayer coordinators train and
communicate with the pastor's personal intercessory teams.

OFFER TRAINING

- Personal intercessors serve best if they know what's expected of
  them. An introductory meeting to share expectations is critical.

When an intercessor joins the team, it is important to give him guidelines on how to pray for a ministry leader.

- If intercessors pray as a group, provide training on small-group and corporate prayer. This will help avoid problems that sometimes arise among intercessors if they don't know how to relate to those who pray differently than they do. Ongoing training in intercessory prayer is important for helping intercessors remain inspired and be refired.

ESTABLISH CHANNELS OF COMMUNICATION

- You will want to communicate prayer requests and answers to prayers to your intercessors, so you'll need efficient ways of communicating. This can be done through letters, e-mails, electronic voice mail, or a password-secured website.
- Clarify with your intercessors how they should handle any word of encouragement, prophecy, or Scripture they receive for the pastor. You may want them to put it in writing and deliver it to you or the church office. Let them know whether or not they have permission to call you or your pastor at home and, if so, during what hours.
- Provide specific prayer requests. You want to avoid overburdening your intercessors, so make prayer requests short and to the point. Limit requests to five or six at a time. These should be updated every two weeks unless urgent requests come up.
- Provide the intercessory prayer team with a packet of general information that requires ongoing intercession. Some examples include the following: general information about the pastor's spouse and children; any special problems they may be facing; and the church's mission statement, goals, and ministry objectives.

QUALITIES OF AN INTERCESSOR

Now let's look at some qualities to consider when selecting the pastor's intercessory team.

- **A heart for the pastor, his family, and his ministry.** At the core of intercession is love. Those who love the pastor will make the sacrifice of time and energy to intercede for him, and love will protect their hearts from criticism.
- **Ability to respect confidential information.** This is a critical attribute of a faithful intercessor. An intercessor needs to be trusted with personal matters that often require the most prayer.
- **Availability.** Those who are overcommitted may have good intentions but in reality may not be able to undergird you in prayer.
- **Humility—not looking for recognition.** Those who seek recognition or greater access to the leader often find themselves disappointed and sometimes become highly critical of the leader and the church. Look for those willing to stay behind the scenes.
- **Strong Christian character.** A person's character is even more important than how much he knows about prayer. People can be taught to pray if they have a committed walk with the Lord and a right heart toward figures of authority.
- **Faithfulness in the local church.** A red flag should go up when you find intercessors who are not accountable to the local church. Like spiritual butterflies, they flit from group to group and church to church. Look for those who are faithful to God and God-ordained authority.

Ideas for recruiting intercessors

Cindy Jacobs gives helpful advice to pastors who desire to raise up personal intercessors. She bases her advice on Jesus' words in Matthew 7:7, "Ask and it will be given to you; seek and you will find; knock and the door will be opened to you."[15]

The first step is to pray and ask the Lord to set aside personal prayer partners for your ministry. Ask Him to guide you to the faithful and confidential people who already are praying for you. Next make a list. As the Lord brings someone to your mind who has demonstrated an interest in praying for you, write down her name.

Prayerfully consider the names on the list. Do they meet the qualifications of a personal intercessor? Call or write each one personally and ask if she would serve on your intercessory prayer team. Be honest about what it entails. Encourage them to answer only after they have prayed and only if they feel God is calling them to be a personal intercessor for you. Most pastors I know ask their intercessors to make a one-year commitment to the prayer team. At the end of the year, they give the intercessors an invitation to recommit.

Dr C. Peter Wagner suggests that inner-circle intercessors should not be recruited but rather the leader should ask the Holy Spirit to sovereignly produce spiritual bonding so there's no question the relationship is of God.[16]

The best way to recruit congregational intercessors is from the pulpit. Although this level of intercessor may not know the intimate details of a pastor's life and may not spend a lengthy time in prayer each day, his prayers nonetheless can have great impact. Sometimes congregational intercessors get so excited about praying that they eventually commit to a deeper level of intercession.

If you're a pastor, you're probably asking the same question Tom Hodge was asking several years ago: "How do I find intercessors who will pray for me like that?" Tom is the pastor of a Southern Baptist church in Venice, Florida. For several years he pastored a church in our city. One day he came to me and asked if I could help him mobilize personal intercessors.

I suggested to Tom that he seek the Lord concerning the number of prayer partners he should have on his team and then pray that God would send them to him. He decided to use the approach of making an announcement in the Sunday morning service that anyone interested in becoming a part of his personal prayer team should come to a training meeting.

As the time of the training session approached, Tom confided in me that he was believing God for fifty people to serve on his personal intercessory team. I gulped! I didn't want to tell him a more realistic number to recruit the first time is more like ten or fifteen people. To my surprise, an astounding forty-eight people showed up for training that afternoon and made a commitment to pray for Tom. Within the next week, two more people dropped by Tom's office to explain they were unable to attend the meeting but wanted to serve on his prayer team.

Tom's approach was simple. He prayed and then unashamedly made the need known. Then by holding an introductory training session right away, Tom was quickly able to secure a commitment from his intercessors.

When Julie Touvell was prayer coordinator for The Valley Cathedral in Phoenix, she told the following story of how she helped her pastor mobilize intercessors:

> It was Sunday morning and the 2,500-seat auditorium was filled almost to capacity. This was Focus on the Family's Clergy Appreciation Day, and Julie realized it was a great opportunity to launch the prayer ministry's Adopt-a-Pastor-in-Prayer initiative.
>
> She shared with the congregation that the best way to honor their pastor and church staff was to pray for them. Then she creatively illustrated the critical need to pray for church leaders with the following demonstration.
>
> Julie asked her pastor to stand alone in front of the pulpit and hold in front of him a large target like the ones used for shooting practice. "We are in a real war," she said to the congregation. "The church is the target, and the pastor is the bull's-eye!" She explained how vulnerable church leaders are when they stand alone. Then she asked a number of the intercessors to come and encircle Pastor Scott. "See," she said. "The target is no longer visible. When we stand with our pastor in prayer, he is shielded from enemy attacks!"
>
> Julie then invited the church members to choose one of the staff pastors to adopt in prayer for the next three months. Following the service, people flooded to the information center in the foyer to sign up to pray. There they found pictures displayed of the church's twelve staff pastors and an enthusiastic volunteer to assist those who were willing to participate. To Julie's surprise, 400 people adopted a pastor in prayer that day.[17]

The former prayer coordinator of First Historic Presbyterian Church in Phoenix, Gina Reinecke, had another great idea. She made up a prayer shield card with a picture of her pastor, Gayle Parker, and Gayle's husband,

Tom. The card included specific requests on how the congregation could pray for Gayle and her family. Gina encouraged church members to put the card in their Bible or attach a magnet and hang it on the refrigerator as a reminder to pray for their pastor.

Other pastors distribute tabletop cards that read, "Have You Prayed for Your Pastor Today?" These can be purchased through Dr. Terry Teykl at Renewal Ministries (www.prayerpointpress.com). The ministry also carries key chains bearing small cards with Scriptures to pray over the pastor. Ideas like these can help entire congregations learn to pray daily for their pastor.

My pastor, Gary Kinnaman, has mobilized seventy men who meet him for prayer every Wednesday at 5:30 A.M. Included in this group is one teenage boy who faithfully attends the meeting before going to school. Perhaps Kinnaman has experienced this kind of success with his prayer team because he personally recruited each man through a letter of invitation and he personally leads each meeting.

Kinnaman also meets for prayer with a smaller group of about ten men and women once a month and communicates with them through a monthly prayer letter. He requires every pastor on staff to mobilize his own Personal Intercessory Team.

THE PASTOR AND PIT CREW RELATIONSHIP

The relationship between the pastor and his inner circle of intercessors is rooted in trust, commitment, and accountability. Some pastors feel confident having inner-circle intercessors from within their church. Others don't feel they can be that vulnerable with anyone in their congregation. They have found their inner-circle intercessors from among other pastors, especially in pastors' prayer groups.

The real issue is that every pastor and pastor's spouse should have someone in their lives they can call when they are experiencing discouragement, temptation, frustration, or marriage and family conflict. As church leaders for over twenty years, my husband and I have depended on our inner-circle intercessors, who have not only seen us at our worst but also have prayed us out of some of the deepest pits of the Enemy and darkest hours of our lives.

"FOR PASTORS ONLY"

Pray For and Encourage Your Prayer Team

Pray for unity among your personal intercessory team, protection for them and their families, and the Holy Spirit's guidance in prayer. However, as a pastor, you are not expected to make the same degree of commitment in prayer to them as they have made to you.

Be sure to thank them often for their investment in your life and ministry. Occasionally send a note, book, tape, or article on prayer as a source of encouragement. For a special treat, plan a dinner for fellowship and prayer.

Most important, remember to provide praise reports. Intercessors are encouraged when they know their prayers are being answered.

HOW TO Pray For Pastors and Ministry Leaders

Now that you realize how much prayer impacts the life and ministry of pastors, you will want to learn how to pray more effectively for them. (Appendix F and the Prayer Tools CD contain a detailed guide to praying for a spiritual leader.) The following are some tips to help you pray for Christian leaders not just in times of crisis or difficulty but in every area of their lives:

Begin with what you know.
Is your pastor preparing to speak in the weekend or midweek service? Then pray for his preparation time. Will there be time for a vacation soon? Pray for safety, good health, weather conditions, on-time flights, rest, and blessings upon family

relationships. Is your pastor ministering out of town? Pray for protection over the family and the church while he is away, good communication with the ministry host, and favor with those to whom he will minister. You may not feel very anointed when you begin to pray for your pastor, but just get started. The Holy Spirit will give you guidance as you step out in faith.

Proclaim Scripture as you pray.

The Word is sharper than any two-edged sword so hold fast to its truth. Pray Scriptures that apply to situations you know about in the pastor's life. A good example is to pray Psalm 91 for protection over the leader's life. Pray the scriptural prayers from the Epistles and allow the Holy Spirit to quicken Scriptures to pray over the leader every day. Some applicable Scriptures are Ephesians 1:17-19, Philippians 1:9-10, and Colossians 1:9-11. One powerful prayer method is to insert your pastor's name in the Scripture verse and pray it back to the Lord.

Be aware of special prayer needs.

While the prayer needs of pastors may differ, there are three times in every leader's life when he needs special prayer coverage: just before, during, and just after a time of ministry.

- *Pray for your pastor before a service or event.* Often before a time of ministry, many distractions will come to crowd out the pastor's ministry preparation time. Sometimes before the delivery of a powerful message, pastors are hit with personal illness or sickness in the family, fatigue, weariness, or lack of motivation. Strife within the home or church staff is another emotionally draining and time-consuming distraction. All of this is an attempt of the Enemy to keep the pastor from receiving God's message for His people. Pray that your pastor will have adequate prayer and study time, for his good health and stamina, and for unity within his family and church staff. Throughout the week, it is important to pray a shield around your pastor's spirit, soul, mind, and body.

- *Pray for your pastor during ministry.* Once pastors receive a message from the Lord, the Enemy will often attempt to steal it away. Pastors tell me they often have negative thoughts just before they get up to speak. They sometimes feel so intimidated that they lose confidence and boldness to deliver the message. Pray for boldness for your pastor as he delivers the Word. Pray that your pastor will bring the Word of the Lord to the people with clarity and authority.

While the pastor is preaching, many distractions may occur. External distractions include babies crying, people getting up and down, or equipment failure. Internal distractions are more subtle and range from the pastor's inability to think or express himself clearly to the congregation feeling apathetic, having wandering thoughts, or being restless. The prayer covering of intercessors often buffers and even annihilates such distractions.

Hundreds of churches are mobilizing intercessors to pray before and during the church service. Sometimes these intercessors pray inconspicuously in the sanctuary. Other times they are praying in another room. These intercessors pray for clarity of mind and anointing for the pastor. They pray that the Word of God spoken from the pastor's mouth will be "sharper than any double-edged sword, . . . dividing soul and spirit, joints and marrow; [judging] the thoughts and attitudes of the heart" (Hebrews 4:12).

During the service, it's most critical that intercessors pray for the salvation of the lost—that the Holy Spirit will draw the unsaved and give them the desire to come to Christ. Additionally, pray for believers to move into an even more intimate relationship with God.

• *Pray for your pastor after a service or event.* Just following a time of ministry, pastors often feel discouragement, depression, a sense of failure, and a desire to quit the ministry. Please do not stop praying for your pastor after the weekend service.

Sunday afternoons and even Mondays are often difficult times in the homes of pastors. There is a joke that the pastor resigns every Monday morning, but this is really no joking matter. It is the retaliation of the Enemy!

One pastor I know stopped taking Mondays off because he

was so depressed he couldn't enjoy the day. A pastor's wife confided in me that she tries to be out of the house on Mondays, her husband's day off, because he is so discouraged. Just following a time of ministry, pastors often are physically weary and don't pray as much, and so pastors and their spouses are the most vulnerable and need more intercession. We must pray against the spirit of retaliation, division, and depression and raise up a prayer shield for the pastor following every time of ministry.

BEYOND THE PIT CREW

Once the pastor and other important church leaders are covered in prayer, you'll be ready to start expanding prayer throughout the church. The next chapter will help you begin motivating the whole church to pray.

---

1. John Maxwell, *Partners in Prayer* (Nashville: Nelson, 1996), pp. 93–94.

2. Terry Teykl, "Raising Up the Pastor's Prayer Shield," *The BridgeBuilder*, January, 1997.

3. Maxwell, p. 79.

4. James Dobson, *Family News from James Dobson*, August 1998.

5. H. B. London, *Pastors at Risk* (Wheaton, Ill.: Victor, 1993), p. 25.

6. London, p. 27.

7. H. B. London, *Clergy Appreciation Month Planning Guide*, p. 5.

8. C. Peter Wagner, *Prayer Shield* (Ventura, Calif.: Regal, 1992), pp. 66–73.

9. E. M. Bounds, *E. M. Bounds on Prayer* (New Kensington, Pa.: Whitaker House, 1977), p. 597.

10. Nancy Pfaff, "Christian Leadership Attributes Dynamic Increase in Effectiveness to the Work of Intercessors," *Church Growth Journal*, p. 81.

11. Rodrick Logan, "Prayer Shielded Son in Deadly Crash," *The Arizona Republic*, January 12, 1998, p. 2.

12. Cindy Jacobs, *Possessing the Gates of the Enemy* (Ventura, Calif.: Regal, 1991), pp. 161–162.

13. Max Lucado, foreword to *Partners in Prayer*, by John Maxwell

14. Deborah Tyrrell, seminar at Covenant Grace Church, Phoenix, September 1990.

15. Jacobs, p. 163.

16. Wagner, p. 122.

17. Cheryl Sacks, "Who Will Help Me Build It?" *My House Shall Be a House of Prayer,* eds. Jonathan Graf and Lani C. Hinkle (Colorado Springs, Colo.: NavPress, 2001), pp. 22–23.

CHAPTER 9

Motivating the Whole Church to Pray

Slam! Jeff Fillis shut the door behind him, locking himself inside his church's prayer room. It was 6:00 P.M. He would not reopen the door until his replacement arrived at 6:00 A.M. With a sense of both anxiety and excitement, he assessed the accommodations where he would spend the next twelve hours. Maps of the community filled the walls. Lists of names to pray over were stacked on a small table in the corner. A cot was available for times he might need to rest. A cassette player filled the room with worship music.

Jeff was the 119th person to sign up for such a stay in the prayer room. For nearly six months now, the prayer room had been occupied by an intercessor twenty-four hours a day. How had this all come about?

Several months before, Pastor Bob Hake of Orangewood Nazarene Church had showed a video called *Transformations* to his congregation. Capturing present-day revivals ignited by the desperate prayers of God's people, this one-hour documentary shares the stories of transformed cities like Cali, Colombia, where the united prayers of believers resulted in the demolition of the Cali drug cartel—the largest, richest, most organized drug cartel in the world.[1] After watching the video, the congregation couldn't be contained. "If prayers can change a city like Cali, prayers can make a difference in our community as well," they exclaimed.

From that meeting emerged several Transformations prayer groups, organized for the sole purpose of praying for the one-mile radius of their church to be changed by the power of God. In addition, the Orangewood prayer ministry developed a plan to mobilize the church family to prayer-walk the perimeter of the targeted neighborhood. They ordered an aerial photograph of the one-mile radius and secured the names of every resident within that location. Intercessors prayed for each person by name. Now for nearly six months, with only a few exceptions, someone had been in the prayer room twenty-four hours a day praying for the salvation of each household.

Orangewood had hit on an effective strategy for increasing the congregation's passion for prayer. Still, one of the questions I hear most frequently is "How can we increase interest in prayer?" Many pastors and prayer leaders say they've tried everything they know to do and still can't get their people involved in prayer and the prayer ministry.

National author and prayer leader Thetus Tenney says, "We must make prayer exciting. This requires thinking outside the box, planning, and creativity. Look what's happened with the use of music, art, and drama in the church in the last decade. It's time to take prayer out of the dusty back room."[2]

> Most pastors who have trouble getting their people to respond to prayer do so because the people haven't been stirred to the point of asking for it.
>
> John Franklin
> A House of Prayer

Heart Preparation

The Bible reveals that whenever God is ready to do a new thing, He always prepares the hearts of His people. One example of this is in His sending John the Baptist to prepare the way for the coming Messiah. Luke 3:15 confirms that John had accomplished his mission of preparing hearts: "The people were waiting expectantly and were all wondering in their hearts if John might possibly be the Christ."[3]

Because the Holy Spirit is the One who fills hearts with spiritual hunger, nothing can take the place of praying for your church members to be filled with desire to spend time with their heavenly Father. I know of some pastors and prayer leaders who meet in the sanctuary during the week to pray over every seat—that each person who attends the weekend worship service would be drawn closer to the Lord and to the place of prayer.

You will know that your congregation's hearts are being awakened when they begin to talk about their desire to become more intimately acquainted with Christ, mention that more prayer is needed in services, suggest starting a class on prayer, or begin to pray spontaneously with others before and after services.

MAXIMIZING THE WORSHIP SERVICE

The weekend worship service is the best place to awaken the whole church with desire to spend time with God. However, in many American worship services today, very little prayer takes place. This need not be the case, for with just a little planning and creativity, talking with God can become an exciting part of your service.

As a prayer leader, you can assist your pastor, worship leaders, and planning team in designing a worship service that incorporates opportunities to address God (praise and adoration), express their needs (petitions and requests), and be led by the Holy Spirit as He helps them pray (listening and reflecting).

During the worship service, pastors are in a unique position to stir desire for prayer in the hearts of their congregations. Following are some ways pastors and worship leaders can do this:

- Share from their own personal prayer life. Let the excitement overflow.
- Preach a sermon series on different aspects of prayer.
- Give pulpit announcements about prayer opportunities.
- Invite children to come into the worship service and to pray blessings over the adults.
- Encourage people to give testimonies to answered prayer in corporate services.
- Many worship songs in actuality are prayers. As you bring this to

the congregation's attention, encourage them to direct their song as words of adoration or petition to the Lord.

- Between verses of a hymn or worship chorus, invite the congregation to pray in small groups, focusing on the lyrics they have just sung.
- Set aside times during worship for individuals to come forward to offer a prayer inspired by a worship song.
- Use introductory remarks to guide the prayer time: "As a sign of our praise and adoration of God, please stand"; or "As a sign of our humility, please kneel (if you are physically able) as we confess our sins"; or "As a sign of our unity in Christ, please form a group with three or four others. We will recite the Lord's Prayer together."
- Invite parents and children to pray together—holding hands, forming circles, or walking together to pray at the altar during worship or the communion service.
- Spend a series of Sundays praying for various church ministries: "This morning, as our Sunday school teachers and workers stand among us, we will pray for them and the people they serve."
- Ask the congregation to respond to the sermon with an appropriate prayer.
- Ask the congregation to stand and form prayer partners to pray for the pastor before he speaks.
- Invite people who have a special need to raise their hands and ask members of the congregation to gather around them and pray.
- Each week guide the congregation in a prayer for a different pastor and church in the community.
- When the children or youth or a specific ministry group sings before the congregation, invite their leaders to come forward after the song; pray for the leaders and the entire group.
- Another way to excite people to the joy of prayer is by introducing a variety of prayer resources. Showing a video in the worship service, introducing a new book on prayer, or playing a worship and prayer CD are all ways to increase their prayer interest.

MAKING MANY TIMES, WAYS, AND PLACES TO PRAY

Ted Haggard, pastor of New Life Church, in Colorado Springs, Colorado, says that the key to getting more people praying in your church is diversity: "To mobilize a praying church, use a broad variety of philosophies and styles because different things will appeal to different people."[4]

Some people enjoy the intimacy of seeking God in small groups. Others are energized in large corporate gatherings. Still others like to intercede for requests sent by e-mail. Many others pray in Sunday school classes. There is no one style.

For years local church prayer occurred mainly in the Wednesday night prayer meeting. Today, families trying to juggle several school and work schedules are looking for a wider variety of times in which they can join with others to seek God.

How many and what kind of prayer activities you offer will depend upon the size and interests of your church. You may start with fewer prayer opportunities and then expand as your church and prayer ministry grow.

SPECIAL INTEREST PRAYER

I like the title of one of Dick Eastman's first books, *Love on Its Knees*. Within the title is prayer's greatest motivator: love. You don't have to coerce a mother to pray when her teenager has not come home yet and it's 3:00 A.M. Nor do you need to give her prayer points so that she will know what requests to lay before the Lord. She simply pours out her heart to God.

Here then is one of the most powerful keys to motivating people to pray in your church: Connect people to pray for the things that stir their heart. Here are some suggestions:

- Enlist parents who have fought the battle for a child on drugs to pray for other families experiencing the same problem. Those who have experienced divorce will likely have a heart to pray for a marriage in crisis.
- Other people will be enthusiastic about lifting before the Lord the needs of the disenfranchised, such as orphans, the homeless, AIDS victims, prostitutes, prisoners, or unreached peoples.
- Connect people in affinity groups such as the medical profession, teachers, business owners, single parents, or those with an unsaved

spouse. My church has just launched sixteen new special interest prayer groups. Some of these include new-believers prayer groups, pastor's prayer shield, prayerwalking groups, groups for foster parents, and prayer accountability groups for couples.

Special Event Prayer

One way to engage a large number of people in prayer is by linking prayer with a special calendar event. For example, when Kurt Cotter was youth pastor at Living Streams Christian Church, he used a Sunday service at the start of a new school year to rally intercession for students. Kurt preached a sermon on the principles of intercessory prayer and the need to pray for the upcoming generation. The youth led every other part of the service—worship, ushering, offering, and testimonies.

At the close of the service, Kurt challenged the congregation to adopt a youth in prayer for a year. As the youth gathered at the front of the church, Kurt spoke to the congregation: "Will you ask God to protect the youth of our church in the upcoming school year? To give them courage to resist ungodly influences? Would you ask the Lord to give our young people a heart to follow after Him, that their lives will make a difference in the kingdom of God?"

Every intercessor who adopted a youth received a picture and a three-by-five card of biographical information with special requests to help him pray more effectively for his student. In addition, the bulletin carried prayer targets on how to pray for a teenager so everyone in the congregation could take home a reminder to pray for the youth of the church.

I've had the privilege of being in a number of church services that successfully used a calendar event to organize prayer for a specific topic. Here are a few you might like to consider:

- **A prayer launch for the pastoral staff.** During Clergy Appreciation Month in October, invite a special speaker to share why pastors and their families need prayer. Give intercessors an opportunity to sign up following the service. One church distributed pictures of the pastoral staff along with a guide on how to pray.

- **Quarterly prayer and fasting events.** Call the whole church to a day of prayer and fasting in connection with such events as the New Year, the Lenten season, National Day of Prayer, and the Thanksgiving season. The church body prays and fasts throughout the day and then gathers for a prayer meeting at the church at the end of the day, followed by a church family meal together to break the fast.
- **Fourth of July prayer for the nation.** Transform each wall of the sanctuary into a prayer station. These may include prayer for the president and national government, the governor and state issues, the city, and the church. Use banners, pictures, maps, or anything else that helps the congregation visualize their prayer target. Ask the congregation to divide into several groups, each going to a different prayer station where a prayer leader awaits them. The groups rotate to new locations every fifteen minutes until everyone has prayed at each station.

Prayer Initiatives

A prayer initiative is a given period of time when the whole church prays for the same thing. The purpose is for saturation prayer with a single focus. People are encouraged to pray in a variety of ways and times such as personal prayer, family devotions, small-group prayer, prayerwalking, twenty-four-hour organized prayer chains, and all-church prayer gatherings.

You can put together your own initiative or use one already in existence. Here are some examples:

- If your pastor is preaching a sermon series, you can develop a prayer guide to go along with what he preached the past week or the upcoming weeks.
- Launch a campaign to pray for the salvation of lost friends and neighbors, and renewal of a passion for Christ among church members.
- One church launched an initiative to pray for cancer patients when several of their church members were diagnosed with the disease several years ago. After gathering information from

doctors and cancer patients, the prayer coordinator drew up prayer targets for which the entire church prayed for a three-month period.

Every time you conduct a new prayer initiative, you will get new people who want to come on board to the prayer ministry. Plan ahead how you will connect these people to the prayer movement in your church.

MakInG Prayer a ParT of every ministry in THE cHurcH

An effective way to encourage the whole church to draw near to God is in settings that center around their existing relationships. These are found in such places as choir, Sunday school, or discipleship groups. Because these persons know one another, they will naturally want to spend time together lifting their friends' burdens before the Lord.[5]

One prayer coordinator made a list of every ministry, event, or meeting that occurs in her church during a calendar year. After each one, she listed how prayer could become a greater value in that setting and how she could help make that happen.

Prayer leader Anita Hensley took the time to meet with every ministry leader in her church. She encouraged each one to make prayer an integral part of their ministry. Then she offered her help in finding resources and in leadership training. Praying churches not only have strong prayer ministries but they also make prayer a part of every ministry in the church.

cHurcH sTaff

Unlike many churches, the staff at Arcade Baptist Church in Sacramento, California, begins each day with one hour of prayer together. When the pastor first instituted this practice, the staff was asking, "How can we get our work done?" However, they soon learned that time spent with God adds hours to the day. Pastor Daniel Henderson says, "Whenever we say we're too busy to pray, it affects everything we do."[6]

BOARD OF DIRECTORS

Some of the most important decisions regarding God's work are made in board meetings. Churches that are saturated in prayer make prayer a first response rather than a last resort. Pastors and board members tell me that whenever they spend substantial time seeking the mind of Christ before approaching business, the meeting runs more smoothly and answers to problems surface more readily.

WORSHIP TEAM/CHOIR

When the worship team or choir gathers for practice, encourage them to spend significant time seeking the Lord for His manifest presence in the upcoming services. Pastor Jim Cymbala tells what happened when his wife and choir director, Carol, set aside time to seek the Lord in the Brooklyn Tabernacle Choir's weekly practice sessions:

> *Carol would begin with a half hour of prayer. Often a spirit of worship fell on the group. Someone might volunteer a testimony or feel impressed to read Scripture. Carol might offer a short exhortation. Many nights there was more prayer and worship than there was practicing; sometimes the choir never got around to singing at all.*
>
> *This experience put people in a whole different frame of mind. The choir wasn't just coming up with two "specials" to sing before the sermon; rather, the members were engaged in full-scale ministry.[7]*

MINISTRY OF HELPS

Some churches are discovering that the ministry of helps—ushers, parking-lot attendants, and janitors—can become powerful prayer teams while on duty. They are inviting ushers to pray before services (that newcomers will feel welcome), during the services (that God will touch each person they serve), and after services (for those with special needs).

Parking lot attendants are in a unique position to see people before they walk into church and put on their "Sunday smile." Encourage attendants to bless those in every car and to ask the Holy Spirit to show them those who need special prayer that day.

As janitors prepare the church physically for the upcoming times of ministry, they simultaneously can prepare the rooms spiritually. Mobilize cleaning teams to invite the presence of God into the rooms where ministry will take place, such as in the nursery and children and youth rooms, Christian education classes, and worship services. You may want to hold an on-the-job training session to teach those in the ministry of helps how to bring the needs of the church family before the Lord.

Married Couples

Encouraging married couples to pray together is a worthwhile goal for any church. There are many benefits for couples seeking the Lord together, one of the most important being that it reduces the divorce rate in the church. Consider the following statistic. The divorce rate among couples who go to church together regularly is 1 out of 2—the same as unbelievers. But the divorce rate among couples who pray together daily is 1 out of 1,152.[8]

I once heard the late Dr. Edwin Louis Cole, best-selling author and unofficial founder of the Christian men's movement, say, "We become intimate with whom we pray, for whom we pray, and to whom we pray."

Here are some suggestions to promote married couples' prayer:

- Hold a weekend couples' retreat. Invite a speaker to share on the power of couples' agreeing together in prayer. Offer instruction, modeling, and time for couples to pray together.
- Invite a speaker to the couples' Sunday school class to teach couples how to pray together.
- Introduce books to assist couples in having devotions together.
- Help couples be creative in finding time to pray together, such as over the phone during the lunch hour; prayerwalks in the evening; weekly prayer dates; and yearly prayer retreats for praying, planning, and goal setting.

Children

The prayer life of children is one of the most untapped resources of the church today. We often do not take children's innocent conversations with God seriously and instead send them to another room during times of corporate prayer. Scripture paints a different picture of times when the whole church comes together to seek the Lord: "Gather the people, consecrate the assembly; bring together the elders, gather the children" (Joel 2:16).

Transgenerational prayer meetings are the norm at Shekinah Church in Blountville, Tennessee. Pastor Sue Curran says,

> *Our children from speaking age (two to three) know that their prayers are welcome in corporate meetings. It is not at all unusual for one or more of them to pray for me and other leaders before we preach or minister in worship services. A capacity to give themselves in prayer was developed in prayer meetings. We "suffered the little children" not forbidding them to come to Jesus, and as we took their prayers seriously, they became pray-ers![9]*

Children will learn they can make Jesus their best friend when their pastors, teachers, and parents model an intimate relationship with the Lord and when they invite children to share in their exciting times of talking with Him.

Because most Sunday school classes have little or no prayer curriculum, consider holding a children's workers seminar on "Teaching Kids to Pray."

I once spoke in a prayer conference to train parents and children's workers how to pray for children. When parents asked if they could bring their kids, we decided to make them a part of the training. At the beginning of the seminar, we dismissed the children to go on a prayer journey. Earlier in the afternoon, we had placed handprints throughout the church building for the children to find. These handprints were stuck to the doors of the pastor's study, the nursery, the youth room, offering baskets, and more. The object was for the children to find the handprints and then place their hand over the larger handprint and pray a blessing for that area of the church. In the meantime, we were equipping adults with children's prayer tools and resources. When the prayer journey was over, the children met us back in the sanctuary to share their experience.

YOUTH

Why do young people come away from conferences like Acquire the Fire and The Call so on fire, so desperate to take their schools for Christ, so hungry for something deeper and more intimate in their Christian walk?

Over and over we hear them say, "We only wish it didn't have to end." The question I would like to pose is this: Why can't the excitement continue when they return to their churches and youth groups?

I'll admit that neither students nor adults can live in a perpetual conference high. Yet as youth workers and prayer leaders, we can nurture rather than quench this new generation's holy dissatisfaction with the status quo. We can give them a place to express their passion for more of God and desire for change—and that's the place of fervent prayer.

If you'd like to ignite the youth in your church to pray, here are a few suggestions that come straight from the mouths of the youth themselves:

- **Let the students lead.** In most churches where youth groups are on fire in prayer, adults see themselves as coaches and raise up student leaders. Young prayer mobilizers Nicole Sacks and Stephanie Seekins say, "The youth have to own it. And believe me, they know when they don't!"[10]
- **Gather the passionate pray-ers.** Find those with a heart to seek God, and bring them together at a time separate from the regular youth group meeting. Encourage their prayer hunger, and they will become the spark that will later ignite a blaze within the entire youth group.
- **Mentor your core group.** This small group will likely become candidates for student leadership.
- **Slowly introduce short times of prayer into the larger group.** Allow your core group to give testimonies of answered prayer and to invite others to join them when they meet.
- **Establish a prayer covering.** Recruit a team of adult intercessors to cover every student in your youth group.
- **Invite youth into the church's corporate prayer meetings.** This makes them feel a part of the church family, and they will learn from the adult models of prayer they see. At the same time, adults will be renewed with passion when they experience the youth's abandonment to the Lord.
- **Spread the fire!** Meeting with other youth groups to pray can

help spread the prayer fire your youth are experiencing or catch from another youth group the fervency your youth group lacks.

In the Phoenix area, teenagers Nicole and Stephanie started a citywide youth prayer meeting called Sacred Edge. Several hundred youth from different churches met the first Friday night of every month to pray for the healing and restoration of their generation. The week before school started, Sacred Edge filled vans and buses with praying teenagers to intercede on location at the city's forty high schools. They asked God to show up in revival on their high school campuses that fall. Later, students reported that God was showing up in extraordinary ways with public repentance of sin and many miraculous salvations.

That fall, several students sensed an urgency to get up early before school and drive to an abortion clinic to pray for God to expose Satan's works of darkness there. Shortly after that, an incident, which the media caught wind of, occurred in the clinic, and within two weeks the clinic was closed.

Men

One of the most-often-asked questions among prayer ministry leaders is, "How can we get more men involved?" In some churches the prayer ministries are so feminine that the men won't respond to them. If you want to attract more men to the prayer meetings, it's important to be intentional about making some of the prayer meetings more masculine in nature.

When local church prayer leader Harvey Cozzens leads men in prayer, he sees himself as a coach. When he teaches those in his prayer group how to pray corporately, he uses sports terminology. He talks about "passing the ball" and "quarterbacking from the podium." This is not a new concept, because the apostle Paul often compared the discipline needed in the Christian walk with that of an athlete.

If you would like to start a prayer meeting that attracts the men in your church, try including some of the following:

- **Passion and Cause.** With men, passion and cause are everything. Many times a guy will not come to a prayer meeting unless he perceives there's a cause. Every guy wants to have an adventure, win a battle. This is the way God made them. His battle might be abortion or a national issue, such as the war in Iraq.

- **Prayer Targets.** Men are task oriented. When you give them specific prayer targets, they walk out feeling like they accomplished something. Because they have prayed specifically, when answers come, everyone knows that God has answered. One idea is to use a Ten Most Wanted list, usually used to list the top ten people for whom you are praying to come to the Lord. (You will find a sample on the Prayer Tools CD.)

- **Five-Minute Chunks.** To hold the attention of many men, you have to keep the prayer meeting moving. Derek Packard, a leader of "The Call to War" prayer meeting in Colorado Springs, Colorado, recommends building your prayer meetings around five-minute chunks of time for each of the following: worship, personal reflection, small-group prayer, and individual-led prayer from the microphone.

- **The Agenda.** Men like to know what's going to happen—who is going to lead prayer next and for what topic. Make an agenda and give it to each man in the meeting, or project the agenda on a screen using an overhead projector or PowerPoint. The more men you can involve in the process, the more they will take ownership.

- **Matching Prayers and Calling.** Get men praying for the things they know about: their careers, passions, and hobbies. If one man is a medical doctor, he can pray for the field of medicine with authority.

- **Leadership.** Strong male leadership draws men to the prayer meeting. In churches where male pastors talk about their own prayer lives and lead exciting prayer meetings, a greater number of men participate. One suggestion is to find three or four influential key men in the church who are already praying. Ask them to form the leadership team to start a men's prayer meeting or to draw more men to an existing prayer meeting.

- **Promotion.** Men won't carry a flier around, but they are accustomed to carrying business cards. Design a business card that has the name and location of the church as well as the time of the prayer meeting. Pass out cards for the next prayer meeting and encourage men to invite a buddy or bring their son to the next meeting.

- **Pray for the Pastors.** If your church isn't quite ready for a men's prayer meeting, try rallying men to form a PIT Crew to pray for the pastor, as discussed in chapter 8.[11]

HOMEBOUND

Some elderly or handicapped church members may not be able to attend prayer meetings. Others in the church can be homebound due to prolonged sickness or having young children. Here are some ways to make church members who pray at home a part of the team:

- Start an e-mail prayer network
- Invite those who pray at home to be a part of the prayer chain
- Send them the prayer requests covered in the small-group and corporate prayer meetings
- Invite them to adopt a youth in prayer or become a part of the pastor's prayer shield
- Set up prayer partners that meet weekly by phone
- Send another intercessor to their home and pray with them there
- For those who could and would come to a prayer meeting if they had a ride, arrange for someone to pick them up

ESTABLISHING PRAYER TRAINING

The biggest mistake we make when teaching on prayer is assuming that people know more than they actually do. We assume people know the basics. Just because the pastor teaches several sermons a year on prayer and a portion of the Sunday school class or small group is spent in prayer doesn't mean that the people in your congregation are equipped to pray. In reality, even those who have been in the church for many years may lack instruction in how to communicate with the Father.

Consider the following topics when planning basic training for prayer:

- What is prayer?
- To whom am I praying? (character of God, names of God, who God is)
- Why should I pray?
- How long do I pray?
- When do I pray?
- Where do I pray?
- What position do I pray in?

Possible intermediate topics include:

- Types of prayer: praise, thanksgiving, confessions, petition, intercession
- Why some prayers go unanswered
- How to hear the voice of God
- Why we pray in the name of Jesus
- How to pray God's promises (they're conditional)

Advanced prayer classes might cover:

- Spiritual warfare
- Fasting
- The prayer of agreement
- Prophetic prayer—to pray what is on God's heart

WHERE WILL WE TEACH PEOPLE ABOUT PRAYER?

After determining what you want your church members to know about prayer, the next consideration is, "Where will prayer training take place?" In this section we will discuss some other ways prayer leaders can establish prayer training programs in their church.

Small Groups and Christian Education Classes

One of the first places people learn to pray is in small groups where they feel safe, whether it be home fellowships or Sunday school classes. Following are some ways prayer leaders can help get more prayer in Christian education classes:

- Meet with the teacher of each class and acquaint him with books and other resources to enhance the classes' prayer curriculum. For example, you might visit the teacher of the young married class and drop off a book on teaching couples to pray together.
- Hold a seminar to train children's workers how to teach children to pray and how to provide creative opportunities for children to learn to talk and listen to God. Introduce books, hands-on prayer tools, and creative prayer ideas to use in their classes.
- Develop a speakers' bureau of those within the church and the community who can teach on various aspects of prayer. List those with a focus on couples, youth, children, and so on. Then distribute this list to the leader of every ministry in your church.
- Encourage teachers to include some time for prayer in every class period.
- Suggest that class members have the opportunity to form prayer partners who meet for prayer in person or by phone once a week.
- Hold a training seminar for small-group leaders in order to teach them how to facilitate small-group prayer.

Personal Prayer Retreats

Personal prayer retreats offer people the opportunity to get alone with God for one or more days in a retreat setting. The retreat begins with everyone coming together with a trained leader to receive guidelines for their time with God. The time ends with the group reconvening to share what the Lord did in their lives during the retreat. Personal prayer retreats help people learn to spend time talking and listening to God.

Specialized Training Events

Holding specialized training events is a good way to spark interest in prayer. Why not plan a Saturday morning event to teach parents, grandparents, and children's workers how to pray for their children and youth? (You can offer a simultaneous children's prayer activity.) How about a class to teach businessmen and women how to intercede for their businesses? Other specialized classes include how to pray for your spouse, your pastor, or governmental leaders. The list is limitless and can be tailor-made for the interests of those in your church.

Prayer Conferences

Holding a prayer conference can boost prayer momentum in any church. If your church can afford it, it's a good idea that the main speaker be someone from outside your church. If your church is small or your prayer budget is small, consider joining with several other churches in your community to host a citywide prayer conference. You may want to have several main sessions and a choice of workshops for participants. Incorporating times of extended worship helps create an atmosphere to both pray and hear from the Lord in a corporate setting.

Schools of Prayer

Schools of prayer are becoming quite popular in Protestant churches throughout the world. Some schools of prayer are held on a Sunday afternoon or Sunday evening once a month or once a quarter. At those times, the pastor or some other speaker teaches on some aspect of prayer. Other schools of prayer offer a college atmosphere with year-round courses on a semester basis.

Classes in a school of prayer can be as simple as assigning a book to read and then going through the book together like a Bible study. The first course of prayer we offered in our prayer classes at Word of Grace was centered on Bill Hybel's book *Too Busy Not to Pray!*

Some years ago, Bjorn Pedersen, the pastor of prayer at Community Church of Joy, developed a college of prayer with more than one hundred prayer courses. Whether your school of prayer is simple or more complex, it is important to think through a systematic approach to laying a prayer foundation in participants.

Everyone's Motivated—Now What?

Hopefully, you're getting a glimpse of the endless possibilities for motivating your whole church to pray. You may find more people volunteering to be church intercessors, or you may be noticing some prayer warriors who would be great additions to your intercessory teams. The next chapter will show you how to recruit, organize, and manage your intercessors.

1. *Transformations*, Global Net Productions, 1999.

2. Personal interview with Thetus Tenney conducted by Cheryl Sacks, July 18, 2003.

3. John Franklin, A *House of Prayer* (Nashville: LifeWay Press, 1999), p. 16.

4. Telephone interview with Ted Haggard conducted by Cheryl Sacks, August 6, 2003.

5. Franklin, p. 25.

6. Daniel Henderson, "Teaching Your Church to Pray," audiotape, Strategies Renewal, 2003.

7. Jim Cymbala, *Fresh Wind, Fresh Fire* (Grand Rapids, Mich.: Zondervan, 1997), p. 32.

8. 1993 Gallup Poll.

9. Sue Curran, *The Praying Church* (Lake Mary, Fla.: Creation House, 2000), p. 69.

10. Nicole Sacks and Stephanie Seekins, "Starting a Citywide, Youth-Led Prayer Movement," *Empowered*, Summer 2002, pp. 18–19.

11. Derek Packard, "Mobilizing Men to Pray," National Association of Local Church Prayer Leaders convention, Colorado Springs, Colo., 2002.

CHAPTER 10

Mobilizing and Managing Intercessors

Dr. Gregory Frizzell is convinced that faithful intercession saved the church he was pastoring in 1984. Surrounded by high crime, gang activity, and rapid community decline, the church was deeply divided and embroiled in a catastrophic legal battle. Fees totaled more than two million dollars. As if that were not enough, the church was plagued with a huge public moral scandal, of such severity that they were in the news every day for five years. As a twenty-six-year-old fresh out of seminary, Frizzell knew that neither he nor his church had any chance of survival (much less growth) unless God powerfully intervened.

For years he and his staff had done everything humanly possible, yet nothing changed. The first turning point came when God led them to organize the church's intercessors and begin a serious time of calling out to God. Eighty people committed to at least thirty minutes a day in personal prayer. They all prayed the same specific points of focus: conversion of those without Christ, unity in the church, financial miracles, and for the church to be cleared of all false charges. The prayer warriors met as a whole once a month for a three-hour prayer rally.

The second turning point came when the church began powerful all-church prayer meetings. The Wednesday night church service, which previously had been mostly Bible study, was converted into a prayer meeting with a strong kingdom focus. They petitioned God for conversion of the lost and revival in the church.

The final turning point came when the church established a prayer group that focused on evangelism and revival. The group consisted of ten people who met once a week to intercede for two or more hours. They adhered to the following schedule:

- Thirty minutes—time alone with Scriptures designed to cleanse the heart and make certain no unconfessed sin or hindrances were in their lives before they started praying.
- Twenty minutes—group worship and exalting the Lord.
- Seventy minutes—focused intercession upon the salvation of sixty unconverted people, deep unity and revival in the church, and God's sending laborers to grow the church.

Four months after the weekly prayer revival group was formed, forty-five of the sixty unconverted people had been saved. Several of these were hard cases in which people had been praying for them for years. Explosive growth occurred in the church, with new people continually visiting and becoming members. A miraculous unity filled the church, drawing the congregation and leadership together in increasing harmony. The church's attorneys, who were not members of any church or committed to the Christian faith, forgave the church a million-dollar debt. Ultimately, the church was completely cleared of all accusations. Pastor Frizzell believes that his impossible situation proves there is glorious hope for any church that commits itself to an organized and focused network of intercessors dedicated to serious prayer.[1]

THE POWER OF INTERCESSION

When Moses called out to God on behalf of his people, God answered by humbling Pharaoh, a world leader. After Daniel interceded for his nation, Israel was released from captivity. When Nehemiah prayed for the city, the broken walls of Jerusalem were rebuilt. Esther called a whole nation to a solemn assembly to fast and pray, and once again God's people were saved.

All intercession is prayer, but not all prayer is intercession. Prayer is talking with God. Intercession is petitioning God for the needs of another.

As we study the Bible, we see examples of men and women who interceded for whole cities and nations, and because of their prayers, history was changed. As Christians have observed the passionate, persistent, and often desperate prayers required to bring change—both in Scripture and in their own lives—the word *intercession* has come to be associated with such characteristics as boldness, fervency, and persistence. Some churches call their intercessors *prayer warriors*.

Author and national prayer leader Dr. Terry Teykl says, "True intercession is not just something you engage in one hour a week; it's a way of life. It is motivated by a heart that can look past unlovable exteriors to see people as God intended them to be, and then pray that picture into existence when everyone else has given up."[2] Many people believe that intercession is a gift.[3]

Biblical intercession has two purposes: petitioning God for divine intervention, and prevailing before God to deliver humanity from sin and destruction. Intercession involves:

- Reminding God of His promises (Isaiah 62:6-7);
- Taking up a case before God on behalf of others (Isaiah 59:15-16);
- Building up a hedge of protection and keeping the Enemy out (Luke 22:31-32, John 17:15);
- Crying out for mercy, averting God's judgment (Ezekiel 22:30-31).

Most Christians incorporate some level of intercession into their personal prayer lives, but a small percentage feel called to spend considerably more time praying for others and with unusual fervency and persistency. How do you recognize these people in your church? In this chapter we'll discuss identifying, organizing, and effectively utilizing these prayer warriors.

UNDERSTANDING INTERCESSORS

Because intercessors spend so much time in God's presence, they sometimes hear His voice clearly in their hearts or have a strong "knowing" in their spirits of God's will regarding a matter. They may have a vivid impression or picture in their minds of a person or situation that needs prayer. It is easy to see how intercessors can be misunderstood by others who don't have the same experiences. Sometimes intercessors themselves don't quite understand what they're experiencing.

I've often had calls from intercessors asking questions about such experiences. Stories range from being awakened in the middle of the night with a burden to pray for someone to weeping uncontrollably during a worship service, not because they are being touched by the sermon but because they're feeling someone's cold or hardened heart toward Christ. These intercessors need a place where they can receive nurture and mentoring.

Many intercessors who have been shoved into a corner and tagged "flaky" could have blossomed if someone had taken time to help them understand and grow in their gifting. Church prayer coordinators can create opportunities for potential and growing intercessors to come together with mature seasoned intercessors to share their prayer burdens. At such times, fledgling intercessors can learn how to biblically discern whether or not their experiences are from the Lord and, if so, what to do with the information they've received.

Types of Intercessors

It's difficult to try and put all intercessors in the same box. Not all pray the same way or have a burden to intercede for the same thing, and not every intercessor has experiences such as those mentioned above. It seems that God has given some intercessors a special prayer focus, such as praying for a particular church, community, leader, or nation. Because of each person's unique personality and gift mix, intercessors' prayer styles vary as well.

To effectively mobilize intercessors, it is important to understand their passions and prayer styles. When intercessors understand their own prayer gifting and that of others, they can flow together more easily in prayer. The following list of types of intercessors is not a means of labeling people but is intended to help you, as the prayer coordinator, understand your intercessors' prayer giftings and better utilize them in prayer assignments. This list is neither conclusive nor exhaustive, and your intercessors might fall into more than one of these categories.[4]

Personal Intercessors

Often God will place a particular person on an intercessor's heart on a regular basis. This is likely the Lord's call to adopt the person in intercession. Mordecai is a biblical example of a personal intercessor as he went before the Lord on Queen Esther's behalf.

Mercy Intercessors

They seem to start crying every time they begin to pray. Like Jeremiah the weeping prophet, they feel the heart of God for a person or situation. Their tears are as prayers. When we don't understand mercy intercessors, we may try to comfort them or shut down their emotional expressions. At such times in our attempts to quiet them, we may quench the Spirit's call to weep over the sins of our nation or some other issue upon the Father's heart. Even Jesus wept over Jerusalem and its spiritually fallen condition.

Crisis Intercessors

They love to pray in a crisis. It's not unusual for them to be awakened by an S.O.S. from God at three in the morning. Author Beth Alves calls crisis intercessors "the paramedics of prayer." You're most likely a crisis intercessor if every time you pass by an auto accident, you start praying for the people in the accident, the ambulance drivers, the doctors in the emergency room, and the family of the people in the accident.

List Intercessors

They function from structure and usually pray from an endless list. Their spiritual gift may be administration (1 Corinthians 12:28). They can pray over the entire church's prayer requests—every health concern, financial crisis, and need for protection—lifting up each one individually and in detail. These are the intercessors to whom you want to give the pastor's schedule when he goes on a trip.

Financial Intercessors

They have faith for large sums of money—usually for other people. They may have little money themselves but can trust God for great financial blessing to be released into the kingdom. They may have the gift of faith (1 Cor. 12:9). These are the people you want to have pray over the offering or for finances to complete projects such as purchasing new buildings and property.

GLOBAL INTERCESSORS

They pray for nations and people groups. They may have a burden to pray for missionaries across the world and for international organizations. Dick Eastman, president of Every Home for Christ, prays for every nation by name every day.

WORSHIP INTERCESSORS

They often sing their prayers. Worship intercessors may want to sing continually in the prayer room. Other intercessors may be thinking, *What's wrong with this person? We're here to pray!* Once I was in the prayer room when someone spontaneously led us in singing "Shine, Jesus, Shine" as an intercessory prayer over the Middle East.

SALVATION INTERCESSORS

Most Christians will intercede for the lost from time to time—even regularly. However, some Christians pray much more and with unusual fervency for those who do not know Christ. In such cases, the person's prayer life may be fueled by their calling as an evangelist (Ephesians 4:11).

GOVERNMENT INTERCESSORS

Some people feel strongly led to ask the Lord to intervene in different kinds of government: church government, city and national government, court decisions and laws. They ask God to change nations. They also are informed. They know the names of government officials and what bills are coming up to be voted upon.

RECOGNIZING WHERE THEY ARE

As you read this list, you are probably recognizing yourself and people you know, and you might recognize that someone you know is a combination of these types. For example, if you're a list and salvation intercessor, you'll have a list of the lost. If you're a salvation and mercy intercessor, you'll weep for the lost.[5]

I'd like to emphasize here that as Christians, we will all from time to time have a concern to pray for our government, people in times of crisis, leaders, and every other subject presented above. Still, because of their gift mix and calling, some intercessors will sense an urgency to pray more for certain people and issues.

For more information on discovering the prayer giftings and passions of intercessors, I recommend Elizabeth Alves' book *Intercessors: Discover Your Prayer Power* (Regal Books).

Networking Intercessors

Intercessors thrive on current information and feedback. Unless you can develop a system for dispersing prayer requests and praise reports, your intercessors may become frustrated and feel they're not needed. With all the available technology today, websites, e-mail, and telephone hotlines have become expedient ways to update intercessors. Yet, keep in mind that *relationship* is key to mobilizing prayer. Strong connections are needed among intercessors as well as between intercessors and church leaders. Technology offers useful tools, but *face-to-face* interaction is vital. One of your tasks will be to set in place a system that regularly brings together intercessors for ongoing prayer, mentoring, and training. Rather than randomly sending out prayer requests and calling prayer meetings from time to time, a system will get everyone organized and focused in the same direction.

The question is, what kind of structure will you use to organize and communicate with your intercessors? I have discovered several models of intercessory prayer networks that churches are using to successfully mobilize their intercessors. These include utilizing prayer captains, setting up prayer rooms as communications centers, and training specialized prayer teams. Larger churches and more sophisticated prayer ministries may use a combination of these systems.

I don't mean to suggest here that these are the only systems for networking intercessors. The key is to identify a system that works for your church and then become intentional about keeping it running smoothly. Regardless of what type of prayer network you use, the following components are essential:

Communication.

You'll need an efficient system for dispersing information to intercessors in a timely manner. Providing specific prayer requests is the key to getting more people praying in the same direction. It's important to share testimonies of how God answered as well. For intercessors, fresh ongoing prayer requests and praise reports are like adding fuel to a fire.

Leadership.

A number of leaders are needed to make a church prayer network effective: pastors to communicate the church's strategic vision and mission, ministry leaders to submit individual ministries' needs, and a church prayer coordinator to keep the communications system running smoothly.

Trained and organized intercessors.

Intercessors function best when they know what's expected of them. They desire answers to such questions as "What specifically do I pray for? Where will I pray, with whom, and for how long?" Providing job descriptions and policies and procedures are helpful. In addition, more powerful intercession results when intercessors receive training for such specialized assignments as altar prayer ministry and prayer for the pastor.

UTILIZING Prayer Captains

When prayer captains oversee the intercessory network, it functions in a similar fashion as an emergency prayer chain. A team captain oversees four to ten prayer warriors. He receives the corporate prayer agenda and any congregational requests from the church prayer coordinator and then communicates them to his assigned intercessors.

An intercessory prayer network is different from an emergency prayer chain in that it involves praying for specific ongoing requests of the church as well as emergency needs. The prayer captain communicates with his assigned intercessors on a regular basis (at least once or twice a month). This produces focused saturation prayer. When everyone begins to pray the same things in agreement, great power is released.

Specific duties of a prayer captain usually include:

- To communicate prayer requests and praise reports to their assigned prayer warriors
- To report back to the church prayer coordinator or network director anything the intercessors are receiving from the Lord that concern the corporate body (especially if more than one person is sensing the same thing)
- To pray daily for their intercessory team
- To affirm intercessors through love, encouragement, and positive relational interaction
- To offer accountability and evaluation through regular calls
- To encourage team participation in church prayer gatherings, training, and recognition events

HOW TO KEEP THE INTERCESSORS KINGDOM FOCUSED

One of the most important responsibilities of the prayer captain is to keep intercessors focused upon specific kingdom requests. By kingdom requests I'm talking about praying for those things we desire to see submitted to the rule and reign of Jesus—churches, schools, neighborhoods, governments, and so forth. As such, intercessors are praying for God's kingdom to come and His will to be done on earth as it is in heaven (see Luke 11:2). I recommend that prayer captains offer intercessors specific requests for the followings areas:[6]

- Specific needs for the church—pastor, staff, and ministries
- The power of the Holy Spirit and a heart for evangelism in the church
- Specific list of those who don't know Christ or who are backslidden
- Nationwide revival of the church and spiritual awakening of the lost
- People in the church with pressing physical or temporal needs

THE Prayer room

A prayer room prepared with prayer targets, prayer guides, and prayer opportunities can become the designated location for organizing intercessors' activities. A prayer room can become a central location for mobilizing intercessors because it makes it possible to schedule time with God in a systematic manner. It provides a place for collecting requests and taking them before the Lord and offers a central location for recording answers to prayer. Prayer rooms offer a place to highlight ongoing needs of the church's ministries and a visible location for posting prayer opportunities. A prayer room can be a location for a telephone hotline, and it offers the opportunity to synchronize prayers with other church prayer rooms through the use of technology.

The first thing to do when setting up a prayer room is to find a location. If possible, select a room set apart from church activities that might intrude upon an intercessor's time with God. However, if your church is short on space, find a classroom, an unused office, a storage room, or a portable building. One congregation put up a tent in its foyer. What your original space looks like is not important. Primary onsiderations are security, access, and functionality.

Consider using a room with an outside entrance. This affords access to the prayer room twenty-four hours a day without requiring the entire building to remain open. If the prayer room is open past office hours, it will need a bathroom, telephone, and a combination door lock. Churches in certain locations may need to hire a security guard as well.

Make the most of whatever resources the Lord has given you, and create a place that is inviting, inspiring, and well-ordered. You will likely need comfortable chairs, lamps, carpet, worship CDs, Bibles, card files, notebooks, maps, pictures, and banners.

A possible format for the prayer room is the use of prayer stations. A prayer station is a section of the room that focuses upon one prayer target. The use of prayer stations greatly increases the consistency, specificity, and depth of prayers offered by those in the prayer room. When possible, use specific names, such as when praying for government officials, gangs, and other churches. Some of the stations might include:

• Prayer for personal preparation

- Congregational prayer request cards (including lists of people who need salvation)
- The pastoral staff and church ministries
- Schools
- Missionaries
- Government officials
- Israel and world issues

I once visited a prayer room where each station was separated by a room divider and provided a place to sit and pray through a detailed prayer guide. Each station was beautifully decorated with pictures, flags, maps, prayer shawls, Scriptures, and quotes.

Thetus Tenney shares that after she set up stations in the prayer room of her church, there was a 25 percent increase in the number of people coming to pray there. Even new converts were coming.[7]

Some church's prayer rooms have grown into prayer centers. Such is the case with The Valley Cathedral. This five-room prayer center houses the church's prayer offices, a central meeting room for corporate prayer (holds about sixty people), a prayer room for personal ministry, a room for personal prayer and worship (nicely decorated with banners and a table set for serving Communion), and a "war room" with prayer stations.

Other prayer rooms, such as the one at North Phoenix Baptist Church, focus upon praying for the needs of others twenty-four hours a day. At NPBC, members pray in the prayer room every hour of the day while others answer a prayer hotline. Approximately 350 prayer warriors from the church spend one hour a week at the prayer center, answering phone calls and praying over calls that have been received previously.

A volunteer or staff person should oversee scheduling, recruiting, training, and maintaining of the prayer room. Organizationally, this person would answer directly to the church prayer coordinator, director of prayer, or pastor of prayer.

SPECIALIZED PRAYER TEAMS

Just as the military prepares their special forces, so prayer ministries need people motivated, trained, and sharply focused for specialized areas of

ministry. Many churches today are utilizing specialized prayer teams. The
most frequent include:

Evangelistic/Revival Prayer Teams

These teams meet regularly to call out to God for the salvation of
unsaved people, name by name. They also pray for the church's
evangelistic outreaches, for the people involved in frontline
evangelism, and for revival in the church. In instances in which
prayer is coupled with evangelism, professions of faith dramati-
cally increase. One example of this is the distribution of the
Jesus video in Colorado Springs. Based upon figures gathered
from previous campaigns, Campus Crusade told churches to
expect 30 percent of homes to accept a video when handing
them out door-to-door; for every two videos distributed there
would be one first-time conversion. When New Life Church
members prayerwalked their thirty assigned precincts before
distributing the *Jesus* video, 70 percent of homes accepted a
video—and in some precincts 90 percent took the video.[8]

Worship Service Intercessors

Many churches are recruiting teams that specialize in praying
for the weekend worship services. Sometimes intercessors meet
in the prayer room before the service or station themselves
throughout the congregation to pray during the service. Others
meet in separate rooms using closed-circuit TV or a speaker
system. These intercessors cover the entire order of service:
worship, offering, sermon, and congregational response. The
great preacher Charles Spurgeon had large groups of intercessors praying in a basement located under his pulpit in each
service and said it was his divine "furnace room."

Altar Prayer Ministry Teams

Every weekend, churches are filled with hurting people who
desperately need a touch from God. Their Sunday smiles hide the
pain of marital strife, straying children, financial hardships, and
terminal illnesses. Dr. Terry Teykl says that so often in church people

hear about God and what He can do, but so often they are never invited to experience Him personally.[9] Altar prayer ministry teams are trained to minister the healing power of God's grace, hope, and salvation to broken people. At designated times during the service, those in the congregation are invited to meet a prayer altar team member and receive ministry for their personal needs. People don't have to go home with the same burdens they arrived with. If you desire to train people on how to minister to others in this way, I recommend Teykl's book *Praying Grace* (Prayer Point Press).

Healing Teams

Dr. C. Peter Wagner reports that "an increasing number of churches, both charismatic and noncharismatic, are now organizing teams of people skilled in praying for physical and emotional healing."[10] Wagner's book *How to Have a Healing Ministry in Any Church* has helped many churches recruit and train people to move into this area. Healing teams are not limited to church services; they may be dispersed to homes, hospitals, or the scene of an accident. Recently, there has been a resurgence of healing rooms in churches. These prayer rooms are dedicated to lifting before the Lord people suffering from illnesses, especially those for whom the medical world has no answers.

RECRUITING TIPS

When people see that the prayer ministry is a priority of the church, recruiting intercessors will be easier than if they consider it just another program. Recruiting is most effective when it occurs continually throughout the year rather than only once or twice a year.

Here are some specific ideas for recruiting:

- Include recruitment of additional intercessors on the list of permanent prayer targets.
- Approach other departments of the church, such as youth,

seniors, or men. Ask them to fill an open time slot in the prayer room or to pray during a worship service.

- Make announcements from the pulpit. Make certain it's on a Sunday when it doesn't conflict with another major event announcement.

- Hold a training event to teach people about the ministry of intercession. Use this as a time to recruit intercessors for various prayer ministries.

- Enroll intercessors in term praying. For example, recruit them to pray one hour a day from June through September. Or ask them to pray for the worship service once every six weeks for a six-month period. This keeps people from getting burned out and gives them a sense of accomplishment. Pray-ers may choose to recommit at the end of their term or allow a fresh recruit to take their place.

While at Arcade Church, Pastor Daniel Henderson said he didn't preach unless there was a substantive number of people in the prayer room. If he found there was a sparse number in the prayer room lifting the service to the Lord, he stood up and announced the need. Because everyone knew the pastor's commitment to prayer, usually many people volunteered quickly.

seLecTinG anD Training inTercessors

Ultimately the secret of an effective prayer ministry is not in its organizational structure but in the lives of the individual intercessors who make up the ministry. Thus, those who volunteer for the prayer ministry need to meet some basic requirements and be trained to pray powerfully and biblically.

Your prayer ministry will want to establish its own guidelines for those who enlist in prayer ministry. The following are a few examples: (1) a genuine desire to serve the Lord through the prayer ministry, (2) a committed member in the church, (3) willingness to attend training sessions, (4) commitment to pray one hour a week, and (5) commitment to confidentiality.

For those who serve in the prayer room, it's important to establish prayer room policies. I suggest Terry Teykl's *Prayer Room Intercessor's Handbook*. Conduct ongoing orientations for all new prayer ministry volunteers. At least

once a year, hold a training conference for your prayer ministry participants
and intercessors.

An Intercessors One-Hour Prayer Model

Sometimes even seasoned intercessors need a model to help them stay
focused for one hour of prayer. Many good models exist. I'd like to invite
you to have a refreshing encounter with Christ as you pray through the
following guide. Why not stop right now and splurge in an extravagant
hour with the Lord?

Prayer Focus—Ten Minutes Each

- Ask God to show you anything that hinders your intimacy with
  Him.
- Use a worship CD or read from the Psalms to worship and adore
  the Lord.
- Pray over a specific list of lost and backslidden people.
- Pray for your local church.
- Pray for the nation and urgent world happenings.
- Petition God for critical concerns in your own life.

WHY INTERCEDE?

Many situations have gone unchanged simply because there was no intercessor, no one to stand in the gap between God and man. Such was the
case when the Lord was looking for an intercessor to stand in the gap for
the sins of Israel. The Lord said, "I looked for a man among them who
would build up the wall and stand before me in the gap on behalf of the
land so I would not have to destroy it, but I found none" (Ezekiel 22:30).
God desired to avoid pouring out judgment. He actually looked for someone to intercede, to ask Him that judgment be averted.

John Wesley said, "God does nothing on earth, save in answer to believing prayer."[11] Knowledge of this truth is what fuels many intercessors to

spend long hours entreating God on behalf of others. Intercession is not just a gift or a nice addition to your church; it is a crucial, biblical necessity if your church is going to fulfill its intended purpose in God's kingdom.

---

1. Telephone interview with Greg Frizzell conducted by Cheryl Sacks, January 10, 2004.

2. Terry Teykl, *Prayer Room Intercessor's Handbook* (Muncie, Ind.: Prayer Point Press, 1999), p. 13.

3. C. Peter Wagner, *Prayer Shield* (Ventura, Calif.: Regal, 1992), p. 48.

4. Elizabeth Alves, Tommi Femrite, and Karen Kauffman, *Intercessors: Discover Your Prayer Power* (Ventura, Calif.: Regal, 2000), p. 127.

5. Alves, Femrite, and Kauffman, pp. 5–7.

6. Greg Frizzell, *How to Build an Evangelistic Prayer Ministry* (Nashville: Baptist Connection, 1999), p. 19.

7. Personal interview with Thetus Tenney conducted by Cheryl Sacks, July 18, 2003.

8. Ted Haggard, *Primary Purpose* (Lake Mary, Fla.: Creation House, 1995), pp. 36–37.

9. Terry Teykl, *Praying Grace* (Muncie, Ind.: Prayer Point Press, 2002), p. 13.

10. C. Peter Wagner, *Churches That Pray* (Ventura, Calif.: Regal, 1993), pp. 100–101.

11. Dutch Sheets, "Does God Really Need Our Prayer?" *Pray!* Issue 11, March/April, p. 15.

CHAPTER 11

Leading Corporate Prayer Gatherings

The Saturday evening service at Southwest Christian Center was just getting under way when the pastor received the update of John's condition. Just earlier, while setting up for the service, John suddenly had suffered a massive cardiac arrest. When workers were unable to resuscitate him, they quickly called 911. Within minutes an ambulance was rushing John to the emergency room.

Now the call had come from the hospital: "After repeated attempts by medical teams, John is not responding to life-saving measures. The doctors are ready to give up."

Immediately the church service turned into a prayer meeting; the congregation broke into intercession in John's behalf. As they called out to God to bring John back from the brink of death, he was resuscitated. Though the doctors said John would most certainly suffer brain damage, intercessors continued to pray for him through his lengthy recovery. Today John is a walking miracle—not only alive but fully restored.

At Southwest Christian Center, corporate prayer is a first response, not just a last resort. With prayer meetings scheduled each weekday at 6:00 A.M., noon, and 7:00 P.M., intercession is the norm for this church family.

The Bible records another corporate prayer meeting attended by people who were startled by God's miracle-working power. The releasing of Peter from prison was so unexpected that some thought they had seen his angel—

even though they had been offering constant prayer to God on his behalf (see Acts 12:5-16).

The people in the Acts church were where they needed to be in a time of crisis—already on their knees in prayer, beseeching God for the miracle they were seeking. Likewise, the people at John's church had already responded to God's call to pray by organizing many regular opportunities throughout the week for people to pray corporately. Both of these churches were prepared for a crisis because they had started the practice of passionate, corporate prayer. God is powerfully present when His people gather corporately to pray, unified in purpose and in His love.

THE SYMPHONY OF CORPORATE PRAYER

So, what is it about corporate prayer that is different from other kinds of praying? When we call a prayer meeting, we're not simply asking people to offer individual prayers in a group setting. Rather, the strength of corporate prayer lies in the unified purpose of the whole group, "the uniting of many hearts with the Spirit of God to pray the mind and will of the Father."[1] Jonathan Graf said it well: "True corporate prayer seeks God's face as on body in one voice about one thing."[2]

> *Corporate intercession means praying together instead of alone. But praying together does not merely refer to physical proximity. It also refers to unified purpose.*
>
> Steve Meeks
> pastor, Calvary Community Church
> Houston

There is a beauty and power of agreement in prayer, not unlike the different harmonies working in concert to produce a symphony. Jesus spoke of this when He said, "I tell you that if two of you on earth agree about anything you ask for, it will be done for you by my Father in heaven" (Matthew 18:19). The word He used, *agree*, means to be in harmony, to be in accord.

Imagine if you went to a concert where everybody played his own melody whenever he wanted to. You would have a harsh, disjointed cacophony. In contrast, prayer that is in agreement involves calling out to God together to make a great symphony of prayer that moves the Father to answer.

The result when people truly join together to pray is a concert of prayer where God's will is accomplished. Jesus prayed, "Your kingdom come, your will be done on earth as it is in heaven" (Matthew 6:10). It seems that corporate praying provides an opportunity for God to fulfill kingdom promises that don't happen by any other means.

corporate prayer in the Bible

If you're still wondering whether you should think about organizing small-group or churchwide prayer meetings, consider the examples in Scripture where corporate prayer brought a greater experience of God's kingdom. Ezra 9 and Nehemiah 8–9 show entire cities coming into confession, repentance, and revival through corporate prayer. Acts 1 records the birth of the church in a prayer meeting as the disciples "all joined together constantly in prayer" (verse 14). Later the new believers "raised their voices together in prayer to God" and in response "they were all filled with the Holy Spirit and spoke the word of God boldly" (Acts 4:24-31). God's will can be accomplished when the church meets for prayer. "The prayer gathering enlarges the channel through which God will bless and give victory to His people; it actually moves us into an entirely different realm of power."[3]

preparing to lead a prayer meeting

In most churches, the worship service is planned in advance. Band members and choirs get together to rehearse, pastors write their sermons, and often a group of intercessors pray over each service. But it might not occur to us to get ready for a prayer meeting with the same intentionality. At High Point Church, the pastor and prayer leader are always getting together and asking, "How can we get more people involved in the prayer meeting? How can we make the prayer meeting better? How can we make this a good experience for those who come?"[4] The following suggestions will help you prepare to lead a large corporate prayer gathering or a small-group prayer meeting.

Prepare spiritually. Effective prayer meetings do not happen by human ingenuity; the Holy Spirit draws people to a place of prayer when He is invited. You (and possibly your pastor and prayer action team) will want to seek the Father's heart for the meeting and pray for the group participants. Pray that the Spirit of prayer will permeate all who participate. "Now the Lord is the Spirit, and where the Spirit of the Lord is, there is freedom" (2 Corinthians 3:17).

Prepare the room. Do what you can to make the place in which you pray conducive to an unhindered encounter with God. It should be quiet, comfortable, free of distractions, and spiritually prepared through prayer. If possible, have a prayer team pray though the room in advance and touch the chairs, asking God to move upon the people who will be sitting there. Make sure the facilities are set up beforehand—chairs, podiums, music equipment, information table.

Prepare resources. Gather prayer requests and praise reports, prepare Scripture readings, and plan the prayer agenda as the Holy Spirit directs. Prayerfully decide how to communicate the mission of the prayer meeting. At your meeting, distribute a brief outline of your prayer agenda and guidelines for participants. Appendix H includes a sample of group prayer principles.

TIPS FOR LEADING A PRAYER MEETING

Many people, even pastors, have never been taught how to lead a prayer meeting, and people often ask me for instruction in this art. The following guidelines will help you lead your group in unity so that you can release focused, unhindered prayers to God.

Begin on time. Waiting for people to arrive only encourages lateness and discourages "ready-to-go" intercessors. Your invitation or announcement might say something like, "We'll gather at 7:00 P.M. and begin praying at 7:15."

Set a unified tone for the prayer meeting. Explain the group's mission, agenda, and how the meeting will work. Because people will be at different levels of maturity and understanding about prayer, you can get everyone "on the same page" by distributing and teaching from a handout of prayer guidelines. Once the meetings have been established, newcomers can easily be briefed by providing them with the handout.

Establish a prayer mindset. Many prayer groups spend the first forty-five minutes talking about their prayer requests, and only the last fifteen minutes in actual prayer. You will be emphasizing that the primary purpose of the prayer meeting is to *pray*—not to fellowship, eat, teach, or counsel. All these things are wonderful and have an important place in the church, but they do not mix well with times of strong prayer. When you guard people's prayer time, the serious pray-ers will return.

Listen for and share God's direction. It is important that you stay open to the direction of the Holy Spirit for God's purpose of the prayer meeting. You'll also want to keep a listening ear toward group members for confirmation of that purpose. At times, the group will discover the direction of the Holy Spirit together as all seek the Lord. Other times, you may sense the Holy Spirit's leading, and as the leader you can gently steer the meeting.

Incorporate ways for everyone to get involved. Praying in one accord doesn't mean people always pray the same way. Utilize different people's strengths by implementing ways to get everyone participating. You can break into partners and then shift to a quarterback praying up front. Have a time of silent prayer. Give opportunities for people to pray on an open microphone. Go to the corners and kneel, do a prayer march, or go prayerwalking. Have a time of worship. Make use of flags or maps. Ask for the mind of the Holy Spirit as you direct prayer activities.

Keep the group on track. Encourage intercessors to pray thoroughly over one request before moving to another one. Allow time for everyone to pray who has something to contribute to that topic. If someone jumps to a new request prematurely, gently bring the group back to the unfinished topic. Usually a short season of silence will alert you that prayer for the subject has finished and it's time to move on.

Try not to let any one person dominate. A good rule of thumb is that the *larger* the group, the *shorter* the prayers of each person should be. Try to draw everyone into the time of prayer. If one person is especially shy or quiet (and you know this person is comfortable praying out loud), you may want to ask him to pray over a specific request.

Be willing to exercise loving, firm control if someone's prayers disrupt the unity of the group. Some methods of prayer that are appropriate for individual praying may not be appropriate in the group setting. God will show you ways to yield to His Spirit in a way that all can remain unified.

Close on time, on a positive note. To be sensitive to people with other commitments, end the prayer meeting on time. Ending on a positive note is important so that people look forward to the next time of prayer. This can be done with a song, prayer, or hearty amen. If the group is experiencing a special move of God that would warrant extending the meeting, stop at the appointed time and release all those who need to leave before continuing.

Model and encourage faith-filled prayers. Expect great things of God! Focus on His faithfulness and ability rather than on the problem. Pray to Him with an attitude of expecting a miraculous answer! Hebrews 11:6 tells us, "Without faith it is impossible to please God, because anyone who comes to him must believe that he exists and that he rewards those who earnestly seek him."

DEALING WITH DISTRACTIONS

Harvey Cozzens, in his teaching on "Nurturing or Quenching a Prayer Meeting," lists the following prayer meeting disruptions.[5] If someone in your group repeatedly makes any of the following errors, you run the risk of frustrating or alienating your intercessors.

Being a ball hog. In sports a "ball hog" gets the ball and won't let go. He will take the ball and start running, dribbling, or shooting while everyone else watches. Team spirit is hindered, which diminishes the likelihood of winning the game. The same is true with prayer. Spiritual ball hogs are not team players.

Sometimes a person who prays the best is the most likely to be the ball hog! Still, when everyone prays as a team, there is a new level of God-driven energy and power. One way to divert the ball hog is to specifically ask different members to pray over certain agenda items or to remind people at the start of the meeting to limit their praying time in order to give everyone a chance. You may also need to have a discreet conversation with the offender after the meeting or during a break.

Bringing a personal prayer agenda. All needs are genuine, but keep in mind that the Holy Spirit may want something else to transpire. Discernment is critical here. Though the Lord may be speaking to someone to pray about something as an individual, it may or may not be what He wants the group to pray about in this particular meeting. If someone's personal or emotional burden continues to weigh heavily, you can ask him if he would like others to pray with him after the meeting has concluded. Ask him if he feels okay continuing in the meeting as you move on to other subjects.

Praying "around the world." This kind of praying goes like this: Someone starts praying for Israel, and the Spirit of the Lord starts bubbling up in you and giving you prayers to pray over Israel. But before you can pray, someone begins to pray for China. You begin to sense what God would have you pray for China, but before you can get a word in edgewise, someone else has started praying for Iraq. This tends to stifle a prayer group. Help your group understand the concept of praying for one subject at a time, and encourage them to be sensitive to whether a topic has been fully prayed for before moving on.

Rushing into the throne room. Some pray-ers may be ready to jump in with petitions right away, before an appropriate period of worship and repentance. As the prayer leader, you may need to model a suitable format. You also can ask some of your more experienced intercessors to offer opening prayers of adoration, thanksgiving, and confession. You'll find that in some prayer meetings, the Lord may direct more time in worship or repentance than at other times. Even if some people are ready to petition immediately, others are not. Each meeting will be different, but it's up to you to sense the leading of the Spirit and guide the meeting accordingly.

Lack of eternal perspective. Your group needs a vision and a focus—a redemptive purpose. Ask, "What is God doing in the big picture? What are the redemptive purposes in our praying? Why are we praying this way?" Instill in your group that they are there to change the world through their prayers. This keeps the group's focus from being too narrow or self-centered and opens the door to true one-accord praying.

Answering some sticky questions

Prayer leaders are occasionally faced with dilemmas that are difficult to handle because of the potential to alienate or offend group members. Often these circumstances arise in the middle of the prayer meeting, requiring discernment and very tactful handling on the part of the leader. Here are a few questions I've heard from leaders of corporate prayer gatherings.

1. **What if someone starts praying theologically unsound prayers? ("Lord, have my angel give me a sign.")**
   As the prayer leader, you should address this kind of problem head-on. Otherwise, your group could mistake your silence as

assent. Turn this obstacle into a brief teaching. Say, "I think it's important we talk about this. While angels do exist and this request was prayed sincerely, it's important for us to understand more clearly how the Lord gives us direction. He guides us through the Word, witness of the Spirit, and witness of elders in the church." Keep your explanation to the point and then swiftly move back to the business of prayer. Bear in mind that the need to instantly correct should be employed only if the prayer is seriously unsound, not just a badly worded prayer.

2. **How do you redirect a misguided prayer without embarrassing the person? ("Lord, please stop Bill and Sandi's wedding so he can marry me.")**
Say something affirming first. Let the person know she is loved and that you appreciate her fervency and her willingness to share the prayer. You could say, "While that issue is important, I feel at this time we need to focus on . . ." For an awkward social situation, you could say, "We thank You, God, that You care about all aspects of our lives. We ask that Your will be done in this matter." If the person seems distressed, offer to minister to her personally later. It's important to realize that if a person has a negative or misguided prayer behavior, the loving thing to do is help her get past that.

If a sincere person is still learning the ways of the Lord, the best way to handle it is to speak with her personally later. Most people in the group will understand your graciousness. A good biblical example is Apollos in the book of Acts. This eloquent Jew was an articulate teacher and fervent servant of the Lord who hadn't yet heard the full message of the gospel. Rather than being singled out publicly, he was taken aside privately to be taught more accurately the ways of God (see Acts 18:26). Had this man been put down publicly, the body of Christ might have lost an excellent spokesperson.

3. **What if there is a large interdenominational prayer gathering where not everyone agrees on the same theological issues?**
Most participants will realize this is the case and be more tolerant.

As the prayer leader, your role will be not to nitpick but to find the common points of faith in Jesus Christ that you can pray about. (Appendix H contains Guidelines for Interdenominational Prayer and Worship Gatherings.)

4. How do you handle normal distractions, such as loud babies or children?

If it's a minor or short-lived situation, it's better to overlook it. Often, sensitive parents deal with problems quickly. But if a baby's soft cries become uncontrollable piercing screams and nothing is being done, direct intervention is necessary. Jack Hayford handles these potentially awkward situations with a statement such as, "Gee, if I were six months old, I'd be bored with Pastor Jack's praying, too. We do have a child ministry location where your baby would be much more comfortable."

5. What if someone starts wailing, weeping, groaning, or laughing?

Sometimes these are genuine responses to a deep move of the Holy Spirit upon a person. At other times, these responses are indicative of a person having difficulty handling his emotions. It's important that you discern what the Lord is doing and be sensitive to its effect on newcomers. Is God calling people to deep repentance, and is this person leading the way? Is this an appropriate time of the meeting to do this? If so, then you can assure the people that this is okay and encourage them to seek the Lord for what He's doing in each of them. If you sense this is a misplaced but sincere display of emotion, then you can say something like, "This person is being touched by the Lord, so let's rejoice with him that the Lord is moving so powerfully in his life." In some cases it may be necessary to ask a team member to accompany the person to another room (the prayer room if you have one) where his expression will not hinder the group. Then encourage a vocal time of praise or worship to shift the focus.

6. If I must give corrective guidance, will I always be able to avoid offending people?

No. Unfortunately, no matter how gentle or gracious you are, not everybody will take your correction well. Don't let that stop you from giving necessary corrective guidance, but let it remind you to be sensitive on the few occasions when you administer it.

If you find giving correction difficult (and most of us do) consider this: When a person is derailing a prayer focus, other people's prayers will be hindered if you *don't* take action and administer the needed correction.

Prayer Meeting Formats

The psalmist said, "Those who hope in the LORD will inherit the land" (Psalm 37:9). And Jesus showed us how: "This, then, is how you should pray: . . . your kingdom come, your will be done on earth as it is in heaven" (Matthew 6:9-10). That's our mission—to advance God's kingdom through our praying.

There are a number of effective prayer models that work as long as we understand their primary purpose: to give people the opportunity to have an encounter with the living Christ so that His kingship is established in their hearts. Any one or a combination of the following prayer meeting formats will provide ways for people to touch God and experience His presence as they pray together.

Prayer and Fasting

The observance of a corporate fast involves a time of special prayer and waiting upon God together. The heart of the fast is this: We need God to move more than we want food or other creature comforts. Jack Hayford says, "The Word of God makes it clear that fasting is an instrument of spiritual power; a key by which bonds of evil are broken, and by which God's counsels are received and established in the affairs of men or women (see Isaiah 58:6-8; Mark 9:29; Acts 13:2, 3). Jesus taught fasting by His own word and example, and He said that in the era following His earthly ministry, after His ascension, it would be a part of the disciplines of His people to fast (see Matthew 4:2, 6:16; Mark 2:20)."⁶

There are many types of fasts. Whether fasting from all food, desserts, TV, or any other thing that involves a sacrifice and commitment to God, fasting increases intensity and clarity in prayer. You may call a fast for a certain number of days, one day each week, or a set time each day. You may call different individuals to fast in shifts until the entire week is covered. The important thing is that people understand that self-denial is not the main focus of fasting and prayer. Rather, our goal is to seek God for the release of His purpose on our planet (see Esther 4:16–9:32).

Prayer Watch

A prayer watch is an "intense, concentrated prayer for a specified time or purpose."⁷ The essential idea is to exercise continual prayer vigilance to guard people from danger, as in rotating military watches (see Isaiah 62:6). The prayer watch concept is taken from Leviticus 6:13, where the priests were to keep the fire burning on the altar on behalf of the people twenty-four hours a day, seven days a week. There are several ways to mobilize prayer teams to ensure unceasing intercession:

- Organize people in one-to-four-hour shifts around the clock for a specified season. Cindy Jacobs suggests three hours is best.⁸
- Host an overnight event in which everyone is encouraged to stay to pray through the night from 10:00 P.M. to 6:00 A.M.
- Set aside a prayer room that is continuously open.
- Establish a communitywide prayer watch in which thirty churches commit to praying one day a month. Then individuals in each church pray that day in shifts.

Creative methods such as these enable intercessors to answer the Lord's call to pray without ceasing (1 Thessalonians 5:17).

Harp and Bowl (Worship and Intercession)

This type of format lends itself to continual prayer through singers, musicians, and intercessors who pray and minister interactively (see Revelation 5:8). Mike Bickle, director of the International House of Prayer of Kansas

City, has organized this prayer model. Each meeting lasts two hours and folds seamlessly into the next. An example of how this works is one intercessor will pray for a few moments; then a singer will paraphrase the same prayer in song. The intercessor then adds to the prayer and pauses to allow the singers to echo the prayer. Psalms, hymns of Revelation, and the prayers recorded in the New Testament are used as models for their praying.

This format can easily be adapted to fit a regular church setting. To do this, you will need a good worship leader and musicians who can flow spontaneously and are sensitive to the Holy Spirit. Instead of the IHOP method of totally creating new songs based on Scripture, you simply need to allow the worship to drive the meeting. Pick songs that are prayers, or pointed worship that focuses on attributes of Jesus Christ or that exalts Him. The worship leader then allows for times of prayer focused on topics that come out of the music. He should also allow for times of worship when everyone sings their own song of praise.

concerts of prayer

The term *concerts of prayer* is derived from powerful and united prayer gatherings in the early 1700s that gave birth to major spiritual awakenings. Throughout the years, the term has been used to describe major prayer movements of united believers preceding new global advances of Christ's kingdom. *Extraordinary Prayer* (Crossway, 2001), by Bob Bakke, is an excellent book that explores the history of this subject.

Central to a concert of prayer is the understanding that believers pray for the things on God's heart and that they pray with all members harmonizing *in concert* with one another. The focus is twofold: (1) To seek Christ's fullness to be revealed in the church for His empowerment to accomplish the task ahead; (2) To pray for the fulfillment of Christ's saving purposes among the nations through an awakened and consecrated church.

In recent years, the ministry of prayer leader David Bryant has been largely responsible for reintroducing this method to the church. Bryant's concerts of prayer have seven basic components: celebration, preparation, dedication, seeking fullness, seeking fulfillment, testimonies, and the grand finale. (Appendix H contains a suggested format for his two-hour concert of prayer.)

WORSHIP-BASED CORPORATE PRAYER

This method, popularized by International Renewal Ministries and the Pastors' Prayer Summit movement, has recently been exploding in churches, thanks largely to the ministry of Daniel Henderson and Strategic Renewal International.

Henderson calls his corporate prayer meetings Fresh Encounter. The idea is that people encounter Jesus instead of simply praying through a list of requests about personal needs. Using a facilitator, this method focuses on a theme (perhaps an attribute of God, such as Provider, Comforter, or Almighty). Participants are able to pray a prayer of praise related to the theme, read a Scripture, or start a song. Sometimes the facilitator gives directions (Let's all pray prayers that finish this sentence: "I love you, Lord, because . . . " This free-flowing meeting can be very exciting and is highly experiential. For more information on how to lead this kind of prayer meeting, I recommend Henderson's book *Fresh Encounter* (NavPress, 2004).

EFFECTIVE CHURCHWIDE CORPORATE PRAYER

Most church prayer meetings focus only on the needs of church members. We review our lists, add requests to them, and pray, making sure to cover everything. These prayer meetings are not heavily attended, because they do not focus on kingdom things. When our prayer meetings turn from seeking added benefits for our people to seeking God, we will see more participation and a greater blessing of God in our midst. But it is not easy to turn the focus around. Most churches need to start a completely new prayer meeting or give those who want to focus on parishoners' needs a different venue where they can focus on them.

One church that made this change effectively was the Syracuse Alliance Church. When Kevin Walzak became senior pastor at Syracuse, a church of six hundred, he knew he wanted to change the format of the Wednesday night prayer meeting. It attracted about thirty intercessors and focused almost exclusively on needs of the church members. But Walzak did not want to alienate these intercessors; their role was important to the body life of the church. So Walzak developed a "one-size-doesn't-fit-all" format. Now his prayer meetings have more than doubled in size. What did he do?

Everyone starts in the sanctuary for a time of worship and sometimes a devotional. After thirty minutes, the participants move to different parts of the building, going to the room that focuses on their need or like. Those in the sanctuary participate in a prayer time similar to Daniel Henderson's Fresh Encounters. Others go to a room where they focus on praying for missions; some go to another room and pray for the needs of the church. There are a number of other rooms, each focusing on a different subject; one room has elders who will pray for your needs.

True corporate prayer is important. It can come in many group sizes and formats, including the ones already described. Churchwide corporate prayer is often the starting place for many churches that seek to make prayer more foundational. It can be easily organized by a new prayer leader or adapted to existing prayer meetings.

IS IT WORTH IT?

Unless God's people humble themselves in fervent, corporate prayer, revival doesn't just happen! Only sustained, consistent, concerted, corporate prayer will release the reign of the Lord—His power and glory over our communities. Read what happened when a lone intercessor began a prayer meeting for businessmen in New York City.

The date was September 23, 1857. An intercessor named Jeremiah Lanphier had posted a sign on the Fulton Street Church building that read, "Prayer Meeting from 12 to 1 o'clock—Stop 5, 10, or 20 minutes, or the whole hour, as your time permits." Jeremiah waited ten minutes, then ten more. By 12:30, no one had come. Then at 12:30, one man entered the room, then another and another until there were six men praying. Nothing extraordinary happened that hour, but the men decided to meet to pray the following week. That time, twenty men came; the next week, forty. Because of the climbing interest in prayer, Jeremiah decided they should meet for prayer daily. Within days of that decision, a financial panic hit the country. Banks began to close and people lost their jobs. Conditions were ripe for a revival. Soon, three thousand people were jamming into the Fulton building to pray. Within six months, twenty thousand pray-ers came and at least twenty other corporate meetings had begun in the city. Corporate prayer movements such as these began to spread quickly across the nation and in different parts of the world.

The years of 1858–1859 became known as the *Annus Mirabulus*—Year of Miracles. During this era, powerful missionary movements were birthed and great leaders such as Dwight Moody, Andrew Murray, and William Booth came to fruitfulness. When Jeremiah and his five prayer partners began their prayer vigil, they had no idea that God would bring an estimated one million persons into His kingdom.

The Fulton Street prayer meeting is just one of thousands of examples of corporate prayer that preceded a major awakening. Gregory Frizzell says, "Corporate prayer is the foundational pattern in nearly all great revivals of history. Though a variety of prayer strategies are certainly important, none can rival the historic role of the corporate prayer meeting."[9] Truly God works through people who pray in one accord for the expansion of His kingdom.

---

1. Sue Curran, *The Praying Church* (Lake Mary, Fla.: Creation House Press, 2000), p. 40.

2. Jonathan Graf, "One Voice, One Focus," *Pray!* Issue 10, January/February 1999, p. 15.

3. Curran, p. 11.

4. Personal telephone interview by Cheryl Sacks with Robert Baxter, High Point Church, Arlington, Texas, January 20, 2004.

5. Harvey Cozzins, "Nurturing or Quenching a Prayer Meeting," NALCPL conference, Colorado Springs, Colo., June 2001.

6. Jack Hayford, "It's Time to Fast" (Van Nuys, Calif.: Living Way Ministries).

7. Cindy Jacobs, *Possessing the Gates of the Enemy,* p. 207.

8. Jacobs, p. 210.

9. Gregory Frizzell, *Biblical Patterns for Powerful Church Prayer Meetings* (Memphis: The Master Design, 1999), introduction.

CHAPTER 12

Praying Outside the Walls of the Church

It's five o'clock in the evening and more than two thousand people are standing outside Calvary Temple Worship Center in Modesto, California. They're not coming to hear the latest Christian recording artist, and most of them are not even churchgoing people. What could be so compelling that it would draw drug addicts, gang members, self-sufficient business leaders, unsaved spouses, and prodigal children all to the house of God?

There's no gimmick, no celebrity. It's quite simply a presentation of the gospel—a drama about heaven and hell.

When the service begins at 7:00 P.M., the sanctuary is packed. Every seat is taken, the aisles are filled, and people are standing four-deep along the walls. During the evening, the crowd laughs, weeps, breaks into applause, and sometimes sits quietly in awe as they see themselves in the actors—standing at the judgment seat of Christ. Probably for the first time, many of them become aware of the gates of heaven open before them on the one hand and the door to an eternal hell on the other.

Moments later, hundreds stream to the altar to give their hearts to Christ, laying down the symbols of their hopeless lives—syringes, guns, knives, colored bandanas, and a river of tears. In the next eight weeks during twenty-eight performances of *Heaven's Gates, Hell's Flames*, eighty-one thousand people pack the sanctuary and thirty-three thousand give their lives to Christ. How did this miracle happen?

"We don't know all the reasons God chose to pour out His Spirit upon us during this season," a staff member confided. But the church did take specific steps to invite God and the people of Modesto into their church. First, they called the congregation to forty days of prayer and fasting. Next, church members gave out fifty thousand tickets to unsaved friends, coworkers, and family members. Three days before the drama, church leaders called for twenty-four-hour prayer. The names of the invited guests were strewn across the altar. Church members came to the building day and night and prayed over the names—that they would come to the drama, and that they would make a commitment to Christ. Before each performance, church staff and performers met for an hour, interceding for God's anointing to be upon the drama and for His Spirit to convict the hearts of the audience.

> *Revival will come when we get the walls down between the church and the community.*
>
> Jack Graham, pastor
> Prestonwood Baptist Church

No one expected phenomenal results. What was to be one week of performances turned into an eight-week run. When volunteers made up new believers' packets, they thought they had enough to last for the entire week. They never imagined every packet would be distributed on the first night.

Pastors and members of other churches also were involved, praying for the drama and bringing their friends and loved ones. As a result, churches all over Modesto expanded overnight. One church with two services immediately found it necessary to add a third. Another church phoned Calvary Temple's office and said, "Please don't send us any more follow-up cards. We can't fit anyone else in our building!"

Maybe you could call this a modern-day counterpart to the church in the book of Acts. It's a simple plan for transforming communities: the power of prayer in partnership with the proclamation of the gospel.

PrayInG For your SPHeres of InFLuence

God has set your church in a particular location. He has placed each member in a certain neighborhood and a specific place of employment by His design (see Acts 17:26). His purpose is that through our Christian influence, we would transform the places where we live and work. Churches can be catalysts for change when they help their members catch a vision outside themselves. Too often we think of the church as being only what happens inside the four walls of the church "building." We forget that the church is the people of God—you and me—and that everyplace we go, we can carry His presence and power.

Communities suffer when God's people fail to take responsibility for the areas in which they live, work, and minister. Through the prophet Jeremiah, the Lord tells us, "It will be made a wasteland, parched and desolate before me; the whole land will be laid waste because there is no one who cares" (Jeremiah 12:11).

By God's design, we each have been given a sphere of influence or spiritual authority. Since Old Testament times, we find that God has assigned His people to territories. This was the case in ancient Israel. While the land was still in enemy hands, each of the twelve tribes was given, according to its size and ability, an allotted inheritance. Each family was required to conquer and maintain its areas of responsibility and then, as an extended family, take possession of the entire land.

The principle of being assigned responsibility for a geographical area is also found in the early days of the church. Paul speaks of "the field God has assigned to us" (2 Corinthians 10:13-16). He taught that God gave individuals geographical areas of responsibility so the gospel could spread abroad and the church could be established. This Scripture helps us understand that we not only have authority in neighborhoods but also in other places where we have influence such as a school where we teach, a church we pastor, or another place of employment. It all starts, however, with taking to heart the assignment we have been given.

I discovered the power of our God-given authority in 1979, when I was a young single high school teacher in Carrollton, Texas. I was attending a growing, dynamic church where every Sunday the pastor told us, "You don't just *come* to church; you *are* the church. Now go out there and change the world." There was no doubt in my mind that my schoolteaching was a special assignment from God. Every morning before school, I prayed over the empty desks, asking the Lord to draw each student to Himself. I prayerwalked the four-block perimeter of my large high school and boldly prayed, *God, somehow use me to bring the gospel to the two thousand students in this school.* I gathered a number of other Christian teachers, and we began to meet during lunch to pray for our faculty and students. In answer to our prayers, the Lord led me to discover a dusty set of books in a closet, dozens of copies of the Christian book *The Cross and the Switchblade.* I assigned all my English classes to read it and then began to pray that the Lord would send the main character, ex-gang leader Nicky Cruz, to speak at my school. Of course, the sharing of the gospel and inviting preachers to speak was strictly forbidden in a public high school, but the Lord opened the door for Nicky to come and tell his story—how Jesus Christ delivered him from drugs and gangs and gave him a new life. My most vivid memory of teaching high school is the standing ovation the students gave Nicky when he finished his story of how Jesus Christ died on the cross for his sins and theirs.

As a pastor or prayer leader, you can help every individual in your congregation develop a lifestyle of praying for those in their sphere of influence. Through Mission America's Lighthouse Movement, thousands of churches are helping their congregations focus upon praying for their unsaved families, friends, and coworkers. A lighthouse is a person, family, church, or any group of people who commit to praying and caring for those in their network who don't know Christ and then sharing the gospel with them as God opens the door.

There are other creative ideas that put praying for the lost in front of a congregation. Some churches use "a miracle mile," where they map out every home, business, and school that sits within a one-mile radius of the church. They get as much information as they can about each home and business: names of people, owners, teachers, principals, and administrators; type of business; and so forth. They have people scan the newspapers each day for more information. Then they keep reminding people to pray for those who are within their miracle mile. Other churches hand out copies of *Paths of Gold* (NavPress, 2002) to adults and teens. This little booklet provides pray-ers with forty-six Scripture-based prayers to pray for a specific lost friend. When coupled with reminders to keep praying, it can be a powerful method to keep people praying in this key area.

TAKING THE FIRST STEPS

If you've been working hard toward a vision of building your church into a house of prayer, you may be overwhelmed with all the details of organizing prayer *inside* your church. In beginning to extend your prayer focus to the community, the nation, and the world, you may want to start with your own personal prayer life and perhaps a small team of intercessors. Begin to pray for something on your heart that is outside your family and church. My recommendation that you personally start here does not supercede what prayer strategies you are working with your pastor and team to raise up in your church. Most churches do not have any plan to focus prayer on the local lost around the church. Before a church can embrace this important concept, its prayer leaders need to be doing it! That's why you should begin making prayer for the lost a lifestyle before you ask others to get on board.

One suggestion is for individuals to pray for the neighbors who live around them. A number of years ago, Hal and I committed to this practice. We were especially drawn to pray for the family who lived behind us, though we didn't know them. Their daughter and our daughter, both about four years old, were beginning to develop a relationship by talking to each other through the fence that separated our backyards. One day (I believe in answer to our prayers) a powerful storm blew in and leveled the fence. Excitedly, the girls ran back and forth between the two houses. In the next few weeks as the dads rebuilt the fence, Hal led our neighbor to the Lord. And in the months that followed, we had the privilege of leading the rest of the family to Christ and seeing them baptized in our church.

PRAYING FOR YOUR COMMUNITY

Kjell Sjoberg, in his book *Winning the Prayer War*, says that "the destiny of a church is bound up in the destiny of its community."[1] This is the same message Jeremiah gave the Jews who were carried away into captivity in Babylon: "Seek the peace and prosperity of the city to which I have carried you into exile. Pray to the LORD for it, because if it prospers, you too will prosper" (Jeremiah 29:7).

The Lord cares deeply for our communities. He is saddened by their decline. He rejoices when they repent, as was the case with the inhabitants of Nineveh. When Christians pray for the Holy Spirit's involvement in their communities, the heavens over an area are opened. The spiritual atmosphere becomes more conducive for unbelievers to receive the gospel. Everyone in the city experiences more safety, peace, and prosperity.

The story of Cali, Colombia, told in the *Transformations* video mentioned in chapter 9, is a prime example. For many years, Colombia has been the world's biggest exporter of cocaine. The Cali cartel, which controlled up to 70 percent of drug trade, has been called the largest, richest, and best-organized criminal organization in history. Until a few years ago, the cartel ran the city. Drug lords murdered up to fifteen people a day who simply got in their way in the streets.

Revolted by the corruption in their city, pastors began to meet and pray together. Then they called their churches to come together for an all-night prayer vigil. More than twenty thousand Christians showed up. Forty-eight hours after the event, the daily newspaper, *El Pais*, headlined, "No homicides!" For the first time in as long as anybody could remember, a twenty-four-hour period passed without a single person being killed. Three days later, the head of the Cali cartel was captured. Within eight weeks, seven of the eight Cali cartel leaders were behind bars.[2]

Almolonga, Guatemala, is another community that was drastically changed by the power of prayer. Typical of many Mayan highland communities, this city was idolatrous, inebriated, and economically depressed. Determined to fight back, a group of intercessors got busy, crying out to God during evening prayer vigils. Almolonga has now become one of the most transformed cities in the world. Fully 90 percent of the town's citizens consider themselves evangelical Christians. As they have renounced their pagan gods, their economy has begun to blossom. Churches are now the dominant feature of Almolonga's landscape.[3]

Truly we are seeing that the united fervent prayers of God's people have the power to renovate communities for Christ. But perhaps you're thinking, *We can't get twenty thousand Christians together for an all-night prayer meeting. What can our church do?* The following section will outline ways your church can start right now to pray for your city's spiritual transformation.

UNITE WITH OTHER CHURCHES

Many churches pray over lists of unsaved people, but they don't pray much for the community as a whole. The multifaceted needs of larger communities can be time-consuming and overwhelming. However, when prayer-saturated churches join together, the task becomes more manageable and the visible, practical unity of the body of Christ is powerful.

Citywide Houses of Prayer

Churches in many cities are establishing citywide prayer rooms or prayer houses to provide twenty-four-hour prayer coverage for their cities. Several churches may purchase or rent a building for use by all the churches in the area. Intercessors or groups of intercessors take different "watches" or three-hour shifts. One example is the International House of Prayer in Kansas City, where Mike Bickle and his staff lead eighty-four prayer meetings each week attended by intercessors from churches throughout the city.

Church Prayer Coordinators' Networks

In a growing number of communities, church prayer coordinators are meeting regularly to pray for one another's pastors and churches, as well as the needs of the city. Through their relational networks, they can easily bring their churches together for systematic saturation prayer of their neighborhoods in a number of creative ways. Border Prayer Network in El Paso, Texas, is successfully drawing together prayer leaders from both sides of the Mexican border to pray for the transformation of their cities. (See appendix B for a guide to starting a local network of church prayer leaders.)

Multichurch Prayer and Worship Gatherings

Something powerful happens when the churches of a city come together in worship and intercession. I've been a part of many multichurch gatherings around the world—one in my own state during PrayerQuake 2000.

At the time of the gathering, Arizona was in the midst of one of the worst droughts in the state's history. Fires were breaking out everywhere; the state was a tinderbox. On Friday night, the worship leader led us in intercessory worship with the song "Open the Heavens." As we sang the chorus over and over, the leader called us to lift up the words as a petition to the Lord, asking Him to send His spiritual *and* physical rain to our state. Later that evening as we left the meeting, much to our surprise and that of the local meteorologists, drops of rain already had begun to fall. Within a few hours there was a deluge. The next day, the weatherman said the rain came out of nowhere. Tuesday's *Arizona Republic* reported the beginning of the earliest monsoon season since 1925.[4]

Mountaintop Prayer

All over the world, individuals and churches are gathering regularly to pray on mountaintops and other high places overlooking their cities. For several years, a number of churches in Arizona, including ours, have started each year by praying for our communities from mountaintops throughout the state. Designated prayer leaders are assigned to each mountain, and scriptural prayer guides are distributed in advance to help coordinate prayer sessions. We started small, with church prayer coordinators simply announcing to their congregations the opportunity to climb their favorite mountain and pray for the city on New Year's morning. Every year the event has grown. Last year the local Christian radio stations even got involved.

One year, Hal and I had gathered with a group on North Mountain, and we began to focus our prayers upon exposing drug trafficking in our city. One intercessor voiced a sense that God was going to answer quickly as a sign of His pleasure for our intercession over the city. Within twenty-four hours, the evening news was reporting the largest drug bust in the history of Phoenix.

TARGET SPECIAL GROUPS

An effective way for your church to begin praying over your community is by adopting target groups in prayer. When Jill Griffith was prayer leader at Second Baptist Church in Houston, Texas, her organized outreach to pray for specific groups in the community became so successful that many other churches joined in. Following are several creative ways your church can structure opportunities to reach out to those who might never receive prayer otherwise.

In Honor Services. These events show appreciation to such people as teachers, police officers and firefighters, government officials, and health care workers. Plan a luncheon or dinner with a program that includes music or drama, words and letters of appreciation, gifts, and a time of prayer.

Adopt-a-Leader. Assign intercessors to pray for state and national governmental leaders and their families. You'll need to prepare prayer guides with names and positions of those in office, along with Scriptures and other practical helps for praying for a governmental leader.

Shield-a-Badge. To establish this program, recruit intercessors willing to make a one-year commitment to pray for a local police officer or firefighter and his or her family. Start by praying for those in your own congregation. Then visit police and fire stations to share your plan and obtain the names of those officers and firefighters who desire to participate. Someone with good computer skills is needed to oversee this ministry in order to do data entry and maintenance.

PrayerCare for the Elderly. Those with a heart for the older generation can pray for those in assisted living programs and their immediate families. Start with church members and their families who have relatives in assisted living programs, and then add others in the community as more intercessors become available.

MediCare. Intercession is especially important for health care professionals who must continually deal with life and death. Identify medical personnel interested in this ministry through existing relationships with those in your church body.

INFORMED INTERCESSION

Statistical data, historical research, and personal interviews can uncover vital information about a city, community, or region. When intercessors are armed with such information, their prayers can be more specific and fervent. Vital information empowers intercessors much the same way that X-rays serve physicians.[5]

Statistical data provides such helpful information as high crime areas, high school drop-out rates, teen pregnancies, and divorce rates. It can help pinpoint concentrated areas of adult bookstores, bars, and occult activity.

Some churches and cities have assembled research teams to gather data that can be used to help intercessors pray intelligently about their communities. When we began to gather statistical data in our city, I was surprised to learn that Phoenix is number one in the nation for citizens running red lights resulting in deaths. That's something to pray about! When I learned that one of the highest crime areas in our city is only a few blocks from my home, I started praying even more fervently for my neighborhood.

PRAYERWALKING

In 1994, Family of God Fellowship was facing a number of challenges. The small Hispanic congregation was increasingly concerned about its south Phoenix neighborhood. Crime was increasing, and within a few short blocks of their church, ten gangs and six crack houses flourished. Pastor Leroy Albo called to ask if I would come and speak to his congregation about prayerwalking. I didn't know what to expect, but the next Saturday morning when I arrived at the church, the entire congregation— all twenty-five of them—was eagerly awaiting the start of the seminar.

During the morning, I explained that prayerwalking involves praying on-site in neighborhoods where you want to see God intervene. It might be the neighborhood near your home or church, or perhaps it's around schools, government buildings, or the business area of your community.

"Listen to the Lord as you walk and He will impress upon you what to pray," I said. "Prayerwalk your designated area on a regular basis. Be persistent and expect to see change."

The next Saturday morning, the members met again—this time to put what they had learned into action. United together in one large group, they began to walk and pray through their neighborhood. One member led the way carrying a large American flag, while to his left, another member carried the Christian flag. Between prayers, the group sang and worshiped the Lord with tambourines and other musical instruments. When the pastor called to give me a report of their first prayerwalking adventure, I realized I'd forgotten to mention something I usually say in prayerwalking seminars: Break into twos and act naturally. Don't do anything to call attention to yourselves.

Clearly this wasn't what the Lord had in mind in this case. The united bold prayers of this group brought immediate results—a swift blow to the Enemy's work. Within one month of the initial prayerwalk, the main crack house across the street from the church burned to the ground. Within another four months, every other crack house disappeared: The city condemned and tore down several, and residents of the other houses just packed up and moved out. The gangs disappeared, too.

"All the gangs either disbanded or moved out of the neighborhood," says Pastor Albo. "That is, all except one."

The pastor went on to explain. The church had opened its doors after school, offering Bible studies and recreation for the neighborhood children. A number of the gang members brought their younger brothers and sisters to participate. At Christmas, the church gave the children gifts, and their older siblings received New Testaments. Overwhelmed by the love the church extended to their families, the gang members gave their lives to the Lord. Now they call themselves the "Jesus Gang." They didn't disband—they just changed their name and their mission.

Also during this time, members of the community began to come to church. Soon the church grew to 158 members with as many as 80 continuing to prayerwalk the neighborhood weekly.

The concept of prayerwalking is not new, though until recently it was somewhat forgotten. An often overlooked passage in the New Testament reveals that Jesus modeled prayerwalking.

"After this the Lord appointed seventy-two others and sent them two by two ahead of him to every town and place where he was about to go" (Luke 10:1). In the next verse, we see that Jesus points out that the harvest is ripe and that the way to prepare for the harvest is through prayer (see Luke 10:2). I would suggest here that Jesus sent His disciples to cities to intercede in advance of His coming, that there might be a great harvest of souls.

Prayerwalking can take on various forms:

Casual. An individual or family may walk and pray over their neighborhood as they go for their early-morning walk or jog.

Organized. Your church can turn Saturday morning into an exciting time of worship and prayerwalking around the vicinity of the church. Participants may break into smaller groups or all join together as they walk, pray, and worship. When churches visibly and openly worship, pray, and declare God's Word over the community, the term *praise march* may more accurately describe the activity.

Systematic. Your church or a number of churches can join together as part of a systematic strategy to saturate an entire city with prayer. Maps and specific assignments of intercessors ensure that the entire city or community is covered.

Praying For The World

As a congregation seeks to discover ways to pray outside the walls of their church, it is important to move from praying just for their own community and nation, to the nations of the earth. There are many creative ways prayer leaders can design opportunities for their congregations to pray for those around the world.

Praying for Your Church's Missionaries.

If missionaries and their families are to survive on the mission field and break through in some of the darkest places on the earth, ongoing prayer support as well as finances are needed from their local church. One idea is to ask your church families to adopt a missionary family in prayer. Correspond with the missionary and ask for specific prayer requests. Children can even get involved by praying for missionaries' children.

One of the best illustrations of the power of intercession for a missionary is found in the story of J. O. Fraser. Fraser was a pioneer missionary to the Lisu tribe of southwest China. As a young missionary, he served with the China Inland Mission in the early 1900s. For several years he preached Christ among the mountain villages, with virtually no outward results. Most of Fraser's few converts soon fell back into the clutches of demonism. Then he himself was attacked by severe depression and thoughts of suicide. He became so defeated that he asked God to take his life rather than allow him to labor on without results.

Meanwhile, on the other side of the world, Fraser's mother started a prayer support group to pray for Fraser. The group consisted of eight to ten Christians who committed to pray faithfully for Fraser and his ministry. At this time Fraser reported that he experienced a tremendous lifting of the cloud over his soul. God seemed suddenly to step in and drive back the forces of darkness.

Soon after the cloud of depression lifted, God's Spirit enabled Fraser to pray "the prayer of faith" for several hundred Lisu families. In the following years, hundreds of Lisu families accepted Christ, and ultimately a movement began to evangelize tens of thousands. As a result, today in southwest China and northern Burma, they are a missionary tribe taking the gospel to neighboring tribes.[6]

Praying for Unreached People Groups.

A number of prayer guides and world prayer maps offer information on how to pray for the most unreached people of the world. One good source for ordering such resources is Every Home for Christ, in Colorado Springs, Colorado. Its maps and prayer guides will be an excellent addition to your prayer room.

In the last decade, millions of Christians have focused their prayers upon the 10/40 Window—a geographical rectangle between 10 and 40 degrees north of the equator, and running from North Africa on the west to Japan on the east. It is estimated that more than 90 percent of those in unreached people groups live in the 10/40 Window. In recent years an emphasis is also being placed upon the 40/70 Window. Another excellent resource is *The Global Prayer Digest.*

Taking Prayer Journeys and Expeditions.

One way to help your church get a heart for praying for nations is to plan a prayer journey to some area of the world. The need for maturity and commitment is much higher for this type of intercession than for prayerwalking a neighborhood. It is recommended that those who sign up for a prayer expedition feel called of God to do so, and raise up personal intercessors to pray for them while they are away. A number of prayer and missions organizations coordinate such trips, and you could learn much by going on one of these trips before attempting to organize your own.

Prayer for the Persecuted Church.

Promoting the International Day of Prayer for the Persecuted Church, held annually in November, is a good way to awaken your church to the need to pray for Christians around the world. Few congregations realize that two hundred million Christians face persecution each day—and 60 percent are children. Every day, three hundred are killed for their faith in Jesus Christ. Various ministries have materials that can help you promote this important day. A simple search of "persecuted church" on the Internet can put you in touch with these ministries.

Praying from Heaven's Perspective

We all know that prayer works, but have you ever thought about how prayer works to change cities, nations, and societies as a whole? The answer is found in understanding the work of the Holy Spirit on the earth today. Scriptures show us that the Holy Spirit guides into all truth (see John 16:13), testifies about Christ (see John 15:26), convicts of sin (see John 14:26), gives life (see John 6:63), and comes to those who ask (see Luke 11:13).

When we pray for someone, our prayers release the divine activity of the Holy Spirit to work in and around the person for whom we are praying. The same is true of the places for which we pray. As we pray in agreement with God's Word and revealed will, He raises up a wall of protection that restrains evil spirits attempting to gain influence over a person's life or place for which we are interceding. Through our prayers, the Holy Spirit is released to neutralize the work of the Enemy and pour out God's blessings, which in turn change the spiritual climate around a person or locale.

As established in chapter 1, these things don't just happen automatically. The Lord answers those who ask. He opens the door to those who knock and comes to those who seek. There is action required on our part.

When prayer is absent, the heavens are closed and demonic and worldly influences have free rein. In his book *Primary Purpose*, Ted Haggard says, "When Christians start praying, the demonic influences can become so weak that a vacuum actually develops and the kingdom of God can be manifested with greater effectiveness. In these places, massive conversions, life-giving church growth, societal improvement and great spiritual encouragement occur."[7]

Prayer always releases the divine activity of the Holy Spirit and thwarts demonic influence. This holds true whether we are praying for the president, our congress, a police officer, or a schoolteacher. The principle works every time—not because we pray in our own authority but because we pray in His name and from the vantage point of heaven.

This bears out in Ephesians 3, when Paul tells us, "His intent was that now, through the church, the manifold wisdom of God should be known to the rulers and authorities in the heavenly realms, according to his eternal purpose which he accomplished in Christ Jesus our Lord" (verses 10-11).

No person can come to Christ unless the Holy Spirit reveals truth to him. Yet Scripture tells us that Satan has blinded the minds of those who do not believe (see 2 Corinthians 4:4). This is where you and I come in. When we pray in Jesus' name, through His blood, we use our position of authority in Christ to make known to demonic rulers the perfect will of God. This is something that only we in the church can do. There is no one else who can change the spiritual climate over communities, who can open the door for people to respond to the gospel.

Jesus left us with this final thought about how we should pray for our communities and world: "Our Father . . . your kingdom come, your will be done on earth as it is in heaven" (Matthew 6:9-10).

1. Kjell Sjoberg, *Winning the Prayer War* (Chichester, England: New Wine Press, 1991), p. 12.

2. George Otis Jr., *Transformations*, videocassette, The Sentinel Group, 1999.

3. Otis.

4. *The Arizona Republic*, June 20, 2000.

5. C. Peter Wagner, *Churches That Pray* (Ventura, Calif.: Regal, 1993), p. 195.

6. John D. Robb, " Prayer As a Strategic Weapon in Frontier Missions," *International Journal on Frontier Missions*, Vol. 8:1, January 1991, p. 23.

7. Ted Haggard, *Primary Purpose* (Orlando, Fla.: Creation House, 1995), p. 159.

If You Build It, I Will Come!

"Fire came out from the presence of the Lord *and consumed the burnt offering . . . on the altar. And when all the people saw it, they shouted for joy and fell facedown"* (Leviticus 9:24).

Throughout the ages, the one characteristic that has distinguished God's house from any other is His tangible presence. True worshipers desire nothing less. At the dedication of the tabernacle in Leviticus 9, God's people presented a sacrifice upon the altar. The miraculous fire that started was a sign, not only of the acceptance of the offerings but also of God's actual residence in the chosen dwelling place.[1]

God's command was that the fire kindled from heaven was to be perpetually preserved and never allowed to go out: The fire on the altar must be kept burning continuously; it must not go out (see Leviticus 6:12)—lest they need to resort to use of common fire. Fire for sacred purposes obtained somewhere other than from the altar was called "strange" or common fire, and for the use of such, the two priests Nadab and Abihu were punished with death by fire from God (see Leviticus 10:1-2; Numbers 3:4, 26:61).[2] God is not pleased when we try and do things in our own way and in our own power.

To keep the fire from ever being extinguished, strict regulations were given to the priests with respect to offering burnt sacrifices. The priests of the Old Testament were given explicit instructions of how to prepare daily sacrifices upon the altar in such a way that the fire was maintained.

As the fire on the altar was to be kept alive continuously, so God calls us to unceasing prayer. Because of the constant succession of burnt offerings during the day, the fire was easily kept alive; the only danger was that the fire would go out at night after the evening sacrifice had been consumed. In our passionate desire for life-changing encounters with God, we must not let our fire go out as we cry out, day and night, for Him.

Just as God called Moses to build the tabernacle, a place for the Lord Himself to dwell, so today He is calling us to build a house for Him. Though that ancient building was assembled with wood and earthly stones, this new structure is being built with living stones: you and me.

Not only has God called us to build something for Him, He has given us instructions for how to build a house worthy of His Presence. Before a church can become a house of prayer, its people must consecrate themselves as living sacrifices and as living stones, committed to spending time in His presence. As people learn to become houses of prayer in their own lives and families, they will begin to come together as a corporate body to become a house of prayer built with many living stones.

Prayer—Our Program, or His Presence?

Throughout the pages of this book, you have received a blueprint for how to build a house of prayer. Yet we must ensure that our churches move beyond "programs" to the place of becoming living altars. Such living altars attract God's glorious presence, which is incomparably better than any program.

We no longer have a temple and no longer build altars and make animal sacrifices. Today when we speak of altars, we speak of a place set aside for man to meet with God. At that altar—in those places of prayer and worship—He still comes with fire.

In the Upper Room, the disciples built an altar of prayer to the Lord, and fire came from heaven. The disciples were to stay until they were clothed with power from on high. When His presence was manifested, they knew it. Their new power came from an intimate encounter with God (see Acts 1:4–2:4).

So great was the disciples' need for Christ's Spirit that they were not to leave Jerusalem until they had it. We are God's disciples today and need His power just as much. He is asking us to remain in the place of prayer until we encounter His fire upon our lives and churches.

I hear the Lord's urgent call, even a promise, to His church today:

"If you will build an altar, I will come!"

My fervent prayer for you is that God's Spirit will come upon you and that together you and He will build your church into a true house of prayer.

---

1. Robert Jamieson, et. al., *A Commentary, Critical and Explanatory, on the Old and New Testaments* (Oak Harbor, Wash.: Logos Research Systems, Inc., 1997), (Leviticus 9:24).

2. William Smith, *Smith's Bible Dictionary* (Nashville: Nelson, 1997).

APPENDIXES

Sample Prayer Coordinator Job Description

(CHAPTER 2: THE ROLE OF THE CHURCH PRAYER COORDINATOR)

This sample job description will give you some ideas for creating your own Prayer Coordinator Job Description. Our sample is quite detailed and sets a very high standard for the position. Your church may have different needs. Remember, this is just a guide. Feel free to adapt it for your church's needs.

Job Title: Churchwide Prayer Coordinator

Reports To: Senior Pastor

Classification: Part-Time Staff

Job Summary:
The prayer coordinator is a member in good standing with
_____ Church whose purpose is to organize, schedule, and provide general leadership for the church's prayer activities.

Prerequisite Qualifications:

A. Membership: Must be an active member and financial supporter of _____ (having attended the membership class).

B. Experience: Two years church attendance at _Church_ and served on the prayer action team for one year.

Skills, Knowledge, Abilities, Qualifications:
- A love for and devotion to prayer
- Ability to lead, organize, and delegate
- Well-grounded in the Word of God
- Ability to teach and train others in prayer
- Ability to facilitate small groups and corporate prayer
- Ability to listen, think clearly and creatively (good judgment)
- Ability to work with people individually and in a group (a team player)
- Sensitivity to different cultures and tolerance of differing theological views
- Friendly and patient approach (nonreactive) to disagreements and differences of opinion
- A committed and caring person
- Flexible attitude and a willingness to learn
- Moral purity, honest with a sense of Christian values
- Spiritual maturity with the ability to give good Christian counsel
- Willing to take direction from immediate supervisor

Duties, Tasks, Responsibilities:
- Pray for and promote opportunities for others to pray for (church name)
- Develop a prayer action team (under Senior Leadership Team approval)
- Develop and train the Pastor's Intercessory Teams (PIT Crews)
- Establish and maintain a prayer room
- Conduct training on prayer

- Assist senior pastor in facilitating weekly staff prayer meeting
- Oversee small-group and corporate intercessory prayer meetings
- Organize days of corporate prayer and fasting (quarterly)
- Conduct "Time with God" personal prayer retreats
- Mobilize strategic prayer for emergencies and in times of crisis
- Conduct all-night prayer meetings as scheduled
- Train, oversee, and maintain the altar prayer ministry team
- Train and resource all department heads to lead and maintain prayer in their respective areas
- Link (church name) with local, national, and international prayer initiatives

(Signed and dated by Pastor and Prayer Coordinator)

How to Start a Church Prayer Leaders Network in Your City or Region

---

(CHAPTER 2: THE ROLE OF THE CHURCH PRAYER COORDINATOR)

Establishing a network of church prayer leaders in your city will help strengthen prayer in the local churches and will help link churches for united fervent prayer for the community, state, nation, and world. The name Church Prayer Leaders Network is being trademarked by *Pray!* magazine, which runs a national network called Church Prayer Leaders Network (CPLN). The CPLN is glad to assist any ministry that seeks to raise up a regional network in its city, and the CPLN would love to have that regional network affiliate with the national organization. Simply contact the CPLN to discuss such an affiliation. When such an arrangement is made, the CPLN is happy to allow use of its name in a regional title (e.g., Greater Phoenix Church Prayer Leaders Network; Boston Metro Church Prayer Leaders Network). Of course you are free to establish a network in your community without any connection to the CPLN; you just need to use a name other than Church Prayer Leaders Network.

Following are suggested steps for establishing a network:

Pray for God's direction and timing.

Secure a commitment of other local church prayer leaders who agree to serve on a task force. Make sure they are pastor-designated church prayer leaders, obtain their pastor's approval to serve, and hold a good reputation in the community. Intercessors who have left churches due to unhappiness with direction or because they struggled to come under the authority of a pastor are not the kind of people you want on your committee.

Include prayer leaders from a broad cross section of Christ-centered churches. It will be difficult to change the character of the network if you don't show inclusivity from the outset. For example: if you are all from charismatic churches or all from noncharismatic churches, it will be almost impossible to get the opposite stream of churches to join in. The same goes for ethnicity. If all the members of your team are white Anglos, it will be hard to gain the trust and participation of black, Asian, or Hispanic churches.

Ask the pastors of the churches represented to serve on an advisory and endorsement board for the network. An alternative suggestion for pastoral involvement is the pastors' prayer network in your city, if one exists.

Pray together as a team for unity, direction, favor, and timing.

Appoint a chairperson and assign responsibilities. (See "Task Force Job Assignments" on page 227 for suggestions.)

Schedule regular team meetings for the rest of the year. We suggest the team meet monthly at the same time and location if possible.

Secure a mailing list of pastors, churches, and prayer leaders in your city, if one exists. If one does not exist, begin to compile one.

Set a date and location and secure a speaker for the first network training event. Plan ongoing training events, such as quarterly training breakfasts in a different Christian church each time from 8:30 A.M. to noon on Saturdays.

Order prayer resources directly relating to mobilizing prayer in the church to sell at the event. Many vendors will allow you to place an order and return what is not sold. If you are unable to secure resources for the first meeting, ask a local bookstore to provide a book table, though you may need to educate them on what to bring because most will have books on personal prayer but very little on prayer in the church.

Send a letter to the pastors of your city explaining your vision and asking them to send a prayer coordinator or prayer representative to the event.

Send a separate letter directly to any church prayer coordinators you know.

Hold the training event. You can serve a light continental breakfast and charge a small fee to help cover the cost of the meal, mailings, printing, speaker honorarium. Ask one of the pastors on your advisory board to be present and participate in the meeting. You may want to invite all the pastors of the city to attend the meetings as well.

Continue to build your database.

Plan remaining events for the year.

Continue to send invitation letters to both the pastors and prayer coordinators for each training event. Even if the pastors don't attend the event, a letter keeps them informed of the training you are providing their church prayer leaders.

The Church Prayer Leaders Network may want to sponsor an annual citywide prayer conference to train intercessors and help unite the churches in prayer. The national CPLN is always looking for locations to hold regional conferences. Contact them for information.

Continue to pray, evaluate, refine, and make adjustments as the Holy Spirit directs.

Starting a Church Prayer Leaders Network: Sample Pastor's Letter

Dear Pastor,

It is extremely commonsensical that every flourishing ministry within a church has a point person (music, youth, children). Prayer ministry is no exception.

Because the position of prayer leader is new to many churches, you may be asking, "How do I select the right person?" or "Where can my prayer leader get training for this specialized task?"

If your "point person" for prayer is involved in (name of local network), then you are already experiencing the benefits firsthand. Hundreds of prayer leaders are learning to raise up pastors' prayer partners, establish prayer rooms, effectively lead corporate prayer, and establish prayer curriculum for Christian education.

Some two hundred pastors, church leaders, and prayer coordinators attended our last training event. We don't want your church to miss out on the next seminar on:

Pastors, Prayer Leaders, and Intercessors
. . . Building the House of Prayer
Saturday, April 20
8:30 A.M. to 12 noon
at Covenant of Grace
906 E. Peoria Ave.
Phoenix, AZ

We have invited Eddie Smith, founder and president of the U.S. Prayer Center in Houston, Texas, to share on the role of this vital team. A former pastor, Eddie is a national prayer mobilizer and author of **Intercessors and Pastors . . . The Emerging Partnership of Watchmen and Gatekeepers** and **Help! I'm Married to an Intercessor!**

Cost for the entire seminar, including breakfast and training, is only $10. To register, call the BridgeBuilders hotline at 602-555-1111, ext. 304. An RSVP is required by Wednesday, April 17, so call today. I look forward to seeing your prayer team there!

In the spirit of united prayer,
Cheryl Sacks

P.S. Please pass the enclosed letter on to your church prayer coordinator/team. And why not offer to pay their registration fee? It would be a wonderful way to show your appreciation for their tireless efforts.

STARTING A CHURCH PRAYER LEADERS NETWORK: TRAINING EVENT—SAMPLE HOST CHURCH CHECKLIST

Thank you for your willingness to host the Greater Phoenix Church Prayer Leaders' Training Event on Saturday, March 4. Dr. Terry Teykl will be our speaker and his subject will be "Establishing a Prayer Room in Your Church."

Approximate times for use of the room (including setup and pack-up) are from 7:30 A.M. to 1:00 P.M. We also would like to do preliminary setup of the room on Friday, March 3, at 2:00 P.M.

Our meeting will go most smoothly if you could provide the following:

- ❑ A well-lit area for the speaker (raised if possible), including microphone and podium.
- ❑ Recorded music playing quietly before the beginning of the program.
- ❑ Large tables (to seat eight to ten people), round if available, covered with tablecloths, arranged close to the speaker. (We usually have between 180-250 people in attendance.)
- ❑ Three long rectangular book tables arranged around the perimeter of the room.
- ❑ Five resource tables arranged around the perimeter of the room.
- ❑ Two registration tables arranged at the entrance of the room, with a smaller table for name tags and information.
- ❑ Two long rectangular tables for buffet service of the breakfast foods.
- ❑ Two servers from your church to serve the food and make sure the platters remain full.
- ❑ Pitchers for water and juice, a 100-cup coffee dispenser, platters for the food, and a container in which to mix the orange juice.
- ❑ Clear, bold, and bright signs strategically placed around the facility and parking lot giving directions to the location of the breakfast.
- ❑ A projector and screen for viewing of a video.

Thank you again for your willingness to be a part of this ministry. If you have any questions, please call _____ at (phone number).

STARTING A CHURCH PRAYER LEADERS NETWORK: GOALS

The Church Prayer Leaders Network is a network of prayer leaders from Christian churches within a city or region. The purpose of the network is to come alongside the local church pastors to start, strengthen, and expand prayer ministries in the local churches. The network's vision is to see every church in the city become a powerful "house of prayer for all nations" (Matthew 21:13).

The goals of the network are to:

- Assist pastors in raising up prayer coordinators and prayer ministries

- Offer ongoing training for church prayer leaders

- Offer opportunities for prayer leaders to network and pray together

- Keep prayer leaders abreast of city, state, national, and global prayer initiatives

- Raise up a prayer shield for pastors and Christian leaders throughout the city

- Assist churches by providing specialized prayer resources

- Assist churches with setting up prayer rooms

- Assist churches in developing prayer strategies

- Encourage cooperation among churches as they pray for their communities

- Promote the linking of strategic prayer with evangelism

STARTING A CHURCH PRAYER LEADERS NETWORK:
TASK FORCE JOB ASSIGNMENTS

The role of the church prayer leaders task force is to give leadership to the citywide Church Prayer Leaders Network. We recommend a task force of six to eight people. Make sure that they are recognized and designated by their pastor and that they have a good reputation in the community.

The following is an example of how a team might function and suggested job descriptions for each task force member. In some cases, one person may take on more than one job assignment.

Chairperson: leads the team meetings and serves as the primary liaison to the pastors, churches, and prayer leaders in the community. It is helpful if this person has some measure of visibility in the community.

Administrative Assistant: assists the chairperson in scheduling task force meetings, facilitating church prayer coordinator training events, taking minutes, and corresponding with speakers.

Books and Resources Manager: orders books, tapes, and resources for the book table; keeps inventory list updated; pays bills related to book purchases; secures and oversees volunteers to man the book table.

Database Manager: assists the chairperson in obtaining mailing lists of pastors, churches, and prayer leaders in the community; updates database or oversees volunteer to update database; runs labels for first-class mailings or makes disk for the mailing service to facilitate bulk-rate or nonprofit mailings.

Prayer Coordinator: mobilizes prayer coverage for the task force. His or her church may also provide the church location for task force meetings.

Phone Secretary: makes calls to remind, notify, or change dates of task force meetings, or to distribute urgent messages or prayer requests to the task force or city prayer coordinators.

Organizing Church Prayer

(CHAPTER 4: BUILDING A PRAYER ACTION TEAM)

Prayer Team Organizational Chart

Pastor

Prayer Coordinator

Prayer Captain | Prayer Captain | Prayer Captain | Prayer Captain | Prayer Captain

see prayer captain's job description on the next page

Sample Job Description
For Prayer Captains

• **Training**—develop ideas and establish prayer training throughout the church

• **Prayer Room**—coordinate prayer room functions/schedule

• **Corporate Prayer**—oversee and schedule weekly or special corporate prayer meetings/Sunday service prayer

• **City/State/National Liaison**—inform and involve local church in city, state and national prayer events

• **Prayer Chain**—organize and implement

• **Special Events**—establish prayer cover for mission outreaches, dramas, and conferences

• **Prayer Coordinator for Cell Groups**—link cell groups in prayer for corporate concerns

House of Prayer Road Map

The Pastor

Solicits support of the staff for the vision of prayer

Casts the vision for prayer to the congregation

Preaches on prayer

Selects and supports the prayer coordinator

The Prayer Coordinator

Serves as the point person for prayer in the church

Assembles and directs the Prayer Action Team

The Prayer Action Team

Develops a comprehensive church prayer strategy

Leads the prayer ministry

The Prayer Ministry

Serves as the hub for all prayer operations

Offers training for those with a special interest in prayer

Seeks to integrate prayer into every ministry in the church

Has a goal to involve every member of the church in prayer

The House of Prayer

Is permeated by the presence of God as a result of the praying church

Sample Prayer Ministry Annual Budget

(CHAPTER 7: DESIGNING A HOUSE OF PRAYER STRATEGY)

Coordinator training at Phoenix quarterly breakfast (Travel expense) 800 miles x $.345	$276
National Day of Prayer (promotion materials, resources)	$100
June 26-29, 2004—PrayerQuake 2004 training registration for 6 prayer leadership people at $80 each, plus motel and meals	$1,120
Van travel expenses to PrayerQuake 2004 200 miles x $.345	$69
Resources for OVCN Prayer Lending Library	$100
Postage and encouragement cards	$300
Annual guest speaker for prayer breakfast	$100
Subscriptions to *Pray!* magazine for 5 pastors and Church Prayer Leaders Network membership for prayer coordinator	$108
Pray! books for leadership team (Qty. 20 @ 30% discount)	$130
Miscellaneous	$100
Total Budget	$2,403

How to Pray for a Spiritual Leader

(CHAPTER 8: RAISING UP THE PASTOR'S PIT CREW)

The outline that follows is for your use as a reference tool while praying for a particular leader. We cannot lay our hands on our manuals and say, "God, do it!" The Holy Spirit must quicken each prayer time. First Corinthians 14:15 tells us to pray with the Spirit and with understanding. We must trust God to give us specifics regarding the needs of the one we are praying for, in addition to the areas mentioned in this manual. It is vital that the insights we receive from the Lord as we pray be used only for intercession and not as an item for discussion with others (Psalm 25:14).

PERSONAL LIFE

Relationship with God
- Sensitive to the Lord
- Openhearted and tender for obedience
- Private times with the Lord to be vital, fresh, and productive
- Fellowship and communion with God remains number-one priority
- Receive personal direction, vision, and teaching

Priorities

- Discernment to know what they are
- Wisdom on how to apportion time
- Discernment and strength to maintain
- Awareness that they are unique to each person
- Open to God's adjustments and changes

Fellowship

- Available on their level of maturity
- Determination to maintain
- Not to be crowded out by responsibilities
- Wisdom not to invest all in one person
- Wisdom and discernment concerning opposite sex
- How to deal with loneliness and aloneness

Wisdom

- Not settling for past wisdom to get by but desiring new wisdom for every situation
- The need for discernment between your wisdom and God's
- Godly wisdom for spiritual, emotional, and physical decisions (Colossians 1:9-12; Proverbs 28:5)
- The Spirit of wisdom (Ephesians 1:17)
- The Holy Spirit would continually remind the leader to seek the Lord's wisdom

Health

- Divine health—emotional, mental, and physical
- Freedom from the effects of weariness
- Supernatural strength—spiritual, emotional, physical (Psalm 68:35)
- Desire to care for physical body
- Ability to rest completely (Psalm 127:2)
- Wisdom and self-control in work, sleep, and eating habits (Philippians 3:19; 1 Corinthians 9:27)
- Time for enjoyable exercise

Temptations

- Bind outside influences, controls, pressures, including ungodly desires of heart

- Not to be trapped by the personal desire to "be somebody"
- That there would be a desire to build God's kingdom and not one's own (Luke 11:2)
- That their hearts' desires would be to serve, not to control, manipulate, or rule (Mark 10:43-45; Philippians 2:3-8)
- Ability to harness ambition
- Revelation of where he and others fit into God's plans

Sexual

- Bind outside influences, controls, and pressures
- Discernment to detect traps of the Enemy
- Strength to resist the spirit of seduction
- Wisdom in knowing the difference between love and lust
- Strength to overcome and wisdom to direct all desires of the flesh (1 Thessalonians 4:3-8)

Financial

- Bind outside influences, controls, and pressures
- Revelation that God alone is provider
- Ability to be content, whether there's little or much (Philippians 4:11-13)

Attitude

- Thoughts and emotions develop attitudes, which become actions
- Discerning wrong attitudes with the courage and ability to change them into godly attitudes (Philippians 3:15)
- Competition to be changed to unity (Philippians 2:2-3)
- Independence to be changed to interdependence (Ephesians 2:21)
- Superiority to be changed to humility (Mark 9:35)
- Defensiveness to be changed to openness for cooperation
- Divisiveness to be changed to embracing of the whole body of Christ (Ephesians 2:14)

Evidence of Holy Spirit

- Graciousness with firmness (2 Timothy 2:24-25)
- Mercy, compassion, and forbearance (Ephesians 4:2)

- Desire to bring restoration to all (2 Corinthians 5:18; Galatians 6:1)

Motives
- Pure (Matthew 5:8)
- Whole and complete in Christ
- Open to God to reveal if not right
- Awareness that God alone knows true motives (Hebrews 4:12; Psalm 139:1)

Appearance
- The glow of Christ (Psalm 34:4,5)
- Reveal the Lord in action, dress, and speech (1 Timothy 3:7; Ephesians 4:1; 1 John 2:6; 2 Corinthians 3:2)

RENEWED VISION
(Proverbs 29:18)

- To be clear and unmixed
- Patience for the fulfillment (Habakkuk 2:3)
- That the Enemy would be unable to cloud, divert, or accelerate
- To stop the mouths of the lions that speak against the vision (Psalm 22:13,21)
- Outreach to others' visions with honest support and encouragement (1 Timothy 2:8; Philippians 2:4)
- A wall of fire to protect (Zechariah 2:5)

THE MINISTRY

Leadership
- Purpose to equip the saints (Ephesians 4:12; 2 Timothy 3:17)
- Revelation and sensitivity in the Word (2 Timothy 2:15)
- Messages that are Spirit and life (John 6:63)
- Anointing to flow
- Communicate with simplicity and clarity (Colossians 4:4)

- Anointing to pray and minister to people with discernment and wisdom (1 Thessalonians 5:14; 2 Timothy 4:2)
- Free flow of the gifts of the Spirit
- Relationship with staff—wisdom to deal with them as individuals (Colossians 4:6)
- Sensitivity in imparting the vision of the ministry
- Ability to delegate—and leave it with the person
- Communicate clearly and completely

Staff
- Desire to understand and share the vision of the ministry
- Faithfulness to their commitment (Colossians 3:23)
- Fulfilled in their own relationship with the Lord
- To enhance and strengthen rather than detract or drain
- Supportive but honest
- That there would be a team attitude (1 Corinthians 3:1-9)
- Anointing to do their job
- Desire to grow spiritually and in job skills

Those Receiving Ministry and Donors
- Open hearts—teachable (1 Thessalonians 2:13; Luke 8:4-15)
- Supportive and responsive (1 Thessalonians 5:12,13)
- Generous and faithful (Philippians 4:15-17)
- Hungry and thirsty for God
- Seekers of God and His will and ways
- Free from dead tradition

FAMILY

Leader
- Responsibility for provision emotionally, physically, and spiritually as well as materially (1 Timothy 5:8)
- Ministry concerns won't crowd out any area of family need
- Sensitivity to recognize needs quickly
- Ability to communicate
- Time to listen to each without divided interest

Family Unit
- Understanding and flow of unity
- No resentment when valid sacrifices have to be made
- Sharing the vision of ministry; comprehending how to be an active part
- Embracing the vision with wisdom and enthusiasm

Spouse
- Desire to complement and complete leader
- True spiritual unity and love flow
- Discernment for what spouse really needs
- Fruit of Spirit to flow
- Fulfillment of own spiritual relationship with God
- Strength to cope with stress and pressures
- Ability to resist trying to live up to others' expectations
- Revelation of their importance in the fulfillment of the call to ministry

Children
- To develop a true and intimate relationship of their own with the Lord
- Love, patience, and understanding
- That their needs would be met with regard to school, studies, friends
- Flexibility
- Good relationship with brothers and sisters
- No resentment or competition with ministry staff
- Security in parents' love
- Strength to cope with stress and pressures
- Ability to resist trying to live up to others' expectations

Financial Provision
- Provision of all needs and some wants (1 Timothy 5:18)
- Family provision not have to be used for the ministry (Philippians 4:19)
- Faith to believe for their own special needs
- Revelation of the joy of giving (1 Chronicles 29:9)

Compiled by Iverna Tompkins Ministries, Scottsdale, Arizona. Used with permission.

Prayer Captain
Mobilization Chart

(CHAPTER 10: MOBILIZING AND MANAGING INTERCESSORS)

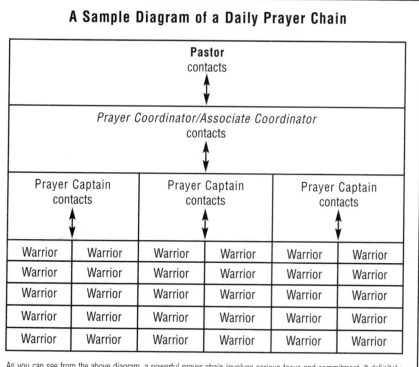

A Sample Diagram of a Daily Prayer Chain

Pastor contacts ↕		
Prayer Coordinator/Associate Coordinator contacts ↕		
Prayer Captain contacts ↕	Prayer Captain contacts ↕	Prayer Captain contacts ↕

Warrior	Warrior	Warrior	Warrior	Warrior	Warrior
Warrior	Warrior	Warrior	Warrior	Warrior	Warrior
Warrior	Warrior	Warrior	Warrior	Warrior	Warrior
Warrior	Warrior	Warrior	Warrior	Warrior	Warrior
Warrior	Warrior	Warrior	Warrior	Warrior	Warrior

As you can see from the above diagram, a powerful prayer chain involves serious focus and commitment. It definitely takes time and attention to call the chain members and send monthly (or quarterly) updates on ongoing requests. Though the process is simple, it requires a deep commitment. Though the flesh and the Devil will fight prayer more than anything else, the results are definitely worth the battle! Indeed there are many advantages of a powerful church prayer chain.

Adapted from *How to Start an Evangelistic Prayer Ministry* by Greg Frizzell. Used with permission.

Guidelines for Participants in Prayer Meetings

(CHAPTER 11: LEADING CORPORATE PRAYER GATHERINGS)

Recognize the appointed leader of the prayer meeting. Look to this person to give direction.

Use prayers that bless, are biblical, and are brief (the 3 Bs).
Bless: Are others built up or torn down? (See 1 Corinthians 14:26.)
Biblical: Does my prayer align itself with the Word of God?
   (See John 15:7.)
Brief: Am I respectful of others who also want to pray?
   (See Matthew 6:7.)

Be sensitive to others in the group who may be from various religious backgrounds, doctrine, and giftings. What is appropriate in your own personal prayer time may not be appropriate when you are praying with others.

Direct prayers God-ward. Avoid prayers that teach, counsel, or give information to others in the group.

Agree in prayer. Bring your thoughts into captivity. Do not let your mind wander. Instead of thinking about what you are going to pray next, listen to the one praying. Giving a sincere word of agreement such as "yes" and "amen" can stir faith in the one praying.

Speak up when leading out in prayer. This enables others to come into spiritual agreement with you. It is important to pray not only with humility but also with boldness and confidence.

Model faith-filled prayers. Pray with an attitude of expecting a miraculous answer. Focus on God's faithfulness and ability rather than the problem.

Flow with the spirit of prayer as you discern the direction of the Holy Spirit (repentance, thanksgiving, praise, warfare). Exercise caution when changing the subject or direction of prayer once a topic or emphasis has been established. Generally speaking, we should saturate a subject in prayer until the level of faith for it has been exhausted. If you are in question about changing the course of prayer, wait for the leader to do so.

Assume that all matters of prayer are confidential. To share even with a close friend or spouse could violate the trust of another person. If you want to share a request outside the prayer group, ask permission from the person who requested prayer.

Guidelines for Interdenominational Prayer and Worship Gatherings: Code of Spiritual Conduct

- The multicultural and religious traditions of each participant will greatly influence the spiritual atmosphere of any prayer meeting. For this reason, our foremost priority must be to focus on the Lordship of Jesus Christ and walk in an attitude of love (1 Corinthians 13) and humility (Philippians 2:1-18). We must endeavor to keep the unity of the Spirit in the bond of peace (Ephesians 4:3).
- We desire that you feel a complete freedom to worship our Lord during this meeting. Feel free to sit, stand, raise your hands,

kneel, or anything else you believe God is leading you to do. We only ask that you be sensitive to the diversity of religious Christian traditions represented at this gathering by keeping all activities both in word and deed on scriptural foundations (1 Corinthians 14:40).

- If your natural style is highly expressive or if you normally use a prayer language, please be considerate of those whose style may be more modest, so as not to distract or offend your brother. We are not expecting one style of worship or prayer to subordinate to another. We are confident that all attending the prayer meeting will conduct themselves in a spirit of humility, regarding one another more important than themselves (Philippians 2:3-4). Our spirituality is measured not by our spiritual giftedness or our doctrinal understanding but in our love expressed toward one another. In all things love is patient, kind, and always forgiving and forbearing (1 Corinthians 13:4-7).

- Be sensitive to the length of your prayers, allowing everyone the opportunity to pray. Please do not counsel, correct, or condemn anyone in your prayers. Let us seek to focus upon the Lord Jesus Christ and to edify one another in love.

THE HARMONY OF INTERDENOMINATIONAL PRAYING

A good way to help people visualize how to pray together was developed by Every Home for Christ (Dick Eastman).

The moment we unite in prayer we become a symphony. As such:

- We blend together in unity respecting the fact that we represent all of Christ's body.
- We realize that like a symphony with its different instruments, there are a wide variety of traditions when it comes to prayer.
- We commit ourselves to accepting one another as we are while disciplining ourselves to use wisdom and caution if we think anything we might do would offend a brother or sister.

Taken from 1999 "Code of Conduct" Arizona Prayer Summit and AD 2000 Movement Memo.

TWO-HOUR CONCERT OF PRAYER SUGGESTED FORMAT

Following the pattern of concerts of prayer over the past 250 years, as well as prayer movements emerging nationwide and worldwide today, here is one model of a format for a two-hour concert of prayer. The approach not only provides a satisfying experience during a concert of prayer but also can be adapted back in the churches, fellowships, and ministries from which we come so that the vision and ministry of united prayer may spread.

Celebration (10 minutes)
- Praise in hymns and choruses, focused on awakening and mission
- Reports of God's answers to prayers offered up during previous concerts
- Prayers of praise for God's faithfulness, for His kingdom, for His Son

Preparation (20 minutes)
- Welcome to the concert
- Overview: Why are we here?
- Biblical perspectives on what we're praying toward (e.g., awakening, mission)
- Preview of the format
- Teaming up in partners and in huddles (With Bryant's concert of prayer, *partners* means a group of three people and a *huddle* refers to two groups of three [six people]. Sometimes you pray with partners and when a huddle is called for, you put two groups of partners together.)

Dedication (5 minutes)
- Commitment: to be servants through prayer and to be used in answer to our prayers
- Thanksgiving: for the privilege of united prayer and for those with whom we unite
- Invitation for Christ to lead the concert and to pray through us
- Hymn of praise

Seeking for Fullness/Awakening in the Church (30 minutes)
- In partners—for personal revival (three people)
- In huddles—for awakening in our local churches and ministries (six people)
- As a whole—for awakening in the church worldwide
- Pause to listen to our Father
- Chorus

Seeking for Fulfillment/Mission Among the Nations (30 minutes)
- In partners—for personal ministries (three people)
- In huddles—for outreach and mission in our city (six people)
- As a whole—for world evangelization
- Pause to listen to our Father
- Chorus

Testimonies: What has God said to us here? (10 minutes)
- On fullness (awakening)
- On fulfillment (mission)

Grand Finale (15 minutes)
- Offering ourselves to be answers to our prayers and also to live accordingly
- Prayer for God's empowerment in our own lives for ministry
- Prayer for prayer movements locally and worldwide
- Offering praise to the Father who will answer our concert of prayer
- Leave to watch and serve "in concert"

Adapted with permisison from Proclaim Hope! P.O. Box 770, New Providence, NJ 07974.

Important Websites

These websites represent ministries that have a heart for prayer in the local church. Each one fills a different role in the global prayer movement. We recommend that you take some time to check out each ministry.

America's National Prayer Committee

Provides information, news, and resources on prayer and revival. Includes U.S. prayer events calendar and links to prayer organizations.
www.nationalprayer.org

BridgeBuilders International Leadership Network

This ministry's purpose is to unite and equip Christian leaders for the advancement of prayer, revival, and city transformation. They offer seminars, conferences, personal consultations, books, and tapes specifically designed to help local church prayer leaders do their job more effectively.
www.bridgebuilder.org

Christian Emergency Network

The purpose of CEN is to share the hope of Jesus Christ in times of national crisis through a joint prayer, care, and share ministry and media response. The website gives prayer coordinators information on how to set up prayer stations at disaster sites, hold corporate prayer services, and mobilize their church's

intercessory groups to pray specifically and strategically.
www.christianemergencynetwork.com

Church Prayer Leaders Network

Provides valuable encouragement and resources for local church
prayer leaders. This site has ideas, links, product reviews,
conference schedules, a speakers' bureau, and many more
resources for local church prayer. Ninety percent of the site is
password protected and available only to CPLN members
(formerly called The National Association of Local Church
Prayer Leaders).
www.prayerleader.com

Harvest Prayer Ministries

Harvest Prayer Ministries, founded by Dave and Kim Butts, seeks to
encourage prayer in the local church. Harvest has a team of
speakers who do prayer weekends in churches as well as
resources to take people deeper into prayer.
www.harvestprayer.com

Intercessors for America

Provides resources to help people pray for the government. This
ministry is also your source for resources and information on
First Friday Prayer, an initiative that encourages prayer for revival
on the first Friday of every month. Hundreds of thousands of
believers and thousands of churches have participated in this
ongoing prayer initiative for more than twenty-five years.
www.ifa-usapray.org

International Renewal Ministries

Best known for being the driving force behind developing Pastors
Prayer Summits, this ministry encourages pastors in communities to pray together. Its website will show you where
summits are being held.
www.prayersummits.net

National Children's Prayer Network

A wonderful ministry to children. It teaches them to effectively pray for national leaders and sponsors the National Children's Prayer Congress each year. Hundreds of children come to Washington, DC, during the week of the National Day of Prayer. Children pray with congressional leaders, prayerwalk around the White House, and participate in a prayer banquet. www.childrensprayernet.net

National Day of Prayer Task Force

The National Day of Prayer is held the first Thursday in May. This organization helps to coordinate events all over the country. Its website provides information on how your church can participate in your area. It also has valuable resources to help you plan and put on an event. www.nationaldayofprayer.org

National Pastors' Prayer Network

This web-based ministry seeks to bring together pastors in communities across the country to pray together. Its website can connect pastors to groups in their area. It also provides a weekly e-mail newsletter of valuable articles, news, and insights. www.nppn.org

Nationally Broadcast Concert of Prayer

Each year on the National Day of Prayer, this three-hour televised concert of prayer beams across the country. Churches in communities across the nation participate via satellite. Its website provides information on how to connect to the broadcast. www.concertofprayer.org

One in a Million

Here you can join thousands who are praying for spiritual awakening in America. Provides inspiration through news of God's activity, a daily devotion written by Henry Blackaby, and a weekly e-mail prayer focus with free resources. This site is sponsored by, but

not limited to, the Southern Baptist Convention.
www.oneinamillionprayer.com

Pray! Magazine

Pray! is a bimonthly magazine that provides practical and challenging articles on prayer. Its website provides a complete archive
of articles from seven years' worth of publishing and excellent
books and booklets on local church prayer.
www.praymag.com

Prayerwalking

If you want information on how to prayerwalk effectively
and—even more important—how to teach your people to pray
effectively for their communities, nation, and world, you need
WayMakers' resources. Its website has valuable Scripture-based
prayer guides. WayMakers also produces and sponsors the Seek
God for the City prayer initiative each spring.
www.waymakers.org

Renewal Ministries/Prayer Point Press

Dr. Terry Teykl is a gifted speaker and author on the subject of
prayer in the local church. His publishing ministry provides
many practical resources for the local church prayer leader.
www.prayerpointpress.com

See You at the Pole

Sponsors the annual student flagpole prayer gatherings. Each year
more than three million teens participate in the annual student
flagpole prayer gatherings. Its website provides news, information,
and resources.
www.syatp.com

Strategic Prayer Network

This national network seeks to unite intercessors across the country.
It has a prophetic edge, seeking God for what's on His heart for

the church in America, and then labors to rally intercessors to pray effectively. It has representatives in each state. www.battleaxe.org/spn.html

Strategic Renewal International

This ministry—founded and run by Dr. Daniel Henderson, a local church pastor—seeks to raise an awareness of the importance of corporate prayer within churches. It provides resources and conferences to train pastors and lay leaders on how to run exciting effective prayer meetings and develop prayer leaders in their churches. www.strategicrenewal.com

U.S. Prayer Center

This ministry of Eddie and Alice Smith, two longtime prayer mobilizers, encourages and challenges pastors and intercessors to work together. Its resources in the area of intercessor/pastor relationships are the best available. www.usprayercenter.org

World Prayer Center

The base of the World Prayer Team, a network of intercessors who pray for concerns all over the world. www.worldprayerteam.org

Recommended Resources

CHAPTER 1: THE CHURCH THAT PRAYER BUILT

Cymbala, Jim. *Fresh Wind, Fresh Fire.* (Grand Rapids, Mich.: Zondervan, 1997).

Damazio, Frank. *The Gate Church.* (Portland, Ore.: City Bible Publishing, 2000).

Graf, Jonathan and Lani C. Hinkle, eds. *My House Shall Be a House of Prayer.* (Colorado Springs, Colo.: NavPress, 2001).

Sheets, Dutch. *Intercessory Prayer.* (Ventura, Calif.: Regal, 1996).

Smith, Eddie and Alice. *Drawing Closer to God's Heart.* (Lake Mary, Fla.: Charisma House, 2001).

Wagner, C. Peter. *Churches That Pray.* (Ventura, Calif.: Regal, 1993).

Wilkerson, Gary. *The Divine Intercessor.* (Lindale, Tex.: David Wilkerson Publications, Inc., 2002).

Whillhite, B.J. *Why Pray?* (Lake Mary, Fla.: Creation House, 1988).

Audio and Video Tapes:

Fuller, Mark. *The House That Prayer Built.* Audiotape. PrayerQuake Conference 2002, BridgeBuilders International Leadership Network, P.O. Box 31415, Phoenix, AZ.

Sacks, Cheryl. *Building a House of Prayer.* Audiotape and Videotape. PrayerQuake Conference 2001, BridgeBuilders International Leadership Network.

CHAPTER 2: THE ROLE OF THE CHURCH PRAYER COORDINATOR

Frizzell, Gregory. *How to Build an Evangelistic Church Prayer Ministry.*(Nashville: Tennessee Baptist Convention, 1999).

Graf, Jonathan and Lani C. Hinkle, eds. *My House Shall Be a House of Prayer.* (Colorado Springs, Colo.: NavPress, 2001).

Smith, Steve. *Building the House of Prayer.* (Berwick, Victoria, Australia: Church Resource Ministries Australia).

Teykl, Terry. *Blueprint for the House of Prayer.* (Muncie, Ind.: Prayer Point Press, 1997).

Audio and Video Tapes:

Ryan, Wendy. *The Role of the Church Prayer Coordinator.* Audiotape. PrayerQuake Conference 2002, BridgeBuilders International Leadership Network.

CHAPTER 3: THE PASTOR/PRAYER LEADER RELATIONSHIP

Franklin, John. *A House of Prayer.* (Nashville: LifeWay Press, 1999).

Graf, Jonathan and Lani C. Hinkle, eds. *My House Shall Be a House of Prayer.* (Colorado Springs, Colo.: NavPress, 2001).

Audio and Video Tapes:

Butts, Dave. *Leadership for a Praying Church*. Videotape, 2001. Harvest Prayer Ministries, 619 Washington Ave., Terre Haute, IN 47802.

Griffin, Leonard. *The Pastor's Role in Mobilizing Prayer*. Audiotape. PrayerQuake Conference 2001, BridgeBuilders International Leadership Network.

Henderson, Daniel. *Fueling Your Pastor's Prayer Vision*. Audiotape, 2003. Strategic Renewal International, P.O. Box 601404, Sacramento, CA 95860.

Vander Griend, Alvin. *The Pastor/Prayer Leader Relationship*. Audiotape. PrayerQuake Conference 2001, BridgeBuilders International Leadership Network.

CHAPTER 4: BUILDING a Prayer ACTION Team

Barna, George. *Building Effective Lay Leadership Teams*. (Ventura, Calif.: Issachar Resources, 2001).

Franklin, John. *A House of Prayer*. (Nashville: LifeWay Press, 1999).

George, Carl and Robert Logan, *Leading and Managing Your Church*. (Old Tappan, N.J.: Revell, 1987).

Maxwell, John C. *Developing the Leaders Around You*. (Nashville: Nelson, 1995).

CHAPTER 5: ASSESSING Your CHURCH'S NEEDS

Frizzell, Gregory. *Returning to Holiness*. (Memphis: The Master Design, 2000).

CHAPTER 6: TAKING YOUR CHURCH TO THE NEXT LEVEL

Anderson, Neil T. *Setting Your Church Free*. (Ventura, Calif.: Regal, 1994).

Franck, Leon. *Helping the Church Become a House of Prayer*. (La Crosse, Wisc.: Valley Press).

Frizzell, Gregory. *Returning to Holiness*. (Memphis: The Master Design, 2000).

Kittle, Onie. *But I Don't Know How to . . . Start a Prayer Ministry*. (Anderson, Ind.: Warner Press, 1999).

Martin, Glen and Dian Ginter, *PowerHouse*. (Nashville: Broadman, Holman, 1994).

Pedersen, Bjorn. *Face to Face with God in Your Church: Establishing a Prayer Ministry*. (Minneapolis: Fortress, 1995).

Vander Griend, Alvin. *How to Coordinate Your Prayer Ministry*. (Grand Rapids, Mich.: CRC Publications, 1997).

Vander Griend, Alvin. *Keys to a Praying Church*. (Grand Rapids, Mich.: CRC Publications, 1996).

CHAPTER 7: DESIGNING A HOUSE OF PRAYER STRATEGY

Developing a Prayer Strategy. (London, England: Dawn Resources).

Graf, Jonathan and Lani C. Hinkle, eds. *My House Shall Be a House of Prayer*. (Colorado Springs, Colo.: NavPress, 2001).

Pedersen, Bjorn. *Face to Face with God in Your Church: Establishing a Prayer Ministry*. (Minneapolis: Fortress, 1995).

Audio and Video Tapes

Covert, Paul. *How to Start a Prayer Ministry in Your Church*. Audiotape. PrayerQuake Conference 2002, BridgeBuilders International Leadership Network.

Hensley, Anita. *Developing a Church Prayer Strategy*. Audiotape. PrayerQuake Conference 2002, BridgeBuilders International Leadership Network.

CHAPTER 8: RAISING UP THE PASTOR'S PIT CREW

Eastman, Dick. *Love on Its Knees*. (Grand Rapids, Mich.: Chosen, 1988).

Jacobs, Cindy. *Possessing the Gates of the Enemy*. (Tarrytown, N.Y.: Revell, 1991).

Maxwell, John. *Partners in Prayer*. (Nashville: Nelson, 1996).

Roberts, Lee. *Praying God's Will for Your Pastor.* (Nashville: Nelson, 1994).

Teykl, Terry. *Preyed On or Prayed For.* (Muncie, Ind.: Prayer Point Press, 1997).

Wagner, C. Peter. *Prayer Shield*. (Ventura, Calif.: Regal, 1992).

CHAPTER 9: MOTIVATING THE WHOLE CHURCH TO PRAY

Alves, Elizabeth. *Families—Praying with Purpose*. Intercessors International, 1997.

Alves, Elizabeth. *Becoming a Prayer Warrior*. (Ventura, Calif.: Regal Books, 1998).

Baker, Brant D. *Teaching Prayer . . . Guidance for Pastors and Church Leaders*. (Nashville: Abingdon, 2001).

Butts, Kim. *The Praying Family: Creative Ways to Pray Together.* (Chicago: Moody, 2003).

Cornwall, Judson. *Praying the Scriptures.* (Lake Mary, Fla.: Creation House, 1988).

Duke, Dee, with Bran Smith: *Prayer Quest.* (Colorado Springs, Colo.: NavPress, 2004).

Dunn, Ronald. *Don't Just Stand There, Pray Something.* (Nashville: Nelson, 1992).

Femrite, Tommi. *Unreached Peoples—Praying with Purpose.* (Bulverde, Tex.: Intercessors International, 1997).

Franch, Leon. *Helping the Church Become a House of Prayer.* (La Crosse, Wisc.: Valley Press).

Franklin, John. *Spiritual Warfare—Biblical Truth for Victory.* (Nashville: LifeWay Press, 2001).

Fuller, Cheri. *When Children Pray.* (Sisters, Ore.: Multnomah, 1998).

Fuller, Cheri. *When Families Pray.* (Sisters, Ore.: Multnomah, 1999).

Fuller, Cheri. *When Mothers Pray.* (Sisters, Ore.: Multnomah, 1997).

Fuller, Cheri. *When Teens Pray.* (Sisters, Ore.: Multnomah, 2002).

Graf, Jonathan. *The Power of Personal Prayer.* (Colorado Springs, Colo.: NavPress, 2002).

Griffith, Jill. *How to Have a Dynamic Church Prayer Ministry.* (Colorado Springs, Colo.: Wagner Publishing, 1999).

Henderson, Daniel with Margaret Saylar. *Fresh Encounter.* (Colorado Springs, Colo.: NavPress, 2004).

Jacobs, Cindy. *The Voice of God.* (Ventura, Calif.: Regal, 1995).

Lemmons, Albert G. *Teach Us to Pray.* (Nashville: Pollock Printing, 1978).

Linamen, Karen Scalf. *The Parent Warrior.* (Wheaton, Ill.: Victor, 1993).

Osborne, Rick. *Teaching Your Child How to Pray.* (Chicago: Moody, 1997).

Sheets, Dutch. *The Beginner's Guide to Intercession.* (Ann Arbor, Mich.: Servant, 2001).

Smith, Eddie and Alice. *Drawing Closer to God's Heart.* (Lake Mary, Fla.: Charisma House, 2001).

Spears, Teri. *Enlarging Your House of Prayer: A Blueprint for Expansion.* (Tioga, La.: Faith Printing, 2002).

Tekyl, Terry. *Acts 29: Fifty Days of Prayer to Invite the Holy Spirit.* (Muncie, Ind.: Prayer Point Press, 1999).

Tekyl, Terry. *Outside the Camp—Beyond the Familiar to Inquire of the Lord.* (Muncie: Ind.: Prayer Point Press, 2001).

Tyre, Jacquie. *Ready for Revival. A 40-Day Heart Journey Toward the Fullness of Christ.* (Colorado Springs, Colo.: *Pray!* Books, 2002).

Vander Griend, Alvin. *The Praying Church Sourcebook.* (Grand Rapids, Mich.: CRC Publications, 1990).

Vickler, Mark. *Communion with God.* (Shippensburg, Pa.: Destiny Image, 1983).

Winger, Mell. *Fight on Your Knees.* (Colorado Springs, Colo.: NavPress, 2002).

Audio and Video Tapes:

Graf, Jon. *Nuts and Bolts of Developing Children in Prayer*. Audiotape.
PrayerQuake Conference 2001, BridgeBuilders International
Leadership Network.

Highlights from The Call. Videotape, 2002, The Call, 1539
E. Howard St., Pasadena, CA 91104.

Henderson, Daniel. *Teaching Your Church to Pray*. Videotape, 2003,
Strategic Renewal International, P.O. Box 601404, Sacramento,
CA 95860.

Ilnisky, Esther. *Mobilizing Children to Pray*. Audio and Video Tape.
PrayerQuake Conference 2001, BridgeBuilders International
Leadership Network.

Kinnaman, Gary. *Mobilizing People Who Don't Want to Pray*. Audiotape.
PrayerQuake Conference 2001, BridgeBuilders International
Leadership Network.

Otis, Jr., George. *Transformations I and II*. Videotapes. The Sentinel
Group, 1999.

Sacks, Nicole. *Igniting Youth to Pray*. Audiotape. PrayerQuake
Conference, 2001, BridgeBuilders International Leadership
Network.

Touvell, Julie. *Developing a School of Prayer*. Audiotape. PrayerQuake
Conference 2001, BridgeBuilders International Leadership
Network.

CHapter 10: MOBILIZING anD Managing Intercessors

Alves, Elizabeth. *Intercessors*. (Ventura, Calif.: Regal, 2000).

Franklin, John. *A House of Prayer*. (Nashville: LifeWay Press, 1999).

Frizzell, Gregory. *How to Build an Evangelistic Church Prayer Ministry.*(Nashville: Tennessee Baptist Convention, 1999).

Graf, Jonathan and Lani C. Hinkle, eds. *My House Shall Be a House of Prayer.* (Colorado Springs, Colo.: NavPress, 2001).

Jacobs, Cindy. *Possessing the Gates of the Enemy.* (Tarrytown, N.Y.: Revell, 1991).

Kamstra, Douglas. *The Praying Church Idea Book.* (Grand Rapids, Mich.: CRC Publications, 2001).

Pedersen, Bjorn. *Face to Face with God in Your Church: Establishing a Prayer Ministry.* (Minneapolis: Fortress, 1995).

Smith, Eddie and Alice. *Intercessors and Pastors.* (Houston, Tex.: SpiriTruth Publishing, 2000).

Tekyl, Terry. *Prayer Room Intercessor's Handbook.* (Muncie, Ind.: Prayer Point Press, 1999).

Tekyl, Terry. *Making Room to Pray.* (Muncie, Ind.: Prayer Point Press, 1992).

Tekyl, Terry. *Praying Grace.* (Muncie, Ind.: Prayer Point Press, 1993).

Audio and Video Tapes:

Alves, Beth. *Pastors and Intercessors.* Audiotape. Arlington Prayer Network, P.O. Box 3503, Arlington, TX 76007, 2001.

CHAPTER 11: LEADING CORPORATE PRAYER GATHERINGS

Chavda, Mahesh. *The Hidden Power of Prayer and Fasting.* (Shippensburg, Pa.: Destiny Image, 1998).

Curran, Sue. *The Praying Church, Principles and Power of Corporate Praying.* (Lake Mary, Fla.: Creation House, 1987).

Eastman, Dick. *Heights of Delight.* (Ventura, Calif.: Regal, 2002).

Franklin, John. *A House of Prayer.* (Nashville: LifeWay Press, 1999).

Frizzell, Gregory. *How to Build an Evangelistic Church Prayer Ministry.*(Nashville: Tennessee Baptist Convention, 1999).

Henderson, Daniel with Margaret Saylar. *Fresh Encounter.* (Colorado Springs, Colo.: NavPress, 2004).

Towns, Elmer. *Fasting for Spiritual Breakthrough.* (Ventura, Calif.: Regal, 1996).

Vander Griend, Alvin. *The Praying Church Sourcebook.* (Grand Rapids, Mich.: CRC Publications, 1990).

Wagner, C. Peter. *Churches That Pray.* (Ventura, Calif.: Regal, 1993).

Audio and Video Tapes:

Franklin, John. *Is the Church Prepared?* Audiotape. Church Prayer Coordinator Seminar, 2003, BridgeBuilders International Leadership Network.

Henderson, Daniel. *Teaching Your Church to Pray.* Audiotape/CD set of three with workbook, 2003, Strategic Renewal International.

Hensley, Anita. *How to Lead Corporate Prayer.* Audiotape. PrayerQuake Conference 2002, BridgeBuilders International Leadership Network.

Ilnisky, Esther. *Leading Corporate Prayer.* Audiotape. PrayerQuake Conference 2001, BridgeBuilders International Leadership Network.

chapter 12: praying outside the walls of the church

Dawson, John. *Taking Our Cities for God.* (Lake Mary, Fla.: Creation House, 1989).

Goll, Jim. *Intercession.* (Shippensburg, Pa.: Destiny Image, 2003).

Gooding, Terry. *Paths of Gold: Praying the Way to Christ for a Lost Friend.* (Colorado Springs, Colo.: NavPress, 2002).

Griffith, Jill. *How to Have a Dynamic Church Prayer Ministry.* (Colorado Springs, Colo.: Wagner Publishing, 1999).

Haggard, Ted. *Primary Purpose.* (Lake Mary, Fla.: Creation House, 1995).

Hardistry, Vance. *Houses of Prayer, Reaching Cities, One Neighbor at a Time.* (Concord, Calif.: Renewal International, 1993).

Hawthorne, Steve. *PrayerWalking: Praying On Site with Insight.* (Lake Mary, Fla.: Creation House, 1993).

Johnson, Bill. *When Heaven Invades Earth.* (Shippensburg, Pa.: Destiny Image Publishers, Inc., 2003).

Malone, Bill and Pam. *How to Make Prayer Exciting!* (St. Petersburg, Fla.: Pray U.S.A., 2000).

Marr, Mary. *Lighting the Way.* (Kansas City, Mo.: Beacon Press, 2000).

Otis, Jr., George. *Informed Intercession.* (Ventura, Calif.: Regal, 1999).

Sheets, Dutch. *How to Pray for Lost Loved Ones.* (Ventura, Calif.: Regal, 2001).

Silvoso, Ed. *That None Should Perish.* (Ventura, Calif.: Regal, 1994).

Tryon, Howard. *Praying for You.* (Grand Rapids, Mich.: Kregel
     Publications, 1996).

Twin Cities Prayer Guide. *Call to Transformation.* Weekly prayer guide
     for a city. Prayer Transformation Ministries, 810 S. 7th St.,
     Minneapolis, MN 55415.

White, Tom. *Citywide Prayer Movements.* (Ann Arbor, Mich.: Servant,
     2001).

Audio and Video Tape:

Miracle in Modesto. Videotape. Calvary Temple Worship Center, 1601
     Coffee Rd., Modesto, CA 95350.

About the Author

CHERYL SACKS is an inspirational speaker, author, and local church prayer consultant. She and her husband, Hal, are cofounders of BridgeBuilders International Leadership Network (www.bridgebuilder.org), a ministry dedicated to the advancement of prayer, revival, and city transformation.

With a heart to see local churches saturated with fervent prayer, Cheryl founded the Greater Phoenix Church Prayer Leaders Network in 1996. Today this model is being successfully transplanted, as Cheryl assists other prayer leaders in establishing similar networks in cities nationwide. She travels extensively to speak in churches, multichurch conferences, and denominational gatherings on the subjects of revival and local church and citywide prayer mobilization. Cheryl's work of mobilizing prayer in local churches began while leading the prayer ministry at Word of Grace, a five-thousand-member church in Mesa, Arizona.

She serves on the advisory board of the Church Prayer Leaders Network (CPLN), facilitated by *Pray!* magazine, and the The National Prayer Committee, and is the southwest regional coordinator for the U.S. Strategic Prayer Network.

Hal and Cheryl's daughter, Nicole, served as a facilitator for The Call DC, an event that drew four hundred thousand youth to fast and pray on the Washington, DC, mall on September 2, 2000. Cheryl and her family reside in Phoenix, Arizona.

Prayer Tools CD Contents

CHAPTER 4:   BUILDING YOUR PRAYER ACTION TEAM

4.1: Organizational Chart (completed)
4.2: Organizational Chart (blank)
4.3: Forming a Team Worksheet
4.4: Organizing a Prayer Team Start-Up Meeting
4.5: Team Contact Information Sheet
4.6: Questionnaire for Assessing Team Goals
4.7: Team Members' Roles and Responsibilities Worksheet
4.8: House of Prayer Road Map

CHAPTER 5:   ASSESSING YOUR CHURCH'S NEEDS

5.1: Evaluating Your Church's Will and Skill
5.2: Analyzing Your Church's Prayer Level
5.3: Identifying Barriers to the Presence of God
5.4: Church Prayer Discovery Guide

CHAPTER 6:   TAKING YOUR CHURCH TO THE NEXT LEVEL

6.1: Steps for Starting a Prayer Ministry

CHAPTER 7:   DESIGNING A HOUSE OF PRAYER STRATEGY

7.1: Seven Categories of a Prayer Budget
7.2: Sample Prayer Ministry Annual Budget
7.3: Prayer Ministry Budget Worksheet
7.4: Sample Prayer Strategy
7.5: Tips for Drafting the Document
7.6: Prayer Strategy Development Template
7.7: Prayer Strategy Checklist
7.8: Pastor's Endorsement Letter

CHAPTER 8: RAISING UP THE PASTOR'S PIT CREW

8.1: Sample Monthly Letter from Prayer Partner Coordinator
8.2: Pastor's Prayer Partners Breakfast Components
8.3: "Colossians Claims" for Christian Workers
8.4: How to Pray for a Spiritual Leader
8.5: PIT Crew Commitment Form

CHAPTer 9:   MOTIVaTInG THe WHOLe CHUrCH TO Pray

9.1: Ten Most Wanted List

9.2: Forty Days, Forty Ways Prayer Initiative Agenda

9.3: A Prayer Covering for Our Youth (bulletin insert)

9.4: How to Start a Men's Prayer Meeting

9.5: Positions of Prayer

9.6: Teaching Children to Pray

9.7: Ways to Incorporate Prayer into the Worship Service

9.8: The Personal Prayer Retreat

9.9: Sample Prayer Conference Agenda

9.10: Adopt-a-Student in Prayer Instruction

9.11: Adopt-a-Student Assignment Form

9.12: Adopt-a-Student Sign-Up Form

9.13: School of Prayer Curriculum

9.14: Sample Prayer Ministry Brochure

CHAPTer 10:   MOBILIZInG anD ManaGInG InTercessors

10.1: Building an Altar Prayer Ministry Team

10.2: Prayer Captain Mobilization Chart

10.3: Intercessory Prayer Captain Role

10.4: "Faithful 100" Prayer Targets Guide

10.5: Prayer Triplets to Pray for the Lost

10.6: 24-7 Prayer Watch Schedule

10.7: Mobilizing Prayer for a Conference

10.8: Sample Prayergram with Instructions

10.9: Praying Through the Worship Service

10.10: Setting Up a Prayer Room

CHAPTer 11:   LeaDInG corporaTe Prayer GaTHerInGs

11.1: Fasting Bookmark Text

11.2: Guidelines for Participants in Prayer Meetings

11.3: Two-Hour Concert of Prayer Format

11.4: Guidelines for Interdenominational Prayer and Worship Gatherings

11.5: Watch of the Lord (How to Hold an All-Night Prayer Meeting)

11.6: Prayer Meeting Template

CHAPTER 12: PRAYING OUTSIDE THE WALLS OF THE CHURCH